Legal Check-up for Medical Practice

Essential Guide for the Health Care Team

"Always do right; this will gratify some people and astound the rest."

"Habit is habit, and not to be flung out of the window by any man, but coaxed down-stairs a step at a time."

Mark Twain

Legal Check-up for Medical Practice

Essential Guide for the Health Care Team

Sal Fiscina, MD, JD

Assistant Clinical Professor
Department of Health Sciences
George Washington Medical Center
Washington, D.C.

Janet B. Seifert, JD

Director, Legal Medicine Center
Adjunct Assistant Professor
Uniformed Services University of Health Sciences
Bethesda, Maryland

Mosby

St. Louis Baltimore Boston Carlsbad Chicago Naples New York Philadelphia Portland
London Madrid Mexico City Singapore Sydney Tokyo Toronto Wiesbaden

Mosby
Dedicated to Publishing Excellence

A Times Mirror
Company

Publisher: Anne S. Patterson
Editor: Susie Baxter
Developmental Editor: Ellen Baker Geisel
Project Manager: Mark Spann
Production Editor: Beth Hayes
Cover Designer: Robert Messick
Manufacturing Supervisor: Linda Ierardi

Printed in the United States of America
Composition by Shepherd, Inc.
Printing/binding by Maple-Vail Book Mfg. Group

Mosby–Year Book, Inc.
11830 Westline Industrial Drive
St. Louis, Missouri 63146

Library of Congress Cataloging in Publication Data
Fiscina, Salvatore Francis
Legal check-up for medical practice : essential guide for the health care team / Sal Fiscina, Janet B. Seifert.
p. cm.
Includes index.
ISBN 0-8151-3302-2
1. Medical laws and legislation—United States. 2. Physicians--Malpractice—United States. 3. Medical jurisprudence—United States I. Seifert, Janet.
KF3821.F57 1996
344.73'041—dc20
[347.30441] 96–10386
CIP

97 98 99 00 01 / 9 8 7 6 5 4 3 2 1

Preface

This is a small book with a simple goal: to explore some appropriate safety measures for legal risks faced in clinical medical practice. Certainly, every practice does not need every protection. Every potential safety factor requires an investment: changes must be established, maintained, and monitored to achieve the benefits of safety.

Whether any change is worth its price in effort, expense, and personal accommodation has to be an individual practice cost-benefit assessment. Comparable safety-cost choices are made every day in financial affairs, automobile purchase and driving, and personal lifestyle and habits. Investment in safety implies anticipation of error or failure and decisions about where margin for error will be allowed. Practice Check-up offers help in making just such decisions.

Practice Check-up rates 10 practice areas of exposure to legal problems. Check-up Files explore legal problems and safeguards in credentials, negligence, consent, communications, confidentiality, office management, consultation, vendors, practice contracts, and legal process. Each Check-up File surveys safety factors to protect both the practice and the practitioner. Medical case vignettes describe clinical risk situations, with suggestions for optimal management.

Practice Check-up and review of Check-up Files can be completed by physicians or practice staff managers or administrators. To use Practice Check-up and Check-up Files:

1. Use Check-up to test practice for problem exposure and management safeguards.
2. Select Check-up Files for areas of low management safety.
3. Evaluate cost-benefit rationale for various protective approaches.
4. Consider adoption of specific measures.

Sal Fiscina and Jan Seifert

Introduction

Why Invest in Safety Factors?

Risk Is Both Proportional and Capricious

A driver may be traveling on a bad road in an old and poorly maintained car in inclement weather, and nothing bad may happen. Or a new, well-maintained, all-safety-equipped car is parked in a driveway and baseball-sized hail destroys it. Maximizing protection is not a guarantee. Engaging in high-risk conduct may not result in the risked loss occurring. Part of protective action is confidence in having done the best risk-control possible. Another part is lessening the actual chance of an adverse event or loss. As engineers know, the forces of nature will find the hidden defect. Depending on the nature of an individual practice, a physician may choose to drive a Yugo or a Rolls Royce, a Geo or a Jeep, a Volvo or a Lexus. Relative safety on the road also depends on how the vehicle is driven and where.

Why Prepare for Failure?

Failure Is Foreseeable

Maximizing protection against risks of failed hardware, people, or management calls for different strategies. Expectations of safety must also be considered. Airline travelers like to think safety is maximized and that staff performance and maintenance do not rely on luck. Airlines engage many checks and inspections, install monitoring devices, and practice for failures. Bridge designers calculate safety factors to allow for unexpected loads and weather. Fail-safe systems keep elevators from falling when mechanical failure occurs. Monitors, alarms, and security systems guard nuclear facilities, and spacecraft are backed by redundant functions. Medical practice offers parallels to other risk-intensive activities. Decisions can be made to widen margins of safety and narrow allowance for error.

Why Must There Be So Much Legal Concern in Medicine?

Legal Safety in Medicine First Prevents or Avoids Adverse Events for Patients

Most physicians' bad medical legal consequences are rooted in patients' bad medical consequences. Because patients present the medical problems, medical outcomes are theirs to accommodate. Choices in medical treatment may be limited to the best among bad alternatives. Choices in medical practice may also put physicians between competing and threatening options: patient safety versus practice survival in the early discharge policy of managed care; parental outrage versus suspected child abuse; risks of malpractice suits versus needed emergency treatment; and patient confidentiality versus danger to nonpatients of patients' human immunodeficiency virus infection. Medical legal choices by practitioners can also be framed to choose the best among available alternatives. Medical legal safeguards can assure that the best alternatives are available when choices must be made.

Contents

Summary of Check-up Recommendations

Assure Dependability of Personal Capabilities and of Technical, Staff, and Collegial Support

Maximize Early Notice of Changes or Problems

Take Systematic Action or Control

If only one change is made in a practice, it should be the establishment of a master calendar system. On the master calendar, every routine, periodic, and single event is scheduled, including patient appointment and callback, prescription duration and follow-up, accounting, business and professional submissions, legal reviews, education requirements, maintenance rotations, recordkeeping deadlines, supplies and equipment purchasing, housekeeping, and other tasks and deadlines. Each is checked off as completed daily, weekly, monthly, semiannually, or annually, or as a singular event. Project management scheduling techniques, used in building construction, research, and manufacturing, assure timeliness, maximize success, and limit problems.

Bottom Line: The right thing, too late, has nearly the same effect as nothing or the wrong thing and is even more disappointing.

Legal Check-up for Medical Practice

Essential Guide for the Health Care Team

Part 1
PRACTICE CHECK-UP

Practice Checklists

Top Ten Risks ☐
Pattern for Risk ☐
Pattern for Safety ☐
Management Questions ☐

The following lists are a quick assay for practice problems. The first list, Top Ten Risks, pinpoints the ten major factors in adverse patient outcomes, claims of improper or unskilled care, practice management problems, and legal disputes and penalties. Each major risk is matched by a Check-up File that explores practice safeguards and management approaches.

The second checklist, Pattern for Risk, identifies practice management approaches that endanger patient and practitioner, reflected in both bad medical outcomes and adverse legal consequences. The third checklist, Pattern for Safety, indicates management routines that protect against foreseeable problems and prepare the practice to deal with unexpected problems. Consistent and appropriate management can also minimize the damage of bad outcomes and practice errors for both practitioner and patient.

The last practice management assessment rates confidence in answering questions about practice judgments and decisions. The questions match Check-up File topics. Consider the Check-up Files for topics that rate a low level of confidence.

☐ Top Ten Risks

Rate potential major risk situations in the practice.

	NEVER	ON OCCASION	OFTEN
1. Practice outside specialty, deviate from written standards	☐	☐	☐
2. Fail to catch errors, practice without necessary skill or knowledge	☐	☐	☐
3. Neglect to acknowledge patient risks, expectations	☐	☐	☐
4. Forego attentive communication	☐	☐	☐
Fail to achieve patient understanding in consent	☐	☐	☐
Document carelessly	☐	☐	☐
5. Ignore or neglect to safeguard medical information	☐	☐	☐
6. Fail to establish communications systems	☐	☐	☐
7. Allow decision-making authority to dissipate	☐	☐	☐
8. Responsibilities delegate to unqualified persons	☐	☐	☐
9. Make naive choices about sophisticated business and legal matters	☐	☐	☐
10. Ignore, deny, or conceal problems	☐	☐	☐

For practice areas of noted risk, consider strategies and approaches in corresponding Check-up Files.

☐ Pattern for Risk

Rate the occurrence of each risk observed in the practice.

	NEVER	ON OCCASION	OFTEN
1. Depend on the undependable. (4, 6, 9)	☐	☐	☐
2. Rely on mental notes. (2, 4, 7, 9)	☐	☐	☐
3. Generally trust that all will go well. (2, 4, 6, 7)	☐	☐	☐
4. Consider mishaps unforeseeable. (2, 4, 6, 7, 8)	☐	☐	☐
5. Gamble that potential risks will not materialize. (4, 6, 7)	☐	☐	☐
6. Rely on a single source or system. (4, 6, 8, 9)	☐	☐	☐
7. Forego checking on expected tasks and events. (2, 4, 6, 7)	☐	☐	☐
8. Work outside mainstream medical guidelines. (1, 2, 3)	☐	☐	☐
9. Neglect maintenance of outdated skills and knowledge. (1, 6, 7)	☐	☐	☐
10. Take profit by compromising patient or public interest. (2, 5, 8)	☐	☐	☐
11. Avoid written confirmation of arrangements and discussions. (4, 6, 7)	☐	☐	☐
12. Allow patients to maintain mistaken impressions. (2, 3, 4, 7)	☐	☐	☐

For noted risks, consider approaches in Check-up Files numbered in parentheses.

	NEVER	ON OCCASION	OFTEN
13. Discuss patients, staff, and colleagues freely. (5, 9)	☐	☐	☐
14. Delegate responsibility liberally to assistants and staff. (6, 7)	☐	☐	☐
15. Trust that prescriptions are safe and effective. (4, 8)	☐	☐	☐

☐ Pattern for Safety

Rate each measure consistently followed in the practice.

	NEVER	ON OCCASION	OFTEN
1. Listen for the whole story	☐	☐	☐
2. Summarize what you've heard	☐	☐	☐
3. See what is there to be seen	☐	☐	☐
4. Confirm by surest method without harm . . .	☐	☐	☐
5. Know what you should know	☐	☐	☐
6. Know what you don't know	☐	☐	☐
7. Say everything important	☐	☐	☐
8. Ask what was understood	☐	☐	☐
9. Keep a copy of what you've heard	☐	☐	☐
10. Give a copy of what you've said	☐	☐	☐
11. Establish a reliable monitor	☐	☐	☐
12. Check later to assure all systems are go	☐	☐	☐
13. Check again even later—just because	☐	☐	☐
14. Reevaluate at any departure from the program	☐	☐	☐
15. Choose the optimal time for any action	☐	☐	☐

Compare risks noted from Top Ten Risks and Pattern for Risk with safety measures followed. Each safety measure can reduce risk in every area of practice.

☐ Management Questions

Rate your confidence in being able to answer the questions. Answers are part of the analysis that follows each Case Study in the Check-up Files.

Check-up File 1: Practice Scope

	DON'T KNOW	UNSURE	CONFIDENT
When is it time to call in more expertise?	☐	☐	☐
What standard is applied to practice outside qualifications?	☐	☐	☐
How and when may a physician utilize experimental treatment?	☐	☐	☐
Can a physician be a Good Samaritan in a hospital?	☐	☐	☐

Check-up File 2: Questioned Practice

	DON'T KNOW	UNSURE	CONFIDENT
What is reasonable knowledge and skill for the circumstances?	☐	☐	☐
Can a physician be wrong in the right way?	☐	☐	☐
When is a physician wrong in the wrong way?	☐	☐	☐
Has a physician offered the patient what medicine has to offer?	☐	☐	☐
When should a physician suspect that a diagnosis is mistaken?	☐	☐	☐

	DON'T KNOW	UNSURE	CONFIDENT
Can a reasonable diagnosis become unreasonable?	☐	☐	☐
How does a physician weigh differential diagnoses when one choice is personally embarrassing or inconvenient?	☐	☐	☐
Can risk-benefit judgment be right even if it is wrong?	☐	☐	☐
How much protection can a lab slip provide for a physician?	☐	☐	☐
When should lab values be considered suspect?	☐	☐	☐
What analytic process supports choices to delay or proceed to surgery?	☐	☐	☐
What knowledge and skill are required in general practice dealing with specialized care?	☐	☐	☐
When does reasonable medical method require diagnostic confirmation?	☐	☐	☐
What factors contribute to claims and questions about care?	☐	☐	☐

Check-up File 3: Patients and Nonpatients

	DON'T KNOW	UNSURE	CONFIDENT
What acts of "diagnosis" establish a physician–patient relationship?	☐	☐	☐
How many physicians can have a duty to treat a patient?	☐	☐	☐

	DON'T KNOW	UNSURE	CONFIDENT
How is transfer of care accomplished?	☐	☐	☐
How may a relationship with a patient in need of urgent treatment be terminated?	☐	☐	☐
Can a hospitalized patient be transferred to another physician's care?	☐	☐	☐
How is specialty care continued after termination?	☐	☐	☐
How is responsibility allocated between patient and physician?	☐	☐	☐
When must a patient's reports be considered suspect?	☐	☐	☐
What responsibility must a patient take for personal safety and health?	☐	☐	☐
What is the physician's duty to warn examinees of abnormal findings?	☐	☐	☐
Can a single examination impose duties to continue treatment?	☐	☐	☐
What duty is owed to nonpatients?	☐	☐	☐

	DON'T KNOW	UNSURE	CONFIDENT

Check-up File 4: Medical Communications

	DON'T KNOW	UNSURE	CONFIDENT
How does optimism differ from promise?	☐	☐	☐
How can physician and patient interests conflict?	☐	☐	☐
When is documented consent not consent?	☐	☐	☐
What is the standard to judge disclosures to patients?	☐	☐	☐
What circumstances justify therapeutic nondisclosure?	☐	☐	☐
Among specialists, who has a duty to disclose and discuss alternatives?	☐	☐	☐
When instructions do not succeed, whose fault is it?	☐	☐	☐
What constitutes reasonable instructions?	☐	☐	☐
How much instruction is needed for patient safety?	☐	☐	☐
Must all medical injuries be disclosed?	☐	☐	☐
How is reasonable misdiagnosis defensible?	☐	☐	☐

	DON'T KNOW	UNSURE	CONFIDENT
What function does recordkeeping perform in claims of malpractice?	☐	☐	☐
How can an operative note reflect nonnegligent injury?	☐	☐	☐
What constitutes a valid refusal of necessary treatment?	☐	☐	☐

Check-up File 5: Medical Disclosures

	DON'T KNOW	UNSURE	CONFIDENT
Does a patient waive confidentiality by suing a physician?	☐	☐	☐
What parts of the medical record should be released?	☐	☐	☐
What interests outweigh patient confidentiality?	☐	☐	☐
When may a physician begin to defend a potential malpractice suit?	☐	☐	☐
Are conservative evaluations of patient conditions for insurers a conflict of interest?	☐	☐	☐
Is a patient's name medical information?	☐	☐	☐
How does a physician comply with patient requests for partial release of record information?	☐	☐	☐

	DON'T KNOW	UNSURE	CONFIDENT
What is the duty of a physician to a patient seeking to misrepresent medical information?	☐	☐	☐

Check-up File 6: Office Support

	DON'T KNOW	UNSURE	CONFIDENT
How can staff support physician instructions to patients?	☐	☐	☐
Can a physician be responsible for failures of facility staff?	☐	☐	☐
May an assistant authorize routine prescriptions?	☐	☐	☐
When does staff practice medicine?	☐	☐	☐
How must staff protect patient privacy?	☐	☐	☐
What is the physician's responsibility to know what staff have been told?	☐	☐	☐

Check-up File 7: Other Providers

	DON'T KNOW	UNSURE	CONFIDENT
What is the importance of a patient's impression of the treatment team?	☐	☐	☐
What is the attending physician's duty to coordinate care?	☐	☐	☐
To what degree may a physician depend on the skills and knowledge of assistants or others?	☐	☐	☐

	DON'T KNOW	UNSURE	CONFIDENT
What is the physician's duty to check and assure that crucial instructions have been followed? . . .	☐	☐	☐
To what degree must a physician check on the work of other practitioners?	☐	☐	☐
What is a physician's duty to evaluate a consultant's advice?	☐	☐	☐
When is a consultant not a consultant?	☐	☐	☐
What capabilities or qualifications should be verified about referral physicians or facilities?	☐	☐	☐
What qualifications must a covering physician offer?	☐	☐	☐
Must a physician check personal characteristics in selecting a covering physician?	☐	☐	☐
Can responsibility for coverage be transferred to another physician?	☐	☐	☐
What capabilities are reasonable to require of coverage practice?	☐	☐	☐
What background or history is appropriate to assure appropriate covering care?	☐	☐	☐
What is a qualified substitute?	☐	☐	☐

	DON'T KNOW	UNSURE	CONFIDENT
What responsibilities in transferring care can be executed by an assistant?	☐	☐	☐
How can coverage monitoring be delegated to nonphysician staff? . . .	☐	☐	☐

Check-up File 8: Vendors and Suppliers

	DON'T KNOW	UNSURE	CONFIDENT
How do patients cause prescription errors?	☐	☐	☐
How does prescription practice pose risks to physicians?	☐	☐	☐
What prescriptions of controlled substances can be considered criminal acts?	☐	☐	☐
What prescriptions of controlled substances can be considered grounds for revocation of license to practice?	☐	☐	☐

Check-up File 9: Practice Setting

	DON'T KNOW	UNSURE	CONFIDENT
What is the responsibility of a physician for failures of hospital personnel?	☐	☐	☐
Does a physician have a right or a duty to control hospital employees?	☐	☐	☐
What must a physician do when payment is denied for necessary patient treatment?	☐	☐	☐

	DON'T KNOW	UNSURE	CONFIDENT
How can an agreement establish employee status or independent contract services?	☐	☐	☐
What process is used to select plan referral specialists?	☐	☐	☐

Check-up File 10: Claims and Legal Process

	DON'T KNOW	UNSURE	CONFIDENT
How can legal process mistakes be corrected?	☐	☐	☐
What physician conduct may invalidate a policy of liability coverage?	☐	☐	☐

Part 2

CHECK-UP FILES

Safeguarding Practice: Basic Approaches

Assure dependability of personal capability and technology, staff, and collegial support.

- ☐ First, expend effort in selection process of practice scope and staff to define functions and verify qualifications and experience.
- ☐ Second, initiate training/probation periods to monitor performance closely, with safety backups for failures and deficiencies.
- ☐ Third, allow verified function to proceed with periodic checks to assess continuing satisfactory performance.

Maximize early notice of changes or problems.

- ☐ First, establish monitors to alert practitioner and staff to signals of foreseeable problems.
- ☐ Second, activate alarms to prompt the earliest preventive or responsive action.
- ☐ Third, learn and choose appropriate actions to avoid or limit harmful consequences.

Take systematic action or control.

- ☐ First, define routine practice to follow for foreseeable events.
- ☐ Second, specify practice events that initiate changes in action to high control.
- ☐ Third, recognize when outside advice or resources are needed.

Check-up File

1 Practice Scope

Qualifications
Legal Requirements
Standards and Guidelines

Indefensible Risks

Unqualified, Outdated, Experimental, Illegal, or Inappropriate Practice

Practice Objectives

Competence, Conformity, Legality, Knowledgability

Pattern for Safety

Skills, Standards, Patient Selection, Monitoring and Review

Approaches to Medical Legal Safety

Management of Practice Scope and Competence

Cases

Limits of Expertise, Experimental Treatment, Volunteered Treatment

Indefensible Risks

Practice outside medical skills or knowledge
Outdated practice
Experimental practice without experimental protocols
Failure to obey laws
Unindicated, inappropriate, or ineffectual treatment

Practice Objectives

- ☐ **Objective:** Practice well within qualifications.

  Rationale: Patient incurs first consequences of lack of knowledge or skill.

- ☐ **Objective:** Relative conformity with respected guidelines.

  Rationale: Practice is confirmed by expert consensus and consultation.

- ☐ **Objective:** Knowledge of specific legal requirements.

  Rationale: Law represents recognition of specific problem and legal solution chosen.

Pattern for Safety

1. Conform practice to verifiable qualifications.
2. Maintain skills with current use.
3. Brush up infrequently used skills in training setting.
4. Design effective continuing and corrective medical education.
5. Act to match patient population to practice and qualifications.
6. Maintain practice within skills by patient selection.
7. Know range and content of guidelines applicable to practice.
8. Depart from protocols and parameters with confirmation.
9. Learn legal requirements applicable to medical practice.
10. Investigate journals and programs for qualification maintenance.
11. Monitor practice for idiosyncratic patterns of care.
12. Conduct unprovoked practice utilization and outcomes review.

Bottom Line: Exceed boundaries only with persuasive justification.

Approaches to Medical Legal Safety

Qualifications

Implicit in the ability to provide acceptable medical services is the documented preparation in knowledge and skills necessary to practice acceptable medicine. Specialization implies a concentration of higher levels of skill and knowledge in a narrowed focus. Qualifications must be maintained. Knowledge and skill have a finite shelf life and some "expiration date" should be observed related to the rate and pattern of change in the specialty.

Going through the motions of keeping up is not sufficient. Others in the profession may be solving similar practice problems. A coherent plan to maintain and expand skills and knowledge includes reading journals in the specific areas of practice, as well as others addressing significant diagnostic or therapeutic activities. Sources and references should be chosen by design, rather than by letting promotional activities influence the choice of continuing medical education (CME) through mailings or product "infomercial" programs.

Lead, do not follow, educational programs. Choose, do not just buy, journals. Consider cross-training by trans-specialty reading. Perspectives from other specialty "turf" will be presented as contrast when questions arise in adverse situations. Expand focus to quality and risk management articles to see what forces are at work to change practice field. Check pathology journals and research summaries to be prepared when a patient presents with confounding diagnostic problems.

Survey practice population and procedures. Before a practice can acquire the right educational material and programs, current and anticipated patient "pathographics" should be defined. Plan to brush up on or eliminate areas of minimal skill or therapeutic expertise. CME should focus on each significant population or pathology in the practice: adolescents, elderly, veterans, trauma, or chronic or infectious disease. Any procedures performed in practice should be continued with sufficient frequency. Advice on a cut-off number for too few procedures to be skillfully done should be considered as a warning to acquire more experience or drop the procedure. Continuing and renewal education are good insurance and will reflect credibility and confidence with patients; this education will support the physician when questions are asked.

Practice limits are best determined before patients seek treatment. These limits, with sound medical justification, can be clearly communicated to patients and others, eliminating the need to make scope-of-practice decisions more than once. Even appropriate-scope patients may be declined unless they are members of a group protected from discrimination. Any patient, even those protected from discrimination, may be refused for appropriate medical practice limitations applied uniformly.

Exceeding the limits of knowledge, skill, or preparation certainly risks adverse outcome. Practice beyond qualifications supports judgments of deficient practice because the standard applied to "stretched" practice is that of the higher-skill specialty. Nonradiologists, for example, do not read radiographs except for personal edification. Important and risky decisions to treat should have readings confirmed by the appropriate specialist.

Any experimental practice raises the duty of disclosure and consent to a higher level. If off-label medication or an innovative procedure or therapeutic regimen is used, the experimental model for disclosures, records, consents, and monitoring of patient care must be utilized. Patient problems that call for treatment outside the scope of practice expertise, unless an emergency makes inaction dangerous, are best managed by summoning practitioners with appropriate skills and knowledge to diagnose or treat.

Legal Requirements

Legal requirements reflect a history of problems that have prompted government to act. Most legal measures direct or forbid or require action, with penalties for failure to comply. Problems continue to arise and evolve, prompting more legal solutions. Compliance is possible only if the requirement is known; therefore, one periodic task must be to discover current legal mandates for medical practice in each jurisdiction in which practice is maintained. Twice yearly review will provide an adequate update on current legal requirements, and an annual review may suffice. Personal counsel, medical society legal or risk management publications, or even a competent law student can provide this type of information. Advice, however, should be sought from qualified counsel specializing in medical legal practice.

Examples of Legal Topics Relating to Medical Practice

Credentials: Licensure and conduct

Patients:
- Emergency care
- Accepting patients
- Consent to treatment
- Reports and disclosures
- Special patients
  - Reproduction patients
  - Child patients
  - Geriatric patients
  - Psychiatric patients
  - Terminal patients
  - Donor and donee patients
  - Fetal interests
- Special disorders, treatments
  - Communicable diseases
  - Dialysis
  - Mental and physical disability

Management:
- Contracts
- Agents and employees
- Dispute resolution
- Hospitals
- Managed care

Pharmaceutical products and devices
Group practice payment plans
Health maintenance organizations
Integrated care

Legal process: Malpractice liability
Risk management
Insurance
Civil disputes or trials
Deaths, bodies
Forensic medical evidence
Forensic pathology

Crimes, ethics: Fraud
Sexual misconduct
False claims
Conspiracy
Unprofessional conduct
Moral turpitude

Standards and Guidelines

In varying patterns of diagnosis and treatment, determination must be made of what is mainstream, what is exceptional, what is borderline, and what is unproved. Guidelines, parameters, and standards are not all created equal, but practice should take notice of any that are offered from a professionally credible source and accepted generally in the specialty. All current guides relevant to the practice must be acquired and evaluated. Priority can be assigned for adherence to those of highest validity. Political gestures in guidelines that primarily operate to maintain exclusive control of therapeutic areas should be distinguished from medically indicated recommendations.

Precise appreciation for the effectiveness and the limits of guidelines allows physicians to use sound discretion in advising medical decisions for patients. Patients are complex and may require exceptional programs of therapy. If nonmainstream treatment appears advisable, confirm with a more conservative practitioner. If a practitioner has many personal "rules of thumb" and individual therapeutic approaches, and mainstream practice is considered constricting, problems with colleagues, payers, utilization review, and patients can be anticipated.

Dedicate a "library" and plan acquisitions to serve defined needs of the practice. Make a curriculum plan for maintenance and improvements in qualifications and then match programs to the plan. For CME documentation and later reference for consultation, keep an education file of every program attended with lists of attenders and contacts. Choose either to vacation or to go to education programs. For travel expense savings, schedule both events back-to-back, but do not schedule simultaneously. Attend 50% national, 30% regional, and 20% local programs.

Examples of Update and Review Notes

Research Reports on Cancer, Cardiology, Malpractice, and Managed Care

Women with early-stage breast cancer, in which the cancer has not spread outside the breast, can almost always safely opt for a lumpectomy followed by radiation, rather than a mastectomy.
1994 National Cancer Institute workshop.

The two popular techniques for treating narrowed heart arteries—angioplasty and bypass surgery—are equally effective in treating (with noted drawbacks or limitations) more than one constricted artery, according to two separate studies.
1994 New England Journal of Medicine.

Slightly increasing the dosage of heparin during the common heart attack almost doubles a patient's risk of stroke.
1994 Circulation.

A group of blood pressure experts assert that US guidelines concerning which drugs physicians should use to treat high blood pressure severely restrict physicians' ability to treat patients. An

advisory panel of the National Institutes of Health recommends that physicians should first try treating hypertension patients with either a diuretic drug or a beta-blocker. Experts argue that the guidelines discourage the use of newer classes of drugs called angiotensin-constricting enzyme inhibitors and calcium-channel blockers, which may work better and with fewer side effects.
1994 American Journal of Hypertension.

Two studies suggest that physicians are more likely to be sued if patients feel they are rude, rush visits, fail to answer questions, or behave in other ways perceived by the patients as insensitive. Both of the studies were done by physicians from Vanderbilt University in Nashville. The first study analyzed 963 obstetric cases to find out what made patients unhappy with their medical care. The other study looked at the relationship between obstetricians with a history of malpractice claims and the quality of the clinical care they provided to patients 5 to 10 years after those claims were filed.
1994 Journal of the American Medical Association.

Two reports regarding heart attack patient care are said to raise new concerns over the managed-care strategy of expanding the role of primary-care physicians in treating many diseases and curbing the use of specialists. In one report, researchers found that primary-care physicians are less informed about and less likely to prescribe effective drugs for heart attack patients than cardiologists and are more likely to order medicines that are not proved to work. In the other report, scientists found that Canadian patients reported being in poorer health than similar US patients a year after having a heart attack. Among other things, the Canadian patients had fewer "high-tech" procedures and less access to heart specialists than did the Americans.
1994 New England Journal of Medicine.

Most women who suffer ectopic pregnancies can be treated without surgery if the problem is diagnosed early enough, according to researchers.
1994 Annual Meeting of the American Fertility Society.

Utilization Review Criteria to Assess Medical Necessity

There is significant variability in the appropriateness review criteria used by Medicare Peer Review Organizations (PROs) to authorize physicians to perform procedures. Forty-eight PROs cover 54 geographic jurisdictions, with each responsible for developing procedure-specific, explicit review criteria. Practice parameters developed by the specialty organizations have been used as reference points for PRO criteria. However, there is wide variability in PRO review criteria and significant differences between the review criteria and many nationally developed practice parameters.

Guideline and Practice Criteria Development Examples

American Medical Association, RAND, and Academic Medical Center Consortium Clinical Appropriateness Studies address: cataract surgery, aortic aneurysm surgery, carotid endarterectomy, coronary bypass surgery, coronary angioplasty, abdominal ultrasound, cholecystectomy, lower extremity bypass graft, electrocardiography, hip replacement, prostatectomy, and laminectomy.

American College of Physicians Clinical Efficacy Assessment Program offers over 70 guidelines covering diagnostic testing, uses of medical technologies, procedures and vaccines, and issues in health policy.

American College of Cardiology Practice Guidelines address clinical intracardiac electrophysiologic studies, ambulatory electrocardiography, percutaneous transluminal coronary angioplasty, coronary angiography, clinical use of cardiac radionuclide imaging, exercise testing, permanent cardiac pacemaker implantation, early management of patients with acute myocardial infarction, coronary artery bypass graft surgery, emergency department management of angina patients, and clinical application of echocardiography.

American Academy of Ophthalmology Preferred Practice Patterns address comprehensive adult eye evaluation, primary open-angle glaucoma, diabetic retinopathy, and cataracts in otherwise healthy eyes.

American Academy of Family Physicians Clinical Policies for Patient Care address antepartum oxytocin privileges, detection and treatment of breast cancer, and others.

RAND Corporation Appropriateness Standards address coronary angioplasty, coronary artery bypass graft surgery, cholecystectomy, upper gastrointestinal endoscopy, colonoscopy, and carotid endarterectomy.

Harvard Community Health Plan clinical algorithms (decision trees) subjects are internal medicine, pediatrics and child mental health, obstetrics and gynecology, and adult mental health.

Blue Cross/Blue Shield Association Medical Necessity Program has Clinical Laboratory Guidelines for diagnostic procedures.

Blue Cross/Blue Shield Association Medical Necessity Guidelines for routine diagnostic testing use Interqual's Intensity of Service/ Severity of Illness guidelines for utilization review and American Psychiatric Association criteria for psychiatric and substance abuse.

Blues Plus Utilization review criteria use Value Health Sciences' approach to review appropriateness.

Aetna Guidelines address outpatient and inpatient procedures, including cataracts, bunionectomy, heart bypass, hysterectomy, prostatectomy, and tonsillectomy.

Provident Life and Accident utilization review criteria for precertification, continued stay and screens for appropriate discharges, inpatient and outpatient medical and surgical procedures and admissions use Interqual's Intensity of Services/Severity of Illness, Surgical Indications Monitoring (SIM III).

Value Health Sciences medical appropriateness criteria address inpatient and outpatient procedures, including spinal fusion operations, hysterectomy, tonsillectomy, cataract extraction, and computed tomography scans.

Societies Publishing Practice Parameters

American Academy of Allergy and Immunology
American Academy of Child and Adolescent Psychiatry
American Academy of Dermatology
American Academy of Family Physicians
American Academy of Ophthalmology
American Academy of Orthopaedic Surgery
American Academy of Otolaryngology–Head and Neck Surgery
American Academy of Pediatrics
American Association of Electromyography and Electrodiagnosis
American College of Cardiology
American College of Emergency Physicians
American College of Obstetricians and Gynecologists
American College of Occupational Medicine
American College of Physicians
American College of Preventive Medicine
American College of Radiology
American College of Rheumatology
American College of Surgeons
American Geriatric Society
American Medical Association
American Psychiatric Association
American Society for Gastrointestinal Endoscopy
American Society of Anesthesiologists
American Thoracic Society
American Urological Association
College of American Pathologists

The American Medical Association tracks development and completion of practice parameters. The information collected by this tracking system is published quarterly in the Practice Parameters Update which includes a section, "Recently Withdrawn Practice Parameters." The section indicates if the withdrawn practice parameter was replaced with another practice parameter, provides the name of the sponsoring organization, and lists a contact person if additional information is needed.

Cases

When Is It Time to Call in More Expertise?

An operating surgeon was about to begin an elective procedure when it became apparent that the Bovie unit was not functioning properly. The surgeon instructed a nurse to try several connections and manipulate numerous controls and settings. When function appeared restored, the surgery was begun. Midway through the procedure, the unit malfunctioned again, with some injury to the patient. Questions about the injury and complications from the surgery were raised. The surgeon was accused of disregard for patient safety by tinkering with a dangerous medical device and proceeding to operate with a hazardous instrument. The hospital claimed the nurse was acting at the surgeon's direction and was not working for the hospital at the time. It was entirely possible that the Bovie could have operated correctly through the entire surgery, but it did not. The surgeon made the choice to risk its malfunction and to use the instrument; that risk materialized and the patient's injury harmed the surgeon as well. Risks of patient interest should not be made without informing the patient and letting the patient take the risk of adverse consequences. No surgeon would ask the patient if surgery should proceed with a faulty instrument; a rare patient would agree if asked, unless some dire alternative made the choice of the faulty Bovie reasonable. No consideration was apparent to make such a choice reasonable here.

The surgeon should have limited practice to surgery and allowed the maintenance and repair of instruments to be done by someone qualified and employed for that task. To inspect and to check was entirely appropriate; to direct an unqualified person to do tasks without qualified direction was very unwise and a negligent failure of medical judgment.

What Standard Is Applied to Practice Outside Qualifications?

A man sustained a gunshot wound in his thigh while on a hunting trip. He was taken to a community hospital where he was examined by a general surgeon who determined that there was injury to the patient's femoral artery. Although the surgeon had no specialized training in vascular surgery, he did not consult with a vascular surgeon about care of the patient's injury. Instead, he anastomosed the severed femoral artery by grafting it with a portion of the saphenous vein. He did not perform a preoperative arteriogram to determine if a thrombus was obstructing circulation of the femoral artery. Circulation was not restored by the operation; therefore, the surgeon performed a second vein graft that was also unsuccessful because of a preoperative arterial thrombosis. As a result of the surgeon's failure to perform a thrombectomy, amputation was required. The man then sued the surgeon for failure to consult a vascular surgeon.

If the general surgeon had substantial clinical experience in managing vascular injuries, his need to obtain consultation would have been lessened. Ordinarily it will not be presumed that a physician who is trained in a certain general area, such as surgery, has the knowledge and experience to adequately manage a patient's specialized problem. Failure to discover the thrombus by use of an arteriogram or some other appropriate diagnostic procedure was indicative of the general surgeon's lack of experience in managing vascular injuries. Under the circumstances, the surgeon had a duty to consult a specialist.

How and When May a Physician Use Experimental Treatment?

A 7-year-old girl had a bike accident in which she sustained a deep laceration to her left leg. Her family practitioner determined that an emergency repair of the laceration was necessary and that local anesthesia would be inadequate. He telephoned the hospital and requested an anesthesiologist. Because of the weekend schedule, an anesthesiologist was not available. Rather than transfer the patient to a neighboring facility where another physician would have to treat her, the physician decided to use intravenous regional anesthesia (IVRA), a technique he had not previously used. He based the decision on recollections from a booklet published by the pharmaceutical company which made lidocaine (Xylocaine). IVRA is a technique in which an entire limb is anesthetized, and a pneumatic cuff is applied to prevent the lidocaine (Xylocaine), which is injected into a vein, from flowing to other parts of the body.

In the operating room, the physician raised the patient's leg so the blood would drain away from the vein injection site. A nurse applied the cuff which was then inflated. The physician performed a saphenous vein cutdown, inserted a catheter, and injected 20 cc of 1% lidocaine (Xylocaine) over approximately 10 minutes. A minute or two later the child had a seizure. The physician assumed the patient was having respiratory failure. In fact, she was exhibiting a toxic reaction to the lidocaine (Xylocaine). The surgeon's diagnosis of the complication was mistaken because he was unaware of the "flow-back" phenomenon associated with IVRA in which lidocaine (Xylocaine) crosses the tourniquet barrier in children. Although the physician initially managed to control the seizures, the seizures resumed when he removed the pneumatic cuff. As a result, the patient sustained permanent brain damage.

As a result of the malpractice case arising from this treatment, the physician's insurer canceled malpractice coverage, barring him from obtaining or maintaining staff privileges at reputable hospitals. The physician sued the pharmaceutical company for laying a "malpractice trap" for him, by enticing him to undertake an experimental treatment and for failure to provide him with adequate warning. A study of electrocardiogram-monitored cases emphasized the risk of lidocaine (Xylocaine) leaking by the tourniquet with resulting cardiotoxic effects, and recommended the technique be abandoned.

After the initial promotion, the company had promoted prilocaine (Citanest) in a mailing to 65,000 physicians as superior to lidocaine (Xylocaine) for regional anesthesia because it was safer. The U.S. Food and Drug Administration directed the company to mail "Dear Doctor" letters stating the procedure was still regarded as experimental, but permitted the company to notify only the 65,000 physicians who had received the Citanest brochure. Although the general practitioner recalled the original brochure, he did not receive the prilocaine (Citanest) mailing and therefore did not receive a letter of warning about the experimental and hazardous nature of this mode of anesthesia.

This physician ignored many warning signs. Without appropriate anesthesia support, referral of the procedure was indicated to an appropriate and fully staffed facility. Not only was the physician working beyond his qualifications, he was in the area of experimental anesthesia. Unless a frank emergency requires that caution be thrown to the winds, caution is required for patient and physician safety.

Can a Physician Be a Good Samaritan in a Hospital?

Several hours after gynecologic surgery, a patient appeared to be having a type of seizure. The page operator broadcast a call for any physician available. An obstetrician on the floor above was not on call for emergencies and was not a member of the hospital cardiopulmonary resuscitation (CPR) team. He also had no previous physician–patient relationship with the patient. At the beeper alarm, he spoke to the page operator and dashed to the floor below where the nurse guided him into the patient's room. There he observed the patient having a grand mal seizure. He injected Valium into the patient's intravenous tubing to control the seizure. The seizure activity stopped but shortly thereafter the patient was noted to be without a pulse. The obstetrician began external cardiac massage and called for a CPR team. Despite the efforts of the team, the patient could not be revived. The patient's estate sued the obstetrician for malpractice, and an expert medical witness opined that the obstetrician's response to the patient's seizure fell below the standard of care. The obstetrician contended that he was protected by the state's "Good Samaritan" statute which stated that "No licensed physician, who in good faith renders emergency care at the scene of the emergency, shall be liable for any civil damages as a result of any of his acts or omissions in rendering the emergency care." The plaintiff claimed the "Good Samaritan" statute did not apply to hospital emergencies.

The Good Samaritan statute applied to emergency care at "the scene of the emergency." Thus it did not preclude a hospital setting. Whether this physician's response to an emergency in a hospital should be protected under the "Good Samaritan" law depends on whether he already owed a duty to respond. If he did not, the need to encourage physicians to render emergency medical care, when they otherwise might not, would prevail over the right of a victim of malpractice to sue for damages. The physician was not on call for emergencies, was not a member of the hospital CPR team, and did not have a previous physician–patient relationship with the patient. Therefore, his response to the emergency situation was as a volunteer and protected under the "Good Samaritan" statute.

Check-up File

2 Questioned Practice

Standards of Practice
Learning from Questioned Care

Indefensible Risks

Unsought Data, Ignorance, Poor Judgment, Self-Interest, Inflexibility

Practice Objectives

Medical Method, Attention, Competence, Direction, Coherence, Anticipation

Pattern for Safety

Professional Conduct, Judgment Priorities, Qualified Method, Reevaluation, Practice Assessment and Review, Growth and Change

Approaches to Medical Legal Safety

Learning Risk-Limiting Methods and Standards from Questioned Care

Cases

Reasonable Knowledge, Method, Skills, Suspicions. Review and Confirmation of Judgment, Testing, Specialized Care, Responses to Adverse Outcomes

Indefensible Risks

Failure to seek important data at patient history
Mistake of medical fact
Inability to correctly weigh available data
Unreasonable choice of delay or haste to serve physician interest
Unwillingness to reevaluate diagnosis or treatment

Practice Objectives

☐ **Objective:** Diagnostic process by the current standards.

Rationale: Misdiagnosis is understandable and nonnegligent if acceptable method is used.

☐ **Objective:** No failures of attention or documentation.

Rationale: Physician lapse is always substandard care.

☐ **Objective:** No practice outside qualifications.

Rationale: A physician must know limits of expertise.

☐ **Objective:** Continued focus on patient treatment and patient interest.

Rationale: Physician interests in care obscure objectivity.

☐ **Objective:** Appropriate and available data are gathered and assessed.

Rationale: Even when mistaken, coherence is defensible.

☐ **Objective:** Every preventable adverse outcome is avoided.

Rationale: No injury, no claim.

Pattern for Safety

1. Avoid all acts considered grounds for license revocation.
2. Assess whether knowledge and skills are sufficient for cases presented in practice.
3. Err on the least harmful side for the patient, no matter what else is involved.
4. Reevaluate and confirm diagnoses and treatment regimens routinely.
5. When diagnosis remains unclear or therapy is not effective, reevaluate data and conclusions.
6. Fit all history, findings, tests, and pathology into coherent analysis.
7. Whenever the physician's interest competes with the patient's, overcompensate on patient side.
8. Support all important choices to act with confirming findings if possible.
9. Obtain clear instructions in limited management role of special problems.
10. When deviation from expectations occurs, reevaluate from early presentation.
11. Trust consultant advice but verify.
12. Seek lessons from which to learn how to maximize medical effectiveness.
13. Seek lessons from which to learn how to prevent patient injuries.
14. Frankly compare practice habits with reports of preventable injuries.

Bottom Line: If possible, be right; if not, be wrong in the right way.

Approaches to Medical Legal Safety

Standards of Practice

The standard by which medical practice is judged remains: What would a reasonable physician be expected to know and to do under the specific circumstances presented? Questionable care is much more prevalent than questioned care. Most questioned care is resolved in favor of the physician. The object is to prevent questionable care, and to foreclose questions about acceptable care.

Clinical practice lessons can be learned from cases of questioned care reported by many sources. Medical societies draw on expert members for practice guidelines, parameters, standards, and consensus reports, including reports of improper practice and outcomes evaluation. Publishers use experts to provide reports of questioned care for physicians and attorneys dealing in medical issues.

Medical licensing boards have accessible reports of misconduct and malpractice. Insurers have files of meritorious and unmeritorious claims of negligent medical care. Pharmaceutical and medical device companies, the government, and the private health care business sector also research and report medical cases.

Learn the right lessons from histories of adverse medical legal cases. Case reports of questioned care have their flaws. Accounts by medical sources often reinforce reactionary fear and loathing of physicians for legal process, and may selectively report egregious cases of persecution of appropriate physician practice. Lessons learned from such stories direct physician attention away from clinical care improvement and toward manipulating encounters to avoid being a victim of patients and attorneys.

Corrections should fit the problem. With appropriate sensibility, the right lessons can be learned from cases of questioned care. Closed claims reports from insurers often compile data from which nothing of clinical value can be learned: "524 out of 1028 primary care claims closed with payment were filed by parents of children under 12 years old, with 200 for children under 7." Nothing can be learned from such factoids. Reports of dollar amounts claimed and jury verdicts likewise teach no medical lessons other than the financial exposure average for a specialty practice.

Stories of medical mishaps often do not distinguish what lesson should be gained from the events. Distinct types of practice failure by physicians and others involved in patient care are recognizable: Lapses, Lacks, Limits, Legalities.

THE LAPSE: someone knew better but did not do better

THE LACK: knowledge or skill insufficient to task presented

THE LIMIT: impairment or disability hinders acceptable practice

THE LEGALITY: actions in violation of specific rules

LAPSES: failures of attention or judgment require correction in motivation, method, or support. Habits are difficult to change, but represent correctable practice.

Failures in	Correction
Attention, Attendance	Monitoring Incentives, Penalties
Diagnostic Process	Analytic and Management Support Conferees and References Proctorship
Documentation	Technical Support, Incentives Penalties

Tools: accountability, checking, redundancy, fail-safe procedures, backup confirmation.

LACKS: failures of knowledge or skill. These deficits are relatively clear and correctable by education and application of learning skills.

Failures in	Correction
Medical Competence	Practice Limits, Revocations
Knowledge, Specialization	Education, Requalification
Skills, Technique	Retraining, Requalification
Communication	Education, Technical Support

Tools: insight, education, training, practice, testing, vigilance, monitoring.

LIMITS: failures of personal capability by involuntary or willful impairment or disability. Willful problems are correctable only with great difficulty and accommodation in all other facets of professional and personal life. Medical impairments can be recognized but must be accommodated without risk or burden to the patient.

Failures in	Correction
Responsibility	Discipline or Disqualification Termination of Activity
Capability	Compensation for Limitation

Tools: restriction to safe practice, rehabilitation, reeducation, requalification.

LEGALITIES: failures of personal choice. These offenses are not notably correctable unless addressed at the first and single instance.

Failures in	Correction
Financial Responsibility	Discipline & Restitution &
Social Responsibility	Disqualification &

Substance Responsibility	Major Civil/Criminal Penalties
Moral Responsibility	

Tools: social-moral awakening and rebirth or perpetual monitoring and punishment.

Learning from Questioned Care

At a minimum, no physician conduct can be defensible if it is unprofessional conduct or grounds for revocation of license to practice medicine. Typical grounds for disciplinary action include:

Unprofessional or dishonorable conduct
Employing any person to solicit patients
Representing to a patient that incurable sickness, disease, or injury can be cured
Obtaining any fee by fraud or misrepresentation
Willfully or negligently divulging a professional secret
Conviction of any offense punishable by incarceration
Habitual or excessive use of intoxicants, drugs, or controlled substances
Fraud or misrepresentation in applying for license to practice
Aiding the practice of medicine by a person not licensed
Using "Dr.," "MD," or "Doctor" in commercial exploitation of any goods, wares, or merchandise
Adjudication of insanity or mental disease or voluntary commitment for treatment or determined by impartial psychiatrists
Gross negligence or repeated negligence in the practice of medicine
Clear incapacity to practice medicine
Suspension or revocation by another state of a license to practice
Failing to report the change of the location of practice
Making a fraudulent claim

Many major practical deficiencies are said to lead to claims of questioned care, some as medically trivial as rudeness or appearance of unconcerned. These "symptoms" may actually reflect more serious underlying practice problems and failures, such as substandard medical process or lack of thorough attention to detail, which actually do cause adverse outcomes, and motivate patients to seek not just compensation, but satisfaction.

Claims can indicate areas of correctable practice. For example, a closed claim study documented malpractice claims against emergency physicians. In all cases, the allegation was failure to diagnose a medical or surgical problem. More than 87% of cases involved chest pain, abdominal pain, wounds, fractures, pediatric fever/meningitis, aortic aneurysm, cerebral and central spinal bleeding, or epiglottitis. Clinical guidelines for the evaluation of these high-risk areas were developed. Of the 87% high-risk claims, it was estimated by physician reviewers that 20% to 45% would have been preventable by the application of high-risk clinical guidelines. If applied, they would have saved patient lives and almost $12 million spent on defending and compensating preventable claims.

A colon cancer study by the Physician Insurers Association of America reported in its data-sharing program showed that claims involving malignant neoplasms of the colon and rectum resulted in indemnity payments of more than $41 million in 1990. The study focused on cases for which an indemnity payment was made for failure to diagnose cancer of the colon. In half of all cases, failure to perform an indicated endoscopic examination was the major reason for delay in diagnosis attributed to the physician. Almost three quarters of all cases were for cancers anatomically diagnosable by using sigmoidoscopy. This indicates a need for increased willingness to advise and perform studies when a suspicion of problem exists. In one third of cases, there was a failure to respond to symptoms or to key indicators, bleeding, change in bowel habits, anemia, and weight loss. A family history of colon cancer was not sought by the treating physician in more than half of the cases, a serious deficiency in history taking, regardless of the patient's complaints.

Cases

What Is Reasonable Knowledge and Skill for the Circumstances?

An infant was repeatedly abused by her mother's boyfriend. When she was 14 months old, her mother took her to the hospital where a spiral fracture of the tibia and fibula was diagnosed. The mother had no explanation for this injury. The infant also had contusions and abrasions. A linear skull fracture was undetected. The infant demonstrated fear and apprehension when approached. The emergency department physician discharged the infant from the hospital, thus returning her to continuing intentional injury by her mother's boyfriend. At 17 months of age the infant was brought to a different physician who immediately diagnosed "battered child syndrome" and reported it to local authorities. The infant was taken into protective custody, hospitalized, and placed with foster parents. After her mother's boyfriend was convicted of child abuse, the infant's guardian sued the first physician, alleging that diagnostic investigation of the infant's condition should have included skeletal radiographs that would have disclosed her fractured skull. The guardian contended that the physician had not properly diagnosed the cause of the infant's condition. If the physician had applied appropriate diagnostic methods, he would have suspected that the infant's injuries were associated with the battered child syndrome. This would have led to placement of the infant in protective custody until her safety was assured.

The physician had a duty to become aware of the facts and circumstances surrounding the patient's condition. He was expected to collect necessary data in a careful, thorough, and organized manner. The physician was required to exhibit the knowledge and skill ordinarily possessed and exercised by other physicians in similar circumstances. This standard of care included that he know how to diagnose the battered child syndrome. A reasonably prudent physician examining this patient would have suspected that she was a victim of "battering" from the injuries and circumstances presented, and would have confirmed that clinical impression by ordering skeletal radiographs. Even without diagnostic studies suggestive of battered child syndrome, the physician could have reported the suspicion to appropriate authorities to prevent further injuries to the child. If fear of controversy prompted the failure to acknowledge the infant's injuries, an even more serious failure had been committed. It is to counter this reluctance that immunity for reporting suspicion of abuse is granted.

Can a Physician Be Wrong in the Right Way?

A mother found her 2-year-old son playing with an empty aspirin bottle and assumed he had ingested the contents. Hours later the child became ill. The father took him to the hospital and told the nurse's aide about the aspirin. The father, however, did not tell the physician about the aspirin even though the physician asked if the child had eaten any medication. The physician diagnosed "croup" and sent the child home. Shortly thereafter the child died as a result of salicylate poisoning. The parents sued the physician, alleging that he had negligently failed to discover the possibility of aspirin ingestion. They contended that the father's failure to alert the physician to possible aspirin ingestion was irrelevant because the physician had a duty to discover relevant data on which to formulate a clinical diagnosis.

The physician was not negligent, because the father failed to inform and advise the physician about the child's aspirin ingestion. Under the circumstances the physician asked but could not have been expected to use information that was never revealed. When matters material to the diagnosis are not disclosed despite the physician's inquiry, misdiagnosis is ordinarily not considered to be the result of negligence. This parent may not have understood the question about medication to include aspirin.

When Is a Physician Wrong in the Wrong Way?

While her mother had the "flu," a 15-month-old child ingested adult aspirin tablets while unobserved by her parents. The child's father took the mother to her physician for treatment and on his return home he was told that his daughter had developed vomiting and diarrhea. The father observed that the child was blue around the lips and breathing deeply. Therefore, he took the child to the physician who had treated the child's mother. The physician noted that the child was "hyperventilating," but that the remainder of the examination was normal. Because the child's mother had just been found to have a viral infection, the physician diagnosed the child's condition as "flu" and prescribed one baby aspirin every 4 hours, a then-permissible prescription. During the night the child was extremely restless and crying. The father took the child to a hospital the next morning where a physician took a blood sample which demonstrated markedly high salicylate level. Despite heroic measures to save the child, she died. Her parents sued the initial treating physician.

The clinical presentation of the patient should have indicated to the physician that the information he received was either inaccurate or incomplete, that it did not "agree" with observed or reported signs. Thus he had a duty to conduct further diagnostic investigation to reconcile these disparate findings. Expert medical testimony established that the child's hyperventilation when she was initially examined should have alerted the physician to the existence of some problem other than the "flu," prompting investigation of the cause of the other problem. The physician was required to investigate further the facts and circumstances of the child's condition because the clinical presentation should have alerted him to the existence of a more serious problem than the same illness as the mother.

Has a Physician Offered the Patient What Medicine Has to Offer?

A woman gave birth to a child with polycystic kidneys who died shortly after birth. When she inquired of her obstetrician about the advisability of future pregnancies, he told her that she did not have any reason to fear that a future pregnancy would result in the birth of another child with congenital defects. Even though there was some genetic likelihood that pregnancy would again result in a child being born with polycystic disease, the physician did not perform tests to ascertain the genetic makeup of the patient and her husband or to rationally ascertain the probability that a subsequent child would be so afflicted. Instead, he told the parents that polycystic kidney disease was not hereditary, without having researched or investigated relevant and available medical information concerning the hereditary nature of polycystic kidney disease. Relying on this advice, the woman became pregnant and delivered a child who was also born with polycystic kidneys. As a result, she and her husband sued the obstetrician, contending that had they been properly advised of the risks of abnormality, they would have elected to terminate the pregnancy.

The physician was negligent because, during the prenatal examination, he negligently failed to evaluate and detect the probability of occurrence of a well-recognized genetic defect in the child. The physician made representations with the pretense of knowledge and did not provide correct factual medicine for the patient's case. If the physician had advised the parents of the risk of bearing a genetically defective child, and of the availability of tests for detecting the disorder, such tests would have revealed the defect, and the parents could have decided to proceed or interrupt the pregnancy.

When Should a Physician Suspect That a Diagnosis Is Mistaken?

An oral surgeon noted an abscess surrounding a mandibular molar that he extracted. Radiographs disclosed destruction of the bone underlying the tooth. The next month, the surgeon observed that the tooth socket was not healing properly. When the tissue within the extraction site bled easily, the surgeon ordered tests to determine if a blood dyscrasia might be affecting the patient's healing. These test results turned out to be negative. He did not perform a tissue biopsy of the extraction site. Over the next 2 months, the tooth next to the extraction site became loose and required extraction; that tissue also did not heal properly and bled easily when probed. Additional radiographs disclosed bone destruction. He prescribed antibiotics for presumed osteomyelitis and took a cytologic smear of the affected area, the results of which were reported as negative. The surgeon did not order a tissue biopsy because he feared that the biopsy incision might possibly cause the infection to spread if the patient had osteomyelitis. During the next few weeks the patient was treated twice by the surgeon for serious hemorrhaging from the base of the socket. Two months later, the surgeon observed a gingival mass; a biopsy of the mass was done, disclosing poorly differentiated epidermoid carcinoma. Surgical and radiation treatments were unsuccessful, and the patient died of the cancer. The patient's estate sued the surgeon for negligent delay in the diagnosis of the patient's cancer. The surgeon contended there were no apparent signs of a gingival tumor before the biopsy, and therefore it was unreasonable to expect him to have diagnosed the cancer earlier.

Certain events should alert a reasonable physician that the clinical picture is not coherent. The analytic "look-again loop" of reexamination was called for when the patient's diagnosis remained in doubt. The physician was required to perform definitive diagnostic investigation to arrive at a reasonably effective treatment plan. There were signs of cancer much earlier, and thus the absence of a visible tumor in and of itself did not relieve the surgeon of negligence. Although the surgeon was aware that some underlying condition was causing the patient's extraction site not to heal properly, he made an insufficient and inadequate attempt to diagnose the cause of this continuing abnormal condition. Although he suspected a systemic problem early on, the surgeon persisted in treatment of osteomyelitis at a time when tissue biopsy would have disclosed the cancer. The method chosen by the surgeon for diagnosis was inadequate. A cytologic smear was not a definitive diagnostic method under circumstances in which other clinical findings are suggestive of cancer. Therefore, to arrive at a definite diagnosis, a tissue biopsy should have been done. The fear of spreading infection was an insufficient reason for not doing a biopsy. The surgeon did not begin treatment for osteomyelitis until 2 and one-half months after he knew there was some underlying cause for delayed healing. Had he embarked on a "therapeutic trial" or course of treatment for osteomyelitis earlier, his patient's lack of response to this treatment would have been highly suggestive of the need to reevaluate the diagnosis and would probably have led to an earlier discovery of the cancer.

Can a Reasonable Diagnosis Become Unreasonable?

No abnormalities were noted by this child's family physician at her 6-week checkup. At 6 months of age, her parents became concerned that she seemed listless, slow growing, and pale. Because of the mother's concern over the child's lack of growth, at 10 months of age the infant was examined by a pediatrician. The pediatrician noted the growth lag on the growth chart, but attributed it to the fact that the mother was a small-statured person. He diagnosed iron deficiency anemia and prescribed oral iron. On the next visit the hemoglobin had risen from 8.8 to 9.1 g; but on the third visit it was 8.6 g. Assuming that the child was not absorbing iron adequately, the pediatrician prescribed iron injections on subsequent visits. On the sixth and last visit at 14 months of age, the child's hemoglobin level had risen to 9.9 g. The physician told the mother that the child's blood count would eventually be back to normal. At 16 months of age the child's condition was diagnosed as congenital hypothyroidism. Appropriate treatment restored her to normal physical development, but it was then too late to restore her mental development. As a result, she is mentally retarded and will never be able to live independently. The parents sued the pediatrician on behalf of the child.

Although this child did not have the classic symptoms and stigmata of cretinism, she did have retarded growth and development. The pediatrician's growth chart signaled a "growth deficiency," which created an obligation to investigate the cause of the deficiency, including tests that would disclose a thyroid deficiency before irreversible effects of mental function occurred. Either the chart was not kept properly or not properly interpreted for significance to the diagnosis. The physician negligently failed to establish or use a data profile to detect developmental deviations early enough to prevent permanent morbidity. These data have become a professional standard; therefore, the physician was required to carefully assess this collected information. The data pattern generated by the growth chart should have been analyzed as an aid to diagnose the patient's problems. Thus the physician's ignorance of this data was negligent.

How Does a Physician Weigh Differential Diagnoses When One Choice Is Personally Embarrassing or Inconvenient?

A patient had been hospitalized several times for treatment of chronic pelvic inflammatory disease. Finally she underwent a total hysterectomy. The disease process had so distorted the location and position of her genitourinary organs that the gynecologist was unable to locate and protect the right ureter. As a result, the ureter was inadvertently sutured during surgery. On the second postoperative day the patient was febrile and complained of right flank pain and tenderness. The gynecologist recorded that these symptoms indicated either a kidney infection or a blockage of the ureter. He noted that an intravenous pyelogram might be indicated. Instead, he decided to treat for kidney infection with antibiotics. He did not consult a urologist or have the intravenous pyelogram performed until the sixth postoperative day. At that time an intravenous pyelogram was performed, disclosing a compromised right ureter. By that time, however, the ureter was so deteriorated that it became necessary to rebuild it. Subsequently, the ureter became blocked and it was necessary to perform a nephrectomy. The patient sued the gynecologist for loss of her kidney.

Here, the diagnostic problem was a surgical complication. While ureter damage at surgery may have been nonnegligent, failure to promptly identify and manage the complication was negligent. There is a sharp distinction between an error of judgment and negligence in the obtaining of factual data essential to arriving at a proper diagnosis. If a physician, as in this case, does not use available tests and procedures to reasonably formulate a diagnosis, the result is not a mere error of judgment, but negligence. Also suspect is the delay in requesting consultation. The physician would have preferred the complication to be infection.

Can Risk-Benefit Judgment Be Right Even If It Is Wrong?

A college student injured in an automobile accident was taken to a hospital where he was attended by a surgeon for fractured ribs and sternum. A chest tube was inserted to drain the fluid that had accumulated in his thoracic cavity. His initial radiograph of the chest disclosed no increase in fluid. Therefore the surgeon felt that the probability of serious mediastinal injury was so minimal that he could not justify subjecting the patient to invasive diagnostic studies, such as an aortogram. In addition, the patient's clinical condition had improved such that he insisted on being allowed to return to college. At the time of discharge his surgeon told him to select a physician in his college town and have that physician call the surgeon. After returning to college, the patient did not consult a physician even though he continued to experience chest pain. Several weeks later, the progression and persistence of pain caused him to consult a physician; that physician examined him and referred him to a cardiovascular surgeon who admitted him to a medical center for immediate surgery. During the operation the aorta ruptured, resulting in uncontrollable hemorrhage and death. The patient's mother sued the surgeon who attended her son immediately after the automobile accident. She contended that an aortogram should have been performed during her son's hospitalization to diagnose the traumatic aortic aneurysm.

Although the surgeon was not required to exhaust all diagnostic procedures in caring for the patient, he chose not to use a potentially beneficial procedure. Therefore, the surgeon would be expected to be able to explain why its use was unwarranted under the circumstances, or why alternative means chosen to manage the patient's condition were reasonable. His justification and choice of treatment should take into account the condition of the patient, and his clinical progress or lack of it. Although an aortogram may be a definitive diagnostic procedure to detect an aortic aneurysm, it is inherently hazardous and should be performed only if clinical findings warrant it. Thus, under the circumstances of this case, an aortogram was reasonably rejected based on its hazard and the absence of clinical indications of the injury for which it was diagnostic.

How Much Protection Can a Laboratory Slip Provide for a Physician?

A woman consulted her physician because of vaginal pruritus. After taking a history and examining the patient, the physician microscopically examined the vaginal discharge using a standard stain technique. He then told the patient that she had gonorrhea, in all probability contracted by sexual contact. Because the pruritus had occurred shortly after sexual intercourse with her husband, the physician told the patient to talk to her husband or, if she preferred, he would talk to him. The husband came in immediately to see the physician. When he was unable to obtain a smear from the husband's urethra because of the absence of a discharge, the physician expressed doubt about whether the husband had gonorrhea. Nevertheless, he told the husband that he was convinced that the wife had gonorrhea and he therefore advised him to commence immediate treatment. The following day, the couple consulted another physician who performed another test method on vaginal and urethral smears. When the laboratory reported that the test results were negative for gonorrhea, the second physician told the couple that neither one of them had the disease. The couple sued the initial treating physician. When he was notified of the suit against him, the physician sent the slide containing the vaginal smear from the wife to two laboratories. Both laboratories reported evidence of gonorrhea. At the time the lawsuit was filed, expert testimony established that it was the ordinary community practice of physicians to use either test in diagnosing gonorrhea.

The physician was not required to make perfect diagnosis, but was only required to apply a degree of skill and learning ordinarily possessed by similarly situated physicians. The physician relied on a standard test for diagnosing certain types of gonorrhea. His interpretation of the test was confirmed. Even though his conclusion may have been in error, he was not negligent in the care and treatment of the patient.

When Should Laboratory Values Be Considered Suspect?

Before an infant was born to an Rh-positive homozygous father and an Rh-negative mother, the mother had a positive Coombs' test result, indicating her sensitivity to her Rh-positive fetus. This information was recorded in the mother's chart. Although the infant appeared healthy at birth, within 2 days of life she developed jaundice, which the pediatrician diagnosed as "physiologic." This diagnosis was based on laboratory tests made a few hours after the infant's birth. The test results reported that the infant's Rh-factor and Coombs' were negative. In fact, these tests were erroneous. In spite of the fact that the second blood count, made on the fourth day postpartum, showed a significant drop in the hemoglobin, no follow-up hemoglobin test was ordered. Relying on the mistaken laboratory tests, the pediatrician ignored the jaundice, ordered no further tests, and allowed the infant to go home. The infant developed kernicterus and permanent brain damage. On behalf of the child, the parents sued the pediatrician. Expert testimony established that an infant of an Rh-positive homozygous father and a sensitized Rh-negative mother would encounter a serious blood incompatibility at birth.

The physician should have known that the accuracy of the results of the diagnostic tests were highly suspicious because they were at odds with the clinical presentation. He was obliged to investigate and to reconcile these discrepancies by repeating the test or ordering a more definitive test. When laboratory test results are unexpected, unlikely, or inconsistent with clinical findings, the laboratory tests should be repeated. A child of an Rh-positive homozygous father and an Rh-negative mother who develops jaundice in the first few days of life requires diagnostic monitoring and follow-up testing. If the physician had repeated the tests, pathologic jaundice could have been established and an exchange transfusion would have been performed to avert brain damage. On the basis of what the physician should have known about blood incompatibility and the clinical findings presented, he should have realized that the tests were in error or incompatible and should be investigated further. The mistaken diagnosis was based on incoherent analysis.

What Analytic Process Supports Choices to Delay or Proceed to Surgery?

A young boy experienced intermittent abdominal cramping, vomiting, diarrhea, and fever. His family physician's examination disclosed hyperactive bowel sounds, and generalized abdominal tenderness, but no rigidity or rebound. The physician's clinical impression was acute gastroenteritis. When vomiting and diarrhea progressed, he hospitalized the boy and ordered intravenous fluids and medication. The boy's white blood cell count was 18,000. There was no vomiting after admission and the abdominal findings remained the same for 24 hours. Although he considered other diagnostic possibilities, including appendicitis, the physician's working diagnosis remained acute gastroenteritis. The next day the white blood cell count was 16,000 and the abdominal findings were unchanged. On the third hospital day the child's condition materially worsened and significantly changed. His abdomen became distended and rigid and his bowel sounds were absent. The physician diagnosed an "acute abdomen" and requested immediate surgical consultation. Radiographs demonstrated distention of the small bowel with air-fluid levels. A laparotomy disclosed a ruptured appendix and peritonitis. The parents, on behalf of their child, sued the family practitioner for negligent misdiagnosis.

At trial, the surgeon expressed the opinion that appendicitis was the most likely diagnosis, considering the patient's age, fever, vomiting, abdominal tenderness, and elevated white blood cell count. The surgeon testified that it was difficult to determine rebound pain, and he did not regard the presence of hyperactive bowel sounds, or the absence of abdominal rigidity or distension, as findings not suggesting appendicitis. The surgeon conceded, however, that symptoms of gastroenteritis would be the same as those noted by the family practitioner.

The physician's failure to effect the patient's complete recovery is not necessarily evidence of negligence. Professional negligent conduct cannot be presumed solely because the patient has an untoward or unsatisfactory result. The findings manifested by the patient during his first 2 days of hospitalization clinically presented a case of acute gastroenteritis. Later in the clinical course and secondary to the gastroenteritis, acute appendicitis developed with resultant rupture of the appendix. As the symptoms normally associated with appendicitis became apparent, surgical consultation for the treatment of an acute abdomen was obtained. Therefore, the physician was not negligent for mistaken diagnosis. The diagnosis of acute gastroenteritis was not an unreasonable working diagnosis. This was probably an atypical case of appendicitis, with peritonitis rapidly developing following rupture of the appendix.

What Knowledge and Skill Are Required in General Practice Dealing with Specialized Care?

An elderly patient injured her hip. Her family physician admitted her to the hospital for evaluation. Radiographs disclosed a comminuted intertrochanteric fracture. The physician called in an orthopedic surgeon who internally fixed the fracture fragments with a Jewett nail. The fixation device was not designed to withstand the unsupported stresses of early full weight-bearing. The family physician was aware that the orthopedic surgeon did not permit full weight-bearing. The orthopedic surgeon's last entry on the patient's progress notes stated the patient was required to use a walker, and that she might go home when her family physician felt her general condition permitted. The patient remained in the hospital in the care of her family physician who was not familiar with the management of patients who had been treated with a Jewett nail. At the time of discharge, he allowed the patient to walk out of the hospital unassisted. Several weeks later, radiographs disclosed that the Jewett nail and bone had fractured due to the patient's prolonged and frequent full weight-bearing, necessitating a second operation to remove the broken device and insert a new one. The patient sued the family physician for improperly allowing her to bear full weight on the device.

A physician is expected to be aware of what he does not know, and incurs liability not for being ignorant about an aspect of a patient's condition but for remaining ignorant. The family physician was required to know enough to conduct a reasonable inquiry about what he did not know, in particular to seek consultation in the treatment of conditions and matters of admitted unfamiliarity. The family physician was aware that the activity instructions given by the orthopedic surgeon had not been revised or countermanded. In spite of this, he did not attempt to obtain advice from, or consult with, the orthopedic surgeon about the advisability of full weight-bearing. Despite admitted personal lack of knowledge about the management of patients with internal fixation devices, the family physician merely assumed, without inquiry, the strength limits of the device, which were unknown to him. His admitted unfamiliarity with fixation devices and his knowledge of the order prohibiting weight-bearing gave rise to an obligation to investigate by seeking advice before allowing or condoning full weight-bearing by his patient.

When Does Reasonable Medical Method Require Diagnostic Confirmation?

An infant manifested stigmata which suggested Down syndrome: hyperglossia, an umbilical hernia, and a heart murmur. Her family physician arranged a consultation for confirmation of his diagnostic impression. After two evaluations 3 months apart, the consultant confirmed the family physician's initial impression, and provided an explanation of prognosis to the family. He expressed the opinion to the family physician that chromosome testing for absolute confirmation was not indicated. The diagnosis of Down syndrome was accepted by both the family and referring physician. Thereafter, the child developed an anemia unresponsive to iron therapy and failed to grow at the expected rate. Several years passed before the physician realized that the child's anemia and failure to thrive were inconsistent with the consultant's diagnosis. He ordered a thyroid function test which disclosed an abnormally low value. When a chromosome test result was normal, it became apparent to the family physician that cretinism had mimicked Down syndrome. Thyroid therapy was begun and the child experienced an acceleration of growth and motor development, closure of the umbilical hernia, disappearance of the heart murmur and decrease in tongue size, with accompanying improved eating patterns and resolution of the anemia. The child, however, remained mentally impaired. On behalf of the child, the parents sued the family physician and his consultant for failure to properly diagnose the child's condition before irreversible brain injury occurred.

The family physician's diagnostic attitude was probably affected by high regard for the opinion and competence of the specialist. Sometimes such deference can cause a generalist to ignore or minimize the significance of certain clinical findings, and to fail to pay attention to appropriate confirmatory process. Obtaining consultation does not necessarily relieve the attending physician from the responsibility of applying proper and expected diagnostic methods in managing and coordinating the care and treatment of the patient. A physician who selects a qualified consultant must apply appropriate analytic process.

What Factors Contribute to Claims and Questions about Care?

A prostate cancer patient was diagnosed early and was in otherwise excellent health. Several hours after surgery for removal of the cancerous gland, the patient died in the recovery room. He was thought to have died as the result of a massive hemorrhage. The family had returned from dinner to have the surgeon inform them the patient had died of a heart attack: "His pressure dropped and [he had] a heart attack. . . . I know for you this is unpleasant, awful, but believe me, for me it's shattering." (This comment appeared to reflect an extreme degree of self-preoccupation, even for a surgeon.)

Suit was filed, according to the patient's wife, to find the answer to the question, "What went wrong?" Records showed that someone failed for 3 critical hours to obtain the results of a hematocrit taken just after surgery that would have signaled a bleeding emergency. A second test after 3 hours showed a dangerously low hematocrit. The patient still was not transfused until after the resuscitation team was summoned, and he died within an hour.

The surgeon was chosen apparently for his charm, literate manner, and by repeated assurances that he could cure the patient. No one asked him how many times he had performed the procedure he proposed or what the outcomes were. Later in the litigation process, records showed that, several weeks before surgery, anesthesiologists spent more than 2 hours unsuccessfully trying to intubate the patient, whose throat became so inflamed that surgery was postponed, and massive doses of steroids were given to reduce the swelling. Although steroids must be tapered to wean patients from the medication, the patient's doses were withdrawn abruptly.

This case resulted in a settlement, and is narrated in a book by the patient's wife. The story recounts medical management errors from which lessons can be learned. It also shows how unsuccessful care comes to be questioned. A landmark study of medical error from 30,000 hospital discharges in New York concluded that only one in seven negligently injured patients claims compensation.

Check-up File

3 Patients and Nonpatients

Indefensible Risks

Unresponsiveness, Ignorance, Abandonment

Practice Objectives

Realistic Success, Recognition of Exceptions

Pattern for Safety

Screening, Communication, Instruction, Special Needs Confirmation of Expectations, Continuity of Care, Informed Patients and Examinees

Approaches to Medical Legal Safety

Patient Selection, Clear Communications

Cases

Patient Acceptance, Duties to Treat, Transferred Care, Reliance on Patients, Warnings

Forms

Communications to Patients of Acceptance, Termination, Limits, Transfers, Patients, Warnings

Indefensible Risks

Failure to respond to current patient's request or need for treatment
Failure to recognize exceptional circumstances
Failure to warn any person of grave danger
Abandonment of a patient
Allowing an unqualified substitute to treat patients

Practice Objectives

☐ **Objective:** Patients accepted with highest probability of success and satisfaction.

Rationale: Patient satisfaction forecloses problems.

☐ **Objective:** Special patients receive special consideration.

Rationale: Standard of care requires appropriate response.

☐ **Objective:** Examinees understand and accept limited relationship.

Rationale: Limited expectations are appropriate for differences in physician duties.

☐ **Objective:** Exceptional responsibilities are fulfilled.

Rationale: Failure of duty to nonpatients often begins with failure of duty to patient.

Pattern for Safety

1. Accept patients only after initial interview.
2. Interview about crucial issues before any examination.
3. Instruct staff in responses to patient and nonpatient contacts.
4. Distinguish risks to patients from risks to practice.
5. Apply practice controls appropriate for foreseeable risks.
6. Provide highest medical risk control to every patient no matter what legal risk is perceived.
7. Know the legal requirements for acceptance and treatment of every type of special patient.
8. Confirm patient contact address, phone, employer, and insurance immediately after acceptance.
9. Confirm to referring physician and to patient limits of acceptance and terms of agreement to treat.
10. Specify and confirm special terms or limits of patient acceptance at the first interview.
11. Provide information about qualifications and experience in introduction to practice.
12. In covering or on-call treatment, transfer multiple records copies.

Bottom Line: Confirm physician and patient expectations to prevent surprise.

Approaches to Medical Legal Safety

Accepting and Terminating Patient Relationships

Patients can be distinguished in terms of need for special medical legal consideration. In one group are regular patients with relatively common or clear conditions, whose treatment proceeds according to expected norms. Normal medical legal practice should suffice in acceptance, attendance, communication, documentation, consent, instructions, and other aspects of practice.

Some patients who represent a diagnostic or a medical legal classification to which heightened practice attention must be paid. Heightened practice controls should be adopted to safeguard practice with special patients. Application of normal or heightened control does not indicate levels of skill or knowledge or quality of care, but relates to the self-protective mechanisms a physician may find advisable. Controlled level medical legal practice or even termination of relationship may be advisable for high medical legal risk patients. High control measures add more safeguards against increased risk of mishap or mistake in practice and provide tighter handling procedures for administrative practice.

Some reports have attempted to identify high legal risk patients, those thought likely to question medical care. These hypotheses would include patients who are:

Over-concerned with costs
Critical of past physicians
Diagnostic conundrums, "symptoms in search of a diagnosis"
Attempting to control multiple medical problems
Self-diagnosed
Having very high expectations for success
Very submissive to medical authority
Demanding as consumers
Noncompliant patients
Pain patients without apparent organic source
Flirtatious patients

These observations were made from groups of patients who have filed claims of medical failure. If every patient in these categories were referred or declined, a drastic drop in patient load could be expected. A number of these qualities can be managed by physician response to encounters with the patients. A few are real indicators of likely failure of the physician–patient relationship—the diagnostic mystery or the very submissive, noncompliant, pain, and flirtatious patients. Such patients could be declined at the outset. Other management measures could treat these patients with heightened practice control, which could include an ultraconservative approach, enhanced charting effort, and super disclosure. Whenever a patient is declined after initial interview or examination, notation of the decision in the "examinee" chart, with advice to consult another physician, is warranted. A letter to the examinee confirming this recommendation is advisable.

A close and frank look at problem patients can pinpoint causes and help address problems that are solvable. Over-concern with costs can be moderated by absolute candor about fees and payment alternatives. Criticism of past physicians may or may not be well-founded. Ask how the treatment problems arose, and isolate correctable similar faults. Avoid any evaluation of past care. Patients with many physicians and no diagnosis are likely candidates for failure and may not even be appropriately treated medically. The challenge of multiple medical problems is a common practice presentation. Unless the condition(s) require referral, appropriate consultation should suffice unless other disqualifying factors exist, such as noncompliance. The self-diagnosed patient should be validated or declined.

There should be few foreseeable legal problems with a "demanding consumer" patient who rationally aids in his or her own medical care. Irrational patients are separate problems and cannot be satisfactorily accepted without guardians. Patients with high expectations of success must be made to grasp the truth of any medical disclosure. Failure to appreciate potential risks or refusal to acknowledge potential consequences of care will leave the physician inevitably on the short end of the surprise adverse outcome. Submissiveness to medical authority—a return to the completely tractable patient—is a fantasy. Submissiveness will interfere with accepting the burden of making medical choices. Patients who submit without question to the physician's advice will later feel they were pressured, especially if the outcome is poor. Feelings of pressure will then yield to suspicion and resentment about what the physician advised or did.

Demanding consumers want to make sure they are not cheated. As patients, they will question and check-up on everything. If care is exercised, they can be very helpful and may be the most rationally compliant patients if given enough respect and information. Noncompliant patients should initially be given extra consideration in communication, cultural sensitivity, cognitive assessment, or other assurances to determine that correctable logistic or communications problems are not the cause. Refusal to follow instructions after all other concerns are met is the best reason to terminate the relationship. For medical care to succeed, patients are the key participants. Pain patients tend to be in the same category as those without a diagnosis. Pain clinics address these symptoms on an empiric medical model; referral is advisable.

Other claimant factors noted in claims and patient disputes include: past history of claim and payment (35% of claimants have sued before); adverse outcome and loss of trust; adverse outcome and absence of physician concern; surprise adverse outcome; and metropolitan setting versus rural.

How can physicians protect against high-legal-risk patients? These factors are amenable to most of the same appropriate protective practice measures. Patients with a past history of claim and payment may be more realistic about medical care. Many claimants have sued before. The case may have had merit and at least those damages have been compensated. Adverse outcome and loss of trust can be prevented by enhanced effort at disclosure and consent, with appropriate use of second opinions and confirmation. Adverse outcome and absence of physician concern can be prevented by heightened disclosure, consent, and attention to patient concerns. Surprise adverse outcome is the specific avoidable problem to which informed consent is addressed. Metropolitan setting versus rural setting is not generally curable by practice management. Imported patients would be likely to follow the statistical norms of the area to which they have moved.

Problem patients and patient problems boil down to some basic conflicts in the relationship: mismatched expectations, competing interests, and undisclosed agendas. Any practice management change that eliminates or reduces these factors will safeguard the practice.

Special Patients

Patients may present special medical legal characteristics that require distinct differences in practice management. These patients include patients with emergencies, minors, incompetent adults, disabled persons, mentally ill patients, terminally ill patients, patients who refuse crucial medical treatment, patients involved in legal disputes, patients with contagious diseases, donor and donee patients, and others, depending on the jurisdiction.

Patient emergency cases must be directed to immediate emergency care. Doubt about whether an emergency exists is resolved by the emergency department physician. Patients presenting urgent nonemergency needs may be treated by phone if the physician has reason to trust the patient's capability to report accurately and no other patient history factors demand actual examination. The small risk of treating the urgent condition by phone and making a prompt appointment for in-person follow-up examination is generally reasonable.

Minor patients require guardian participation in all but emergency or legally excepted care such as contraception or venereal disease treatment. Any doubt about patient age must be resolved by conclusive proof, especially for major nonemergency care. Consent is presumed to save life or limb, for minors as well as adults.

Patients with cognitive deficits require rational determination of cognitive status as an essential to medical legal security. Legal mechanisms operate very differently for "responsible" persons and for "nonresponsible" persons. Medical practice requires clear awareness of the jurisdiction's rules on mental or emotional deficiencies and medical and legal thresholds for determination of competence.

Other Special Patients

Legal counsel's advice will be needed to designate all the special considerations for each type of special patient in the practice.

Patients Being Discharged from Treatment

Termination of relationships with patients should be completed with clear formality. Unless all patients are being notified of discontinuation of practice, the patient is informed, in person, that treatment has been completed, or patient condition has progressed to require treatment by another source, or noncompliance requires ending the relationship.

The degree to which the patient requires continuing treatment is reflected by the period of notice and the effort offered to find an appropriate substitute physician. Patients must be made aware of any continuing need for treatment, especially the noncompliant patient. Hospitalized patients must be treated until another physician has taken up the responsibility of care. Noncompliant patients can be notified of termination of treatment, with time to secure necessary attention from another source.

A patient request for a specific diagnostic work-up or treatment calls for specific response. The request is recorded, and refusal documented, with rationale. At refused treatment, an offer to refer or terminate the care is appropriate.

Referral is a termination, temporary or permanent, of the physician–patient relationship. Appropriate formality recognizing the transfer of relationship to referral physician and patient can clarify expectations for all participants. Formality includes: notification, repetition, request for acknowledgment, and documentation to all involved.

Nonpatient Examinees

Examinees can be distinguished from patients by specific facts. Examination is not at the request of the examinee. Examination is paid for by the one requesting its performance. Evaluation from the examination is transmitted to the requestor. No expectation of treatment or reliance is offered to the examinee.

Several small duties to examinees have been recognized by legal decision. When an examination discloses a condition that poses a danger to the examinee or demonstrates a need for diagnosis or treatment, communication should be made to the examinee by the examiner-physician that an unusual or exceptional test result or condition has been noted. The communication, confirmed in writing, should recommend to the patient that a **treating** physician evaluate the record of examination, with a request for the name, address, and phone number of the physician to whom the record should be sent. Examinees who wish a copy of the record of an examination should be directed to the requestor. Another responsibility of physician to examinee requires that a physician conduct an examination in a manner which does not actually harm the examinee, such as manipulation of an injured limb or spine which itself causes damage.

Nonpatients

Nonpatient emergency cases present the situation of gratuitous medical attention. By observation of reasonable self-protection, physicians risk little exposure. Check for greater or better expertise available; do all that conditions allow; relinquish care at earliest moment; and record events and facts. Even if the singular outcome is adverse, the historical role of physicians to aid those in need of emergency care is of immense and universal value.

Nonpatients have no expectations of contact or help from physicians except through the acts of patients. A small duty to warn identified persons of a clear and definite threat from a patient is the most extended obligation currently recognized in some places. Where reports are required to protect nonpatients, agencies receiving reports have the duty to contact and warn. Most protection of nonpatients by physicians is accomplished by instructions and warnings to the patient.

Cases

What Acts of "Diagnosis" Establish a Physician–Patient Relationship?

When a woman developed sudden, intense headache, neck stiffness, and nausea, her family physician diagnosed a viral infection. Later, when her condition did not improve, her husband called the hospital trying to reach her physician to ask that she be admitted, but was connected with another physician on the floor. The husband recited his wife's symptoms, and the physician asked what the family physician had diagnosed. The husband replied, "He said it was a virus." The physician replied, "If your doctor said it is a virus, it is probably a virus." When the husband told the physician that he wanted his wife hospitalized for a checkup, the physician replied that the woman could not be admitted unless arrangements were made by her family physician. Subsequently, it was determined that the woman had sustained a subarachnoid hemorrhage with serious and permanent neurologic damage. The woman sued the hospital physician for failing to render proper medical assistance to her. She contended that the physician undertook to render medical services when, in response to her husband's questions and concerns, he confirmed the family physician's medical diagnosis.

If contact between a physician and a person seeking medical attention constitutes an "undertaking" to provide medical care, a physician–patient relationship will have been formed. Withdrawal by the physician after the relationship is formed is subject to conditions discussed in other cases. An "undertaking to treat" establishes, by legal implication, the physician–patient relationship, and a duty to treat and diagnose in a reasonable manner. This physician requested sufficient information to inform the patient of the hospital's procedures for admission. The facts in this case were found insufficient to establish a physician–patient relationship. The only meaningful contact between the husband and the physician was the telephone call in which the physician informed the husband of the hospital's policies. This did not constitute an "undertaking to treat," and therefore no physician–patient relationship was formed.

How Many Physicians Can Have a Duty to Treat a Patient?

A patient with diabetes had been examined by her private physician because she was feeling lethargic. The following evening the patient became unconscious as a result of diabetic ketoacidosis and was brought to a hospital emergency department. The hospital maintained an emergency department staffed on a rotating "on-call" basis by physicians who comprised the entire complement of physicians with clinical staff privileges at the hospital. Under state law, any hospital providing emergency department services was obligated to provide emergency services to everyone in need of them. When the emergency department contacted an on-call physician, he refused to come in and treat the patient. Instead, he referred the emergency department nurse to the patient's private physician, who was also a member of the hospital staff. The private physician insisted that the on-call physician respond to the patient's emergency situation. When the emergency department nurse again telephoned the on-call physician and asked him to see the patient, he again refused. The hospital chief of staff was notified of the situation and came into the hospital and attended the patient. Despite his therapeutic efforts, the patient died as a result of complications of ketoacidosis. The estate of the deceased patient then sued the on-call physician and the attending physician for failing to treat the patient. Expert testimony established that the delay in initiating treatment contributed to the patient's death.

The on-call physician had agreed to staff the emergency department on an on-call basis; therefore he had a duty to render care for patients coming into the emergency department needing urgent care. Even though he would generally be free to refuse to treat a person who was not a patient, the on-call physician in this case had a contractual obligation to treat the patient based on agreement with the hospital. The hospital was obligated to treat all patients who presented themselves in the emergency department. The patient's personal physician had a duty to secure qualified coverage for his patients' care, which would have been satisfied if the on-call physician had not responded.

How Is Transfer of Care Accomplished?

A young man had consulted a general practitioner because of anxiety, loneliness, and insomnia. The physician prescribed some calmative medication to palliate the patient's anxiety. He then recommended psychiatric care directly to the patient and referred him to a psychiatric clinic for further treatment. He also made a similar recommendation in a note which the patient took home to his family. Thereafter, the general practitioner was repeatedly called for assistance by the man and his family, but responded that he could not comply with their requests. Several days later the patient was treated at an emergency department. Two days afterwards, he was admitted to the hospital and there he committed suicide. The patient's mother sued the physician claiming that the general practitioner had improperly withdrawn from care of the patient.

The physician's treatment of the patient effectively terminated when he recommended to the patient and his family that the patient seek psychiatric help and referred the patient to a psychiatric clinic. When faced with a specialized problem, a generalist should not be faulted because he referred his patient to a specialist. A physician employed for a specific service is ordinarily under no duty to continue treatment after that service has been rendered. The patient visited the physician only one time; the physician determined that he was incapable of providing the requested and needed services. He explained this to the patient and his family and referred him to a proper care facility. He had no further obligation to treat the patient.

How May a Relationship with a Patient in Urgent Need of Treatment Be Terminated?

A woman on three-times-a-week dialysis was a source of extreme irritation and disruption at the clinic where she was treated. The care was paid for by Medicaid. The clinic notified her that her behavior would not be tolerated and she would have to comply with clinic rules or leave treatment. She continued to harass the staff and other patients and was notified of her termination with time to arrange for other dialysis services. She was transferred in this way among several clinics until finally each had informed her that she was no longer welcome. She petitioned for an order to a clinic or all the clinics to provide her with treatment, alleging that by terminating her access to treatment, she was being sentenced to death by collective abandonment. An order was issued to all the accessible clinics that the burden of this patient was to be shared in turn.

Although the right to turn away patients for noncompliance is usually recognized, here it was a complete denial of treatment anywhere. The patient was treated serially by each clinic by court order until her death.

Can a Hospitalized Patient Be Transferred to Another Physician's Care?

A surgeon performed a hernioplasty on his patient. Subsequently, the patient experienced groin pain which radiated into the scrotum. When the groin pain persisted, the patient consulted his surgeon who recommended a period of "watching and waiting." Several months later when he returned to the surgeon with the same complaint at the site of the hernioplasty, the surgeon operated through the old incision to "rebuild the external inguinal ring." Postoperatively the patient continued to experience groin pain. After his discharge from the hospital, his complaints continued and the surgeon finally rehospitalized him. While the patient was in the hospital, the surgeon became frustrated by the patient's incessant complaints and discharged him as his patient by telling him that he "was sick of the whole situation" and that the patient "was imagining things." Shortly thereafter, the patient consulted another surgeon who performed a third operation in which he discovered that the reconstruction of the external inguinal ring had been so tight that it compromised the circulation and the flow of secretions to and from the testicle. The patient then sued the original surgeon for abandonment.

Once a physician undertakes to provide treatment to a patient, in the absence of an agreement or specific arrangement limiting the nature of his or her employment, a physician is required to continue attendance of the patient as long as the patient's condition requires attention. Abandonment can be negligent where the physician should be aware that the patient needs care. When a physician improperly withdraws from the relationship, the duties inherent in the relationship may be breached. Under these circumstances, the surgeon's manner of withdrawing from the physician–patient relationship by informing the patient that there was nothing wrong, when in fact the patient was experiencing a complication of surgery performed by the physician was improper, and constituted abandonment.

How Is Specialty Care Continued after Termination?

A patient sustained a leg fracture in an automobile accident and was taken to a general hospital. There an orthopedic surgeon reduced the fracture and instructed her not to place any weight on the leg. Before being dismissed from the hospital, the patient developed a traumatic psychosis, and therefore was transferred to a mental hospital. The orthopedic surgeon did not medically attend her while she was in the mental hospital but did provide current information on her condition to the subsequent treating physician. He resumed care of the patient when she was transferred back to the general hospital for complications of her leg fracture. The patient claimed she was forced to walk on her injured leg while in the mental hospital, thereby allegedly causing additional injury to her leg, and she sued her orthopedist for abandoning her.

A situation may arise where withdrawal of medical attention is required of the physician by circumstances beyond the physician's control. The orthopedic surgeon was not obligated to continue to attend the patient at the mental hospital. Moreover, the specialist had no right to do so because he was not a member of the mental hospital staff and was presumably not qualified to provide psychiatric services. He had made information on his patient available to the physicians at the mental hospital and was not liable for their failure to follow them.

How Is Responsibility Allocated between Patient and Physician?

A woman remarried and moved to an apartment. The next month, she selected a physician from a telephone directory and consulted him to obtain a contraceptive device. She told the physician that she worked at a local university. As a routine matter in assessing her for the contraceptive device, the physician obtained a Papanicolaou smear and sent it to a laboratory. It was returned 2 weeks later with a report that it was "suspicious for malignancy." The physician attempted on numerous occasions to reach the patient to advise her of the report and to recommend further procedures. He tried to reach her through the university but was unsuccessful because she had never worked there. He also attempted several times to reach her at her home without success because she had moved to another address. Six months later the patient came to the physician's office to pay the bill for his medical services. He then informed her of the test result, and took another Papanicolaou smear which again was "suspicious for malignancy." A biopsy disclosed a cancerous lesion. The patient sued the physician for failing to notify her promptly of her condition, which she alleged caused her to undergo more drastic surgery to prevent further progression of the cancer than would have been required if she had been promptly notified of the test result.

Although the physician had a duty to take whatever steps are reasonable to notify the patient of a significantly abnormal test result, the patient had a corresponding duty to avoid intentionally hampering the physician's effort to accomplish this duty. The patient furnished the physician with misleading information as to her status and address. This was inconsistent with the conduct expected from an ordinarily prudent patient; therefore, the patient's own negligent conduct contributed to the delay in her treatment.

When Must a Patient's Reports Be Considered Suspect?

Shortly before being taken into police custody, the patient had consumed beer and Librium. The patient and a companion were taken to an emergency department, where they claimed to be heroin addicts suffering withdrawal symptoms and requested medication for this discomfort. The patient did not tell the physician of his consumption of Librium. The physician asked the patient whether he had attended the methadone clinic and the patient responded that he had participated in the program for 4 months, but had dropped out because he found a new supply source of heroin. The patient manifested signs and symptoms consistent with withdrawal syndrome, rolling his head, clutching his abdomen, and complaining of severe abdominal pain. His eyes appeared glassy and he seemed agitated. After taking a history and observing their behavior, the physician ordered a dose of methadone for the patient and for his companion. Although his companion calmed down thereafter, the patient began to beat his head against a wall claiming that he was still sick and needed more methadone. Consequently, the physician ordered a second dose of methadone to be given to the patient. Shortly after receiving the second dose, the patient calmed down and was taken to a jail by the police officers. The following morning he was found dead in his cell as a result of multiple drug intoxication. It was subsequently determined that the patient had never been an addict although his companion was, in fact, a heroin addict. When his family learned of the manner of the patient's death, they sued the physician, alleging that his negligent treatment of the patient caused the patient's death.

The patient has a duty to be reasonably truthful in describing symptoms to the physician. Such intentional deception would bar recovery from the physician for harm that results from the misinformation supplied by the patient. The patient's conduct contributed to his death; thus no damages were recoverable, even if the physician was assumed to be negligent by not doing more to determine the truth of the patient's assertions. For unexplained reasons, the patient put on an effective act in the emergency department that induced the physician to provide relief from heroin withdrawal discomfort. The patient demonstrated clinical symptoms associated with addiction withdrawal and confirmed the clinical presentation by insisting that he was an addict. He continued to contribute to his own destruction by failing to tell the physician that he was not an addict, and that he had been drinking alcohol and taking Librium. He took the medication offered by the physician, and continued to act out a deception to obtain another dose. Thus he materially contributed to his own death.

What Responsibility Must a Patient Take for Personal Safety and Health?

During convalescence from a complicated hysterectomy, a woman experienced severe lower abdominal pain and was administered morphine frequently. Because she continued to complain of severe pain after her discharge from the hospital, her family asked the physician about the possibility of having pain-relieving medication administered to her at home. The physician agreed and provided the medication and prescriptions. Therefore, her husband and children administered morphine by injections to alleviate her pain. When the patient would complain of pain, her family would telephone the physician who would issue a prescription for morphine, with quantities ranging from 10 to 30 doses. At some point, the patient began to use the medication for "nervousness" and "just to feel good." To obtain a prescription, she complained of pain when none was present. Her family became apprehensive of her behavior and discussed the possibility of addiction with her physician. He assured them that they had no cause for alarm because the pain was so severe it would "counteract the effect of the morphine." He also felt since she was improving physically, she would have less future need for the medication. Finally, her family decided that she was not recovering properly from her illness and consulted a general surgeon concerning the cause of her persistent abdominal pain. This physician performed an exploratory operation, which disclosed adhesions and partial intestinal obstruction. After corrective surgery, the patient's tolerance to pain was so low that it aroused the surgeon's suspicion about her use of narcotics. When he determined she had been receiving morphine about every 3 hours, day and night, he confronted the patient with the issue. The patient then confided in him the amount of morphine she had taken over the past months. At his request, she undertook a program of withdrawal from the narcotics. The patient then sued her family physician for causing her addiction, charging that, instead of attempting to discover the cause of her pain and relieving it, he continually gave her morphine to palliate her discomfort, with the result that she became an addict. The family physician answered that all morphine prescribed was on the insistent demands of the patient and her family who were responding to the patient's pretenses. He argued that even if he were negligent, the patient and her family actually caused her addiction.

It was not unreasonable for the patient to have trust and confidence in the capacity and skill of her attending physician to prescribe pain-relieving medication. The patient and her family were not required to set their judgment against that of the medical expert whom they had employed for treatment, or even to appeal to other physicians to ascertain if the physician was providing proper treatment. It would require extraordinary circumstances to hold a patient responsible for an injury simply because the patient had accepted the physician's advice and followed the physician's prescribed treatment. The patient and the family had a right to rely on the physician's instructions and assumed superior medical knowledge. Neither the family nor the patient was required to determine at what point addiction was beginning. Nor were they expected to be aware that they should, at any time before addiction became a fact, cease to rely on the attending physician's knowledge of the amount of drugs that could safely be taken over a given period of time.

What Is the Physician's Duty to Warn Examinees of Abnormal Findings?

A man sought disability benefits. The disability determination department ordered an examination, and a physician was employed by the department to conduct the examination. The man did not select or pay the physician, nor had he ever been treated by the physician before or afterwards. Radiographs were taken during examination. After the man had left the physician's office, a study of the radiograph revealed, in the physician's opinion, probable pulmonary malignancy. That same evening the physician dictated his report by telephone to the department transcription service, specifically stating his impression that the man had a probable pulmonary malignancy, and strongly recommended that the department examiner contact the man so that he could contact his personal physician and that he be advised to follow up this problem. The department failed to contact the man and inform him of the abnormality observed and reported by the physician. The man did not discover the fact that he had a malignancy until months later, when his claim for disability benefits was denied.

Department Medical Examination Guidelines for Consultative Physicians contained this language:

It is considered desirable to make significant medical information from consultative examinations available to the attending physician or medical institution for treatment purposes, provided the individual authorizes such release. Referral to the claimant's treating source is particularly important where the information reveals a previously undiagnosed condition that may require immediate treatment. Our agency is responsible for making prompt identification and referral of consultative examination reports to attending physicians when the examination reflects diagnostic information or test results which would be of significance to the claimant's treatment. However, you, the consultative physician are requested to notify the examiner handling the case immediately if you suspect a life-threatening condition, and we will immediately take steps to notify a treating physician. You may, at your discretion, advise the claimant, while he is still in your office, when you feel he or she should see a treating physician for additional diagnostic studies.

The physician contended that, because there was no physician–patient relationship between the man and the physician, he cannot be liable as a result of the failure of the department to notify the man of his findings in a timely manner. The plaintiff conceded that there was no physician–patient relationship, but asserted that some duty was owed by the physician to the examinee outside of the physician–patient relationship.

This case explores the issue of whether, in the absence of a traditional physician–patient relationship, a physician hired to examine an individual owes a duty to disclose a life-threatening condition that is unknown to the examinee. Although the physician had no duty to examine the man beyond the needs of the disability determination agency, once a life-threatening condition unknown to the examinee was discovered, a duty to disclose arose, because once the radiograph of the chest was taken, the man had a reasonable expectation of being advised of any abnormal findings. Although the physician did not have a duty to diagnose, treat, or advise the examinee, he could have been expected to inform the patient that the test showed suspicious findings and that the results could be sent to the examinee's physician for discussion within a patient context. Rather than contact the examinee, the physician left a recorded message of his findings with the department in the expectation that they would tell the man that he needed to seek immediate treatment. The agency did not relay the message and months passed. The physician had a limited duty which he failed to fulfill.

Can a Single Examination Impose Duties to Continue Treatment?

A private physician not a hospital employee examined a pregnant woman in the emergency department 2 hours before the delivery of the woman's child. The physician observed no problems with the mother's labor at that time, although the physician was aware, from the labor record, that a large baby was anticipated and therefore delivery problems were possible. The physician left the hospital before the delivery, leaving the woman in the care of a resident physician. The physician was not the supervising physician of the resident physician. She had no further involvement with the woman, nor was she at any time summoned to aid in the subsequent delivery during which the woman and her infant sustained injury as a result of dystocia. The mother and infant sued the physician, contending that she had the duty to remain at the hospital, or to take some further specific course of action to avert possible delivery problems.

The physician was under no obligation to personally supervise the delivery of the woman by the resident physician. The woman did not have a right to expect treatment from any particular physician. The only duty that the physician owed the woman was to conduct her examination in a professionally proper manner. The physician did not cause injury to the woman or her infant during the performance of her examination. She fully and properly discharged her duty of professional care in examining the woman. This single examination did not create a further duty to personally supervise or participate in the delivery of the infant which occurred 2 hours later. The physician did not assume responsibility for the woman's care subsequent to the examination, nor was she legally obligated to do so under the circumstances. Rather, she was entitled to rely on the resident physician and other hospital personnel, as well as on the fact that the woman's labor record set forth the possibility of problems in the delivery for the other physicians to see.

What Duty Is Owed to Nonpatients?

While receiving outpatient therapy at a university clinic, a young man disclosed to his psychotherapist that he wanted to kill his girlfriend who lived nearby with her parents, but who was at that time away on a summer trip. The therapist reported the matter to the campus police, requesting detention and commitment of the man for observation. Satisfied that he was rational, the police released him on his promise to stay away from his girlfriend. When the police reported their action to the therapist, he asked for the return of his letter to the police, and destroyed it. The man did not return for therapy. A month later, shortly after his girlfriend returned from her trip, he went to her home and killed her. The victim's parents brought suit against the therapist for negligence in failing to warn their daughter or them of the impending danger. The parents contended that since the therapist knew the patient was at large and dangerous, failure to warn his intended victim or to tell others likely to apprise her of the dangers constituted a breach of his duty to exercise reasonable care to protect the victim. The therapist contended that he owed no duty to the victim or her parents.

The therapist, by virtue of his relationship with the patient, had a derivative duty to warn a reasonably identifiable third party who might be harmed foreseeably by the patient's actions. Thus the physician owed a duty of care to persons who were foreseeably endangered by the physician's failure to act reasonably. To avoid foreseeable harm to a third party, the physician was required to control the behavior of the patient or to warn another of such conduct. By entering into a physician–patient relationship, the physician became sufficiently involved in the clinical management of his patient to assume some responsibility for the safety of an identifiable third person whom the physician knew to be threatened by the patient. The physician could not avoid liability for negligence merely because a victim was not his patient. The physician determined that his patient presented a serious danger to another; therefore he incurred an obligation to use reasonable care to protect the intended victim against such danger. The discharge of this duty required him to take only reasonable and necessary steps to warn the intended victim or others likely to apprise the victim of the danger.

Forms

Attention to processing forms can obscure their actual function. Many sources provide excellent medical legal forms, some with explanations of the forms' purpose and implications. Forms and checklists included here are examples of recording important understandings and events. Many different variations could operate as effective communication and recording as long as each form fulfills its specific purpose.

Useful Forms for Patient Acceptance and Discharge

Patient Registration Data Record
Patient Acceptance and Practice Introduction
Request to Consultant/Referral Physician
Acceptance Report of Consultation/Referral Patient
Consultation/Referral Patient Limitations
Episodic Treatment Record for One-Time Patients
Patient Acknowledgment of Limited Emergency Treatment
Withdrawal from Patient Care
Withdrawal from Practice
Recognizing Patient Withdrawal from Treatment
Request for Limited Examination Evaluation
Acceptance of Limited Examination Evaluation
Authorization for Release of Examination/Evaluation Records and Findings

An additional log copy of any document can be filed in the appropriate future date folder of the master calendar for note of response or return of requested action or report.

Example Form: Patient Registration Data Record

Identity Data

Name, birth date, marital status, social security number.

Location Data

Address, business, phones, fax.

Personal Contact Data

Person(s) to notify:

Designated guardian/decision maker.

Family members with whom treatment may be discussed.

Durable power of attorney for health care decisions.

Medical Contact Data

Referring physician.

Other physician(s) currently treating.

Insurance Data

Payment plan, numbers, agency, authorization source.

Release Authorization for Medical Information

Discussion.

Access to medical records information.

Reimbursement documentation.

Reports documenting medical status.

Check for changes at each date patient seen.

Example Form: Patient Acceptance and Practice Introduction

This notification could be a letter, or a letter with practice brochure.

Full contact letterhead, names and numbers, office hours.

Formal acknowledgment of acceptance as patient.

Restated patient purpose for seeking physician contact.

Expectation of diagnosis, treatment, evaluation, or other medical services.

Contacts for coordination with other providers.

Recitation of practice services, hospital affiliations, exceptions to use of specific sites.

Names of associated providers patient can expect to encounter.

Important contact instructions for foreseeable patient needs.

Map to office, other sites for treatment, hospital, emergency facility.

Major limits of patient care.

Assurance of qualifications and commitment to assure appropriate care.

Example Form: Request to Consultant/Referral Physician

Date of referral/recommended consultation.

Identity data, name, birth date, address, phone.

Brief outline of physician contact prompting consult or referral history, examination, impression, diagnosis medications, allergies, tests, radiographs.

Transfer intended: referral, with care by transferring physician ended.
- for specialized treatment
- assume all care

consultation for advisory purpose
- for evaluation or diagnosis
- confirm diagnosis
- treatment plan

consultation for joint purpose or procedure
- treatment
- diagnostic process
- surgery

consultation for separate purpose or procedure
- treatment
- diagnostic process
- surgery

Requested actions from consulted/referred physician.
meeting, conference, joint treatment
phone report, written report
instructions to patient

Enclosures and transferred documents, specimens.
records, tests, radiograph copies (enclosed or with patient)
source of other data

Copy to patient, chart, log.

Example Form: Acceptance Report of Consultation/Referral Patient

Date of consultation/referral acceptance.

Acknowledgment of transfer request noted by date, identity data, name, birth date, address, phone.

Statement of understanding of purpose of transfer intended.

- referral, with care by transferring physician ended
  - for specialized treatment
  - assume all care
- consultation for advisory purpose
  - for evaluation or diagnosis
  - confirm diagnosis
  - treatment plan
- consultation for joint purpose or procedure
  - treatment
  - diagnostic process
  - surgery
- consultation for separate purpose or procedure
  - treatment
  - diagnostic process
  - surgery

Report of completed action.

- separate history, physical findings, impression, treatment, disposition, recommendations, advice to patient

Commitment to action by consulted/referred physician.

- meeting, conference, joint treatment
- further referral/consultation
- diagnostic, treatment procedure
- phone report, written report
- disclosures and/or instructions to patient

Enclosures and transferred documents, specimens
records, tests, radiograph copies (enclosed or with patient)
source of other data

Copy to patient, chart, log.

Example Form: Consultation/Referral Limitations

Agreement of Physician and Patient to Conditions of Treatment

Note of discussion between physician and patient, stating that care and treatment of the patient will be accepted by the physician under the following conditions:

Brief history with note of problems to be addressed by this agreement. Medical history, surgery, treatment by other physician, origin of problems (noncompliance, prescription abuse, self-endangerment, endangerment of others, misrepresentation, concealment).

Statement of office policy and medical policy regarding noted problem(s).

Statement of commitment and limits of physician treatment: for example, treatment will be provided for convalescence from spinal surgery; however, nonnarcotic medications only will be prescribed.

Statement of patient commitment to adhere to limits and conditions of treatment: for example, patient will not obtain medications from any other physicians except with physician consent, will enroll in recommended therapeutic course at pain clinic and counseling, including testing to verify compliance.

Statement of physician limit of expertise in management of complications, and commitment to refer for specialized care.

Statement of consequences of noncompliance by the patient: for example, termination of physician–patient relationship.

Example Form: Treatment Record for One-Time Patients

Date of contact.

Patient identification data, name, birth date, address, phone.

Contact context, coverage, on-call, partner/group, emergency.

Contact data, visit, phone call, encounter, time, location.

Report of patient presentation, complaint.

Note of prior information available or provided on patient from practice covered, facility record.

Note history given of allergies, medication, medical conditions of importance, note any confirmation sought.

Inquiries pursued, observations made.

Examination performed.

Impression, conclusion, differential consideration.

Treatment administered or medication prescribed.

Action, advice, and instructions.

Confirmation of patient understanding and compliance.

Enclosures and transferred documents, specimens records, tests, radiograph copies (enclosed or with patient) source of other data.

Copy to patient, chart, log, other providers.

Example Form: Acknowledgment of Limited Emergency Treatment

Date of contact.

Patient identification data, name, birth date, address, phone.

Contact context, coverage, on-call, partner/group, emergency.

Contact data, visit, phone call, encounter, time, location.

Brief summary of patient encounter, including history given of allergies, medication, medical conditions of importance.

Patient impression of treatment administered or medication prescribed, advice and instructions.

Confirmation by patient of single nature of physician contact with understanding of need to obtain follow-up or continuing treatment by other physician.

Acknowledgment of received written instructions, copies of test results, radiographs, prescription to continue care with other physician.

Copy to patient, chart, log, other providers.

Example Form: Withdrawal from Patient Care

Date of withdrawal notice.

Patient identity data (for minors, add parental identity data).

Recall discussion between physician and patient or parent regarding care and treatment of the patient under past conditions.

Brief history with note of conditions prompting withdrawal. Medical history, surgery, treatment, events occurring which require withdrawal.

Statement of commitment and limits of physician treatment: necessary treatment will be available, for example, for 30 days. Time allowed to find other care depends on locale, medical resources, patient condition.

Commitment to transfer records copies and advise new physician of patient history and treatment.

Statement of patient condition and current need for medical treatment, with instructions to seek care by another physician. Emphasis must be expressed for necessary care and consequences of patient failure to seek treatment for identified problems.

Advice for management of emergencies until other treatment obtained.

Enclose authorization to release records to new physician. Authorization acknowledges receipt of notice of withdrawal.

Example Form: Withdrawal from Practice

Date of withdrawal notice.

Patient identity data (for minors, add parental identity data).

Brief note of conditions prompting withdrawal.

Statement of commitment and limits of physician treatment: necessary treatment will be available, for example, for 30 days.

Commitment to transfer records copies and advise new physician of patient history and treatment.

Advice for management of emergencies until other treatment obtained.

Enclose authorization to release records to new physician. Authorization acknowledges receipt of notice of withdrawal.

Example Form: Recognizing Patient Withdrawal from Treatment

Date of acknowledgment.

Patient identity data (for minors, add parental identity data).

Recall discussion between physician and patient or parent regarding care and treatment of the patient under past conditions, and brief note of patient conduct or notice of discharge.

Commitment to transfer records copies and advise new physician of patient history and treatment.

Statement of patient condition and current need for medical treatment, with instructions to seek care by another physician. Emphasis must be expressed for necessary care and consequences of patient failure to seek treatment for identified problems.

Advice for management of emergencies until other treatment obtained.

Enclose authorization to release records to new physician. Authorization acknowledges receipt of notice of withdrawal.

Example Form: Request for Limited Examination Evaluation

Date of request for examination evaluation.

Identity of requestor, corporate and contact individual with title.

Patient/Examinee identity data, name, birth date, address, phone.

Brief outline of purpose for examination evaluation.

evaluation or diagnosis, general or specific

confirm diagnosis

treatment plan

prognosis

disability/impairment assessment

specific findings requested

Requested actions from examining physician.

meeting, conference, testimony

phone report, written report

Enclosures and transferred documents, specimens.

records, tests, radiograph copies (enclosed or with patient)

source of other data

Permission for copy to patient/examinee.

Example Form: Acceptance of Limited Examination Evaluation

Date of acceptance of examinee.

Identity of requestor, corporate and contact individual with title.

Identity data, name, birth date, address, phone, date of evaluation.

Acknowledge enclosures and transferred documents, specimens

- records, tests, radiograph copies (enclosed or with patient)
- source of other data

Acknowledge brief history and understanding of purpose of examination evaluation.

- evaluation or diagnosis, general or specific
- confirm diagnosis
- treatment plan
- prognosis
- disability/impairment assessment
- specific findings requested

Commitment or action by examining physician.

- meeting, conference, testimony
- phone report, written report

Report of completed action.

separate history, physical findings, impression

note of tests and specimens

Enclosures and returned or transferred documents, specimens

records, tests, radiograph copies (enclosed or with patient)

source of other data

Copy furnished to requestor, patient/examinee as permitted, agency, chart, log.

Copy of examinee authorization enclosed.

Example Form: Authorization for Release of Examination/Evaluation Records and Findings

Date of examination evaluation.

Date of release authorization.

Identity data, name, birth date, address, phone.

Identity of corporate and contact individual with title.

Examinee's stated or written understanding of purpose for examination evaluation and recitation of examination by physician.

Permission for disclosure to specific persons of findings of examination, including testimony about records and findings as necessary.

Patient/examinee statement of understanding that confidentiality is waived for the purposes authorized in the release.

Patient/examinee statement of understanding that examination is not for patient diagnosis or treatment and that findings are limited to the purposes for which examination was conducted.

Documents that are anticipated to require legal enforcement or legal interpretation are best drafted by legal counsel.

Check-up File

4 Medical Communications

Patient Interviews and Discussions
Disclosure for Consent
Documentation of Consent Disclosure and Discussion
Instructions and Monitoring
Discussion with Family, Others
Medical Records

Indefensible Risks

Patient Ignorance, Insufficient Records, Uninformed Consent or Refusal, Failed Instructions

Practice Objectives

Full Patient Disclosure and Understanding, Effective Instructions, Clear Documentation

Pattern for Safety

Listening, Summary, Confirmation, Disclosure, Documentation, Review, Reevaluation

Approaches to Medical Legal Safety

Maximize Communications and Documentation

Cases

Promises, Interest Conflicts, Disclosures, Instructions, Errors, Records, Refusal of Treatment

Forms

Consents and Refusals

Indefensible Risks

Patient ignorance of potential serious risk of treatment
Patient ignorance of alternatives to recommended treatment
Patient ignorance of consequences of no treatment
Performance of indicated but unconsented treatment
Performance of treatment unindicated by records
Performance of refused treatment
Discharge without information about further need for treatment
Concealment of treatment error or injury

Practice Objectives

☐ **Objective:** Patients are given every opportunity to communicate about care.

Rationale: Undisclosed expectations and misunderstandings mislead physician and patient.

☐ **Objective:** Full patient understanding and acceptance of treatment risks and consequences.

Rationale: Patient or physician will bear the burden of medical outcomes.

☐ **Objective:** Effective instructions to assure patient return and to signal complications or side effects.

Rationale: Instructions must make layman patient a functioning medical monitor.

☐ **Objective:** Patient controls involvement of others in care.

Rationale: Physician should not sort out patient relationships.

☐ **Objective:** Records support physician in all important functions.

Rationale: Patient and physician safety are directly proportional to records effectiveness.

Pattern for Safety

1. Assure treatment is indicated before requesting consent.
2. Confirm patient understanding of all communications about care.
3. Disclose and discuss every aspect of care important to a patient.
4. Assure patients are not surprised at adverse outcomes.
5. Obtain informed consent for tests and prescriptions.
6. Heighten consent procedures for appropriate conditions and patients.
7. Use disclosure and discussion to help reluctant patients come to their own decisions.
8. Conform instructions for reliable use by the individual patient.
9. Ask patients with whom their care may be discussed.
10. Ask patients if communication would be helped by communication and monitoring from a family member or other person.
11. Try to achieve a one-to-one ratio between desire for medical legal protection and effective completion of medical records.
12. Remove barriers to communication from patients.

Bottom Line: Method is more dependable than luck.

Approaches to Medical Legal Safety

Pattern for communications safety:

Listen for the whole story.
Summarize what you've heard.
See what is there to be seen.
Confirm by surest method without harm.
Know what you should know.
Say everything important.
Avoid any misrepresentation, even for a good reason.
Ask what was understood.
Keep a copy of what you've heard.
Give a copy of what you've said.
Check later to assure all systems go.
Check again even later—just because.
Reevaluate when anticipated progress is interrupted.
Choose the optimal time for any action.

Patient Interviews and Discussions

Communication problems complicate every other issue. If communication is flawed, then history is garbled, diagnosis is misunderstood, instructions are neglected, and compliance is impossible. In short, discuss, summarize, confirm, copy, and check. To make decisions involving treatment, patients must be aware of costs and alternatives. Fees should be discussed early and frankly. Unless there is an emergency, payment can be discussed in the first interview and the patient's commitment to pay confirmed.

Discussion with patients can settle basic approaches of patient and physician to the medical encounter. For example:

The patient bears the burden of medical problems and consequences with physician as guide and source.
Medical advice may include concerns with payment, but not determination of cost-benefit.
Patient danger to others must balance decisions to safeguard patient interest with duties to others.

Patient confirms commitment to comply and cooperate with, as well as augment, medical effort.

Patient confirms willingness to disclose fully and frankly necessary information related to care.

Communication in medical practice can begin at first contact with staff when a request for interview or examination is made. When a patient arrives, accessibility and comfort of facilities may also reflect consideration or disregard of patient ease, comfort, and privacy. Hallways, stairs, elevators, entryway, furniture, and examining rooms all send a certain message. Administrative procedures can also communicate consideration or assembly-line impressions.

Routine medical encounters challenge physician attention spans. Listening is polite but superficial. Distractions are many. Focus may move from speaker's message to speaker's style. Only landmark facts or reports are gathered. Notes replace listening. Patients perceive the automatic pilot and may respond with anxiety or anger. The patient is very interested in the encounter. Success in relationships, whether business, entertainment, social, or personal, has often been linked to the ability to pay attention to the matter at hand. People say of whoever is a participant, "when we talked, he gave me his complete attention. . . . When we spoke, she was doing nothing else." The ability to direct and maintain attention should be practiced. Commitment is the word for this attention.

Many angry plaintiffs are said to have sued physicians for lack of personal warmth or curt treatment. They likely did not sue for curtness; they interpreted the lack of communication or interest as inattentive treatment, a lack of thought for their case. Many such patients have been negligently, inappropriately, or needlessly treated. The lack of manners is often accompanied by an unwillingness to adequately prepare the patient for what must be faced. Perceived lack of attention to the case, plus a surprise bad outcome, yields questions—if not blame—for the physician.

Physicians can establish a patient understanding of what is and what is not being offered by medicine. Asking what a patient expects or hopes for from the encounter is sometimes enlightening.

Establishing mutual understanding with each patient, including wide differences in value and philosophy, is often seen as "touchy-feely," not really the practice of medicine, or as a waste of time. Nevertheless, it is the surprised or disappointed patient who blames the physician for even unavoidable bad outcomes.

Any communication problems must be solved at the outset of patient care. Communication aids may be interpreters, hearing aids or amplification, a note taker for memory aid, or cultural counselor-advocate. It is before crucial decisions must be made in urgent circumstances that patient attitudes and wishes can be discovered and documented. Questions about organ donation, terminal treatment, euthanasia, religious limits on acceptable treatment, substituted consent, guardian appointment, durable powers of attorney for health care, and others should be resolved early.

Time, place, and opportunity should be given to patients for extra questions even if not seen as contributing to the diagnosis and treatment at hand. A sure sign a patient is being given short shrift is when questions are posed to staff and assistants after examination or treatment by the physician. Someone is giving the patient the impression that the physician has no time or inclination to hear patients' concerns.

Pathways to the physician and to patient's records should capture medically significant data offered. Patients may report facts or events to staff and assume the information is somehow transferred to the physician. Often patients will not complain about serious problems of the practice, insufficient explanation of diagnosis or treatment, inconsiderate staff, or lack of privacy unless they are asked about such matters in a frank and nonthreatening way. Asking for patient comment involves more than a check-off form; questions must be framed well, asked in the right setting, and an open-ended opportunity to reply given. The use of car-repair- postcard-type patient satisfaction queries underscores a failure of personal attention. Few patients will write anything of value to practice management until anger outweighs reticence. Most will comment on schedule or payment problems on forms, if at all.

Disclosure for Consent

Consent after disclosure of risks transfers the burden of adverse outcomes to the patient. The risk of physician negligence is not transferable, even with disclosures. Patients cannot consent to be treated negligently; nor can a patient consent to unindicated treatment. Unindicated treatment is always at the risk of the physician, since the patient is misled about necessity for treatment.

Consent forms should reflect disclosure and agreement of patient to consequences. Releases of liability in consent forms, or those executed before care or adverse outcome, are generally unenforceable. Nonnegligent treatment without consent leaves the burden of all consequences on the physician. Extension of a consented procedure to undiscussed treatment is excusable if an emergency occurs, requiring action to save life, limb, or major function. Discussion about what may be encountered and wishes of the patient for extensions or other treatment choices is best done before procedures.

Evidence of consent must also contain evidence of disclosure. Disclosure framed selectively to induce agreement for some physician benefit is fraudulent. All reasonable alternatives to proposed treatment, as well as the consequences of no treatment, should be disclosed. Disclosure is measured by patient understanding and need to decide. Disclosure may be made to the patient and others designated by the patient. Only the patient or the patient's guardian is able to give valid consent. More than one physician may be required to obtain consent to treatment.

Documentation of Consent Disclosure and Discussion

Diagnosis or diagnostic goal
Prognosis
Proposed treatment
  Anticipated benefit
  Anticipated risks
  Anticipated experience

Alternative treatments
  Anticipated benefit
  Anticipated risks
  Anticipated experience
Patient prognosis if no treatment undertaken
Patient expectation of effort, suffering, impairment
Residual changes if successful, unsuccessful
Costs

Signals for heightened consent process include: consent for physician project, lecture, book, rounds, study requiring patient record; observers or participants in treatment; autopsy; use of tissue, sample, or specimen taken from patient; variation on standard treatment, special consent issues, and rationale; and refusal of consent. For minors, unless a frank emergency occurs, even if blanket consent has been given, a parent should be informed and specific consent received. For reluctant patients, consent is not the main issue; disclosure and acceptance of consequences are. Consent forms will not work where more discussion is needed.

A physician's communication to patients that consent and consent forms are for the lawyers undermines the actual function of informed consent. Consent transfers the risks and consequences of nonnegligent medical care from the physician to the patient. The burden of consequences due to negligence cannot be transferred. Liability can be waived or released, but generally only after the fact and in exchange for value.

Risks and consequences are transferred by disclosure. Disclosure is the limit of the consent, except for common knowledge and unimportant matters. The general measure of sufficient disclosure is, what would a reasonable patient in this circumstance need to know to make a decision about diagnosis or treatment? Disclosure is measured also by its receipt. If the patient did not understand, the consent is ineffectual. Because it is the patient who will later complain of failed communication, it is the patient who must say, I understand completely. Many variations of consent forms exist, but forms can be no better than disclosure and consent. Because consequences are expected to be the patient's burden, knowledge of what consequences may occur is essential to effective consent.

Standards for disclosure include reasonable expectations from treatment or prognosis with no treatment. Patients need to be informed of the realities of their situation. Techniques such as disease staging and clinical outcomes assessment offer data for placing an individual patient in the right pathology and therapy "ballpark." Where the individual physician's outcome experience varies from the national or regional data, that divergence may have to be disclosed to provide the patient an appropriate basis for decision making. For example, a study shows that 6-month survival for Whipple surgeries vary from facility to facility. Disclosure of the current standards and guidelines and explanation of the patients' individual characteristics that fit or do not fit the standard profile for treatment may be useful communications. Disease staging is a concomitant of Diagnostic-Related Groups payment plans. Only by documenting the divergence of a specific patient's condition can appropriate compensation be achieved.

Both outcomes management and reimbursement accuracy can be aided by disease staging, which classifies the first and foremost determinant of therapeutic effectiveness: the biologic health of the patient. In disease staging, Stage 1 describes conditions with no complications or problems of minimal severity. Stage 2 relates to problems limited to one organ or system, but with significantly increased risk of complication. Stage 3 designates multiple site involvement, generalized systemic involvement, and poor prognosis.

Other means of communicating how seriously ill a patient may be include Acute Physiology and Chronic Health Evaluation (APACHE II), Computerized Severity Index (CSI), MedisGroups, and Patient Management Categories (PMCs). Disease Staging, CSI, and PMCs are diagnosis specific; MedisGroups and APACHE II are diagnosis independent. As utilization review and pretreatment certification activities increase, more use of diagnostic, severity, and treatment statistics can be anticipated. Disease staging defines casemix in practice and can be used to indicate appropriateness of care by connection with hospital admissions. For example, for a condition such as appendicitis, hospitalization is appropriate at the earliest stage; hypertension rarely requires hospitalization in early stage.

Outcomes assessment distinguishes between timely admission and preventable admission by use of stage data. Admission of a patient with Stage 1 appendicitis is timely and not preventable. Appropriateness of care is not at issue. Admission of a patient with Stage 2+ diabetes mellitus and cellulitis is also timely, but implies a question of preventable admission. Progression to this stage could have been averted by appropriate outpatient treatment. Patient admission for acute cholecystitis and gangrene of the gallbladder may also have been prevented. Evaluation of advanced stage treatment can reflect physician-related problems such as incorrect or delayed diagnosis, patient failure to seek treatment, insufficient access to prompt early treatment, or simply rapid progression of the disease process. A personal and private outcomes evaluation could be advisable in any practice.

Disclosure by patients is another key to appropriate consent procedure. Disclosure of patient values, perceptions, and anxieties can contribute importantly to the patient's agreement to real risks and consequences. Many practices move patients along to keep on schedule, and time for the physician to listen for real matters of concern or uncertainty is not allotted. Any matter of reluctance on the patient's part must be clarified. Patient reluctance is a sign that insufficient basis has been communicated. The patient may proceed, but without confidence in the decisions being made and unwillingness to take the burden of potential adverse outcomes. A reluctant patient is proceeding on trust and hope that nothing will go wrong, and transfers judgment to the physician. Later, the reluctant patient is angry for having ignored "better judgment" and blames the physician for being too persuasive.

Reassurance must have factual basis. Hope can exist in small statistical chances. However, the reality of possible and probable outcomes must be faced. Diagnostic or therapeutic statistics place the patient in a specific prognostic ballpark. Where in that space any one patient will be is speculative. Any patient can achieve the best prognostic outcome in the park.

Patient understanding is really the standard of disclosure. Once dependable communication is established, understanding can be presumed by the physician. New patients, or those whose backgrounds differ from the physician, may require more thorough exploration of circumstances and consequences of care.

Therapeutic nondisclosure offers physicians the option of not telling a patient about risks of diagnostic or therapeutic efforts. Protection is recognized if the physician documents appropriate reasons to forego disclosure. Reasons include the severity of the condition presented, the danger of the procedure or treatment, the certainty of the patient's inability to deal with disclosure, and the urgency of need to proceed with treatment. Withholding disclosure from a patient should be confirmed as appropriate by someone who knows the patient well and would agree that disclosure is more dangerous than the risks of the proposed treatment. The confirmation by the communications contact is not of the decision to proceed but the judgement to forego disclosure of risks. The patient must agree to discussion with the person consulted.

An enforceable guarantee may be established if a physician is found to have promised a result. A guarantee is measured by the patient's reasonable inference from physician disclosure. Part of disclosure and consent discussions should be a frank discussion of what physician and patient regard as "success." Nonclinical aspects may be important, such as a preferred activity, independence, and well-being, as compared with medical "success."

The role of staff and assistants in consent is the physician's delegation to staff of demonstration or education tasks. Staff cannot relieve physicians of the duty to obtain informed consent, nor take any share of blame for failure to obtain informed consent by ineffectual disclosure. Staff assistance can relieve physicians of some of the tasks that take time in disclosure, such as showing videotapes or films, distributing books or pamphlets, and introducing patients to support groups or advisory agencies. After all the educational and informational input, the physician still must discuss the medical indications, recommendations, alternatives, consequences, and prognoses and obtain the patient's knowing agreement to proceed. Records of standard education experiences, film, handouts, pictures, books, and tapes can be routinely given to patients with specific diagnosis, and as evidence of aids to disclosure, will show depth and detail of disclosures. Physician time is saved to answer questions and address uncertainties.

As diagnostic or treatment process continues, a duty to disclose and obtain consent continues. Reports of test results, positive or negative, should be prompt and interpreted. Assurance is needed by the physician that the patient continues to acquiesce to the therapeutic plan. Any unanticipated changes require new disclosure and a new plan. Implied in the communications between physician and patient is a presumption that a physician will not conceal any information that relates to the patient's state of health. This reliance by the patient is based on the trust relationship and prompts the physician's duty to disclose treatment error, whether personal or by others. Although malpractice is a legal term, and no legal conclusions are required of physicians, error that affects the patient's condition, therapy, or prognosis must be disclosed. Coverage of liability for negligent injuries is the purpose of liability insurance. Concealment of error may be an intentional injury for which liability insurance coverage will be denied.

Instructions and Monitoring

Instructions to patients must work. Warnings and instructions operate to install a monitor on therapy for complications and side effects. If the patient does not understand, instructions have not been presented properly. Patient questions to staff and assistants about treatment after seeing the physician, or calls to clarify instructions, are signs that physician discussion has not been effective. Instructions to patients must cover prescribed therapy, monitoring for complications, and reporting side effects. These tasks are being assigned to a medically unsophisticated layman. One advantage in the assignment is the motivation and priority attention the task will likely receive. Information, direction, and guidance, however, come from the physician. Patient failure to follow instructions can be a personal responsibility only if the transfer from physician to patient of the burden of compliance is effective. Protection of nonpatients is also largely the function of patient warnings and instructions. Potential complications must be divulged and direction given to report specific changes. Patient charts must reflect instructions and warnings and note receipt of copies of instructions and warnings by the patient.

Like disclosure for consent, instructions and warnings must be effective in terms of language, literacy, culture, or cognitive status. Follow-up appointments must be impressed on the patient with appropriate importance. The risk of not obtaining follow-up is transferred to the patient by disclosure of the reason for later examination or treatment. Warnings and instructions to largely competent patients suffering from mental lapses or those treated for substance abuse may require asking the patient to designate a "safety officer" a family member or friend, to help remind and comply with care requirements.

Discussion with Family, Others

Contact with third parties is only with the patient's permission. Answers to the most common queries and comments to staff should be prepared and used uniformly. Policy for answering or deferring unusual questions should be established.

Any contact or communication with third parties about patients is limited by the patient's consent to discussion and disclosure. With intrafamily tensions common in social and medical situations, only the patient determines with whom any facts or details of diagnosis or treatment can be shared. While communication to family or others about patients is limited, communication from others that may help in patient care should be valued. When family complains about care, some consideration must be paid to verify or correct the matter. Any negative comments or complaints to staff should be logged and communicated to the physician.

Medical Records

An effective record accomplishes both medical and administrative goals. Although many records tasks can be delegated, responsibility cannot. An illegible record is documented lack of care. Tasks that can be made routine by protocols written once, leaving only exceptions to be recorded. Other features and content of records may include:

Direct quotes from patients
Facts
Reporter identity
Tentative impressions marked as such
Standard abbreviations
Date and time stamped by automatic device
Errors and omissions dated and corrected clearly, by identified agent
Warning systems to alert physician when data record rising hazard
Records made while events fresh
All patient participation or failure recorded
No gossip
No politics
No blame
Medical coherence

To support defensible practice, records must demonstrate a coherent process leading to reasonable judgment. Medical history "quotes" the patient. Examination is appropriate for the presentation. Individual patient characteristics are noted, such as allergies and previous medical events. A diagnosis or diagnostic process fits the facts of the presentation. Notes of discussions with patients reveal appropriate facts as basis for decisions. Disclosures and instructions are given appropriately to continue and monitor treatment.

While the medical analytic process that prompts records cannot be delegated or preformatted, record keeping can be simplified,

organized, and automated. Flowcharts support specific diagnostic and therapeutic programs. Computers and checklist records prompt completion and accuracy. Because acquiring a new records system is similar to marriage, time and effort to get acquainted before purchase are advisable. A few weeks of this effort would be repaid later.

Every patient encounter is documentable in medical practice. Phone calls are remote medical visits. The priority of function is patient care; however, records protect and support physician, patient, staff, consultants, and payment agencies.

In questioned care, some common findings related to records have been noted. Physicians often fail in disclosure of risks of prescribed medications. Patients can establish physician liability for known side effects of prescription medication that are not disclosed and warned of.

A record of reasonable diagnostic and therapeutic process allows for a range of prognostic error. Medical records must document instructions sufficient for patient protection. Disclosure and instruction from the physician can enable the patient to avoid or detect complications. A physician cannot avoid the duty to record and communicate orders.

Records allow fulfillment of duties to contact current and former patients about hazards. Records demonstrate physician awareness and provide notice to check that instructions were followed. Failure of written notation is not evidence of negligence but will make claims of negligence difficult to defend. Records prompt a duty to follow up orders given. Records support a physician's differential diagnostic process by showing a diagnosis supported by recorded clinical findings and evidence of monitoring or note of abnormal anatomy.

Absent records imply at best a failure of attention and care. At worst, lost records raise a suspicion that records would show error. Record alteration demonstrates intentional effort at concealment.

Although records are important defense tools, the major importance of records is for patient care. Excessive concern by physicians on legal forms and witnesses and impatience with recordkeeping lets patients know medical thoroughness is not a priority. If physician protection devices are established, and many should be, they should not be made central to the treatment encounter. Tape records of consent disclosures may be less intrusive and more economical of staff time than presence of "witnesses."

Fees should not be kept for surprise. Discuss costs in routine communications, and specifically for special and expensive procedures or treatment. If patients cannot pay and cannot be cared for without payment, transfer of care must be made to a physician or facility where free or limited payment benefits are acceptable. Repeated billing requests should avoid the tone of red stickers and computer form reminders. Medical practice is a personal contact and billing reminders should be also. If possible, encourage credit card use. Staff must have a script for contacts with patients about bills. Bill collection activities should also be personally evaluated by the physician if treatment is not successful or by physician and legal counsel if there is any question of negligence. Records must never be held hostage for payment of outstanding bills.

Cases

How Does Optimism Differ from Promise?

The patient experienced recurrent hemorrhage from a peptic ulcer; the latest episode had been associated with shock. His family physician admitted him to the hospital and obtained consultation with a surgeon who told him that there was "no danger at all" in the operation, that the operation "takes care of all your troubles," that he could "throw his pillbox and Maalox away," and that he would be able to return to work in "approximately 3 to 4 weeks at the most." A gastrectomy and vagotomy were performed but the surgery was complicated by a perforated esophagus and a resultant mediastinitis. When three subsequent reparative operations were required, thus prolonging the hospitalization, the patient sued the surgeon charging that the promised cure was not delivered under the contract for medical services. The surgeon denied he had promised a cure.

A physician and patient are at liberty to contract with respect to their relationship. The physician–patient relationship, however, is different because a physician's therapeutic reassurance to the patient is usually not converted by a disappointed patient into a binding promise. Loose or exaggerated language, however, when presented in a manner that a patient would reasonably accept at face value, may be sufficient to establish a binding promise. Furthermore, where a physician expressly or implicitly enters into a special agreement for a certain result, he may be liable under a breach of warranty theory if the specified result is not effected, even if the physician exercised extraordinary skill and care.

The determination of whether the surgeon and the patient had entered into a "special agreement to cure" depends on the factual intent and characterization of the words that were spoken, and the circumstances under which they were spoken. As in all contract cases for personal services, to find for the plaintiff, the jury must find from the evidence that the physician made a specific, clear, and express promise to cure or to effect a specific result. The promise must have been relied on by the patient. In this case the jury could reasonably have inferred that such a promise had been made.

How Can Physician and Patient Interests Conflict?

The scar tissue on the patient's hand was the result of a severe electrical burn that he had received years before he consulted a surgeon about treatment for the hand. On several occasions, the surgeon strongly recommended an operation that would involve removing the scar tissue from the palm of the patient's hand and then grafting skin from his chest. Before the operation was decided on, the patient went to the surgeon's office and asked, "How long will I be in the hospital?" The surgeon said, "Three or 4 days, not more than 4; then you can go home, and in a few days you will go back to work with a good hand." The surgeon also said, "I will make that hand a 100% good hand." Eventually, the surgeon persuaded the patient to consent to the operation. The grafting procedure went poorly, producing a dysfunctional hand. In addition, as a result of the complications of the procedure, the patient also was required to stay in the hospital well beyond 4 days. The patient sued the physician, charging a breach of contract both in terms of the hospitalization period and the functional result of the operation. The surgeon contended that even if he did utter the words that he would make a "good hand," a reasonable person would understand the words were not used with the intention of entering into a contractual relationship. The surgeon argued that common knowledge of the uncertainty that attends all surgical operations and the improbability that a surgeon would ever contract to make a damaged part of the human body "100%," should have been decisive in this case.

Circumstances in this case tend to support the patient's contention that certain results were guaranteed by the surgeon. The surgeon repeatedly solicited from the patient the opportunity to perform the operation. This conduct raises the inference that the surgeon sought to perform skin grafting to enhance his clinical experience in those procedures. Thus if the surgeon in fact spoke the words attributed to him, it might reasonably be inferred that he did so with the intention that his words should be accepted at face value as an inducement for the granting of consent to the operation by the patient. The legal question of whether a contract existed was properly submitted to the jury.

When Is Documented Consent Not Consent?

A man consulted a surgeon because he noticed a lump on his abdomen. The surgeon diagnosed a ventral hernia and recommended surgery. The patient stated that if repair of the hernia in any way involved surgery on a recent ileostomy that he had had performed in another city, he wanted to return to that city for the operation. The patient signed a surgical permission form for a "repair of ventral hernia." The evening before surgery, after he had been asleep, he was awakened by a nurse who told him that the consent form had to be completed. She pointed to a paper where the patient was to sign. The patient complied by signing another consent form for a repair of a ventral hernia and revision of ileostomy. Later, the patient could not specifically recall signing this form. When the surgeon discovered that the hernia protruded from the same opening in the abdominal wall as the ileostomy, he concluded that relocation or revision of the ileostomy was required. Accordingly, he repaired the hernia and revised the ileostomy. The patient developed complications that required additional surgery and a protracted course of treatment. He then sued the surgeon for performing unauthorized surgery on his ileostomy.

The surgeon should not have proceeded with an operation that the patient had refused, unless at a time when fully oriented, the patient had changed his mind and consented to its performance. When the patient "consented" to the additional procedure he was not fully aware of what he was signing. By performing an unconsented procedure, the surgeon became liable for all consequences of the procedure.

What Is the Standard to Judge Disclosures to Patients?

Before the birth of her fifth child, for which a caesarean section was contemplated, the patient informed her physician that she did not want more children because she could not afford any more. The physician recommended sterilization. The physician did not inform her of the various methods available for tubal ligation because he believed it was adequate to merely inform the patient that a tubal ligation was to be the method of sterilization. Moreover, he felt that the final choice about which technique to use should be made by the surgeon only after the surgeon has entered the abdominal cavity and observed the condition of the uterus. At the time the procedure was performed there were several methods in common use for sterilization by tubal ligation. The physician used a technique that was the simplest, but had a higher risk of failure when performed at the time of a caesarean delivery than other available methods. The failure rates for the various methods were never discussed with the patient, nor was it explained that the failure rates for all the procedures diminished drastically when performed at a time other than when a caesarean section is performed. The sterilization procedure proved ineffective, and the patient became pregnant with her sixth child. She sued the physician, charging that he failed to obtain her informed consent for the type of procedure and was therefore responsible for the damages sustained as a result of its ineffectiveness.

The information withheld from the patient was material to the decision that a reasonable person with the patient's concerns would have about having another child. The patient would have attached significance to the selected technique's projected risk of failure, the relative risk of continuing fertility of other techniques, and the increased risk of failure inherent in sterilization performed at Caesarean section. Without this information, the patient was denied the opportunity of deciding whether to undergo the sterilization at delivery or at a later date when the risk of failure would have been reduced significantly, even if the risk of second surgery had to be faced.

If disclosure of material risks would not have changed the decision of a reasonable person in the patient's position, there is no causal connection between disclosure and damage. In this case, however, the patient's decision to undergo sterilization was prompted by the high concern to avoid a subsequent pregnancy. Thus the effectiveness of the operation would have been a very important factor in her decision-making process.

What Circumstances Justify Therapeutic Nondisclosure?

The patient had a history of hypertension and chronic renal disease and a recently diagnosed abdominal aortic aneurysm. His cardiologist proposed an aortogram to better define the aneurysm. He explained the procedure to the patient, relating that his femoral artery would be opened, a tube placed in the artery, and dye injected through the tube. The physician said nothing to the patient, however, about the attendant collateral risk of paralysis because the patient was very frightened and apprehensive about his condition and was experiencing chest pain. The cardiologist wished to reassure him and said, "This simply is an injection of material into your circulation so we can outline the swelling or widening of your aorta." The cardiologist thought that full disclosure would not be in the patient's best medical interest in view of the patient's psychologic condition, and that the chance of the collateral risk materializing was relatively minimal. As a result of the procedure, the patient was paraplegic. He sued, claiming that he had not been properly informed of the risk of the treatment. The patient's wife contended that if the patient could not be told, she should have been told about the risk of paralysis.

A physician is not required to disclose alarming risks of an urgently needed procedure if in the physician's best clinical judgment disclosure would be harmful to the patient. From the explanation given to him, the patient had an understanding of the general nature and purpose of the procedure. The physician's omission of the risk of paralysis was within the exception to the duty of full disclosure which excuses the withholding of information for therapeutic reasons. A responsible physician would not disclose information that was likely to induce an adverse psychogenic reaction in a patient highly apprehensive of his condition.

The duty of a physician to make full disclosure is one that originates from the physician–patient relationship and thus it is owed to the patient and not to a relative. If, in situations in which the patient could not be told, a physician has to obtain consent from a spouse, the necessary corollary of that requirement would be that the spouse could refuse consent to the proposed treatment. Such a situation would be incongruous because a spouse does not have the legal right to withhold consent to medical services. When withholding important information from a patient is called for by therapeutic considerations, full disclosure to a family member may help the physician in deciding his or her course of action, because of the family's knowledge of the patient's reaction patterns. Nevertheless, a physician does not have a legal duty to make such a disclosure to the family.

Among Specialists, Who Has a Duty to Disclose and Discuss Alternatives?

When conization of the cervix disclosed early invasive carcinoma, a woman's gynecologist advised her to undergo a radium implantation, and set up a referral to the radiation therapy department. Neither the gynecologist nor the radiation therapist explained to the patient that a hysterectomy was an alternative therapeutic modality to the radium implant procedure. After implantation the radiation therapist visited her and inquired how she was feeling. After discharge from the hospital, the patient experienced persistent vaginal burning and diarrhea and developed a radiation-induced rectoureterovaginal fistula, requiring a radical hysterectomy and a bowel resection. Later, the patient sued the radiation therapist for failure to obtain her informed consent for the radiation therapy. The patient testified that she was not told of any of the unpleasant aftereffects or possible complications. If she had been informed that a hysterectomy was an alternative to radiation, she would have elected to have the hysterectomy. The radiation therapist contended that he was only called into the case as a "consultant," and that the gynecologist was the patient's attending physician; therefore, it was the gynecologist's responsibility to obtain an informed consent for the procedure. He testified that when he was first contacted about treating the patient, he assumed that the gynecologist had fully discussed the procedure with his patient.

The radiation therapist performed the implantation and therefore was required to disclose the nature and need for the procedure, certain risks associated with its performance, and the clinical alternatives to the proposed treatment. The radiation therapist was an independent treating physician responsible for care of the patient. The gynecologist and the patient reasonably assumed that the radiation therapist would be responsible for the implantation. Therefore, the radiation therapist did not adhere to the medical standards when he "assumed" consent had been obtained by the referring physician and failed to obtain the informed consent for himself. It was the gynecologist's duty to discuss alternatives, such as hysterectomy, with the patient. Both had a duty to discuss risks and hazards of radiation.

When Instructions Do Not Succeed, Whose Fault Is It?

The patient underwent abdominal surgery. She experienced a wound dehiscence shortly after the sutures were removed. Her surgeon resutured the incision. After her discharge from the hospital, she returned to him on several occasions for treatment and finally for removal of the sutures. Subsequently, she moved to another city where she was hospitalized because the surgical wound had become infected. A surgeon reopened, cleaned, and packed the wound with iodoform gauze. It was repacked, and the patient was discharged from the hospital 2 days later. The following day she returned to the hospital, and the wound was again repacked. Several days later, the surgeon told her that he had unpacked the incision and that she should go home and take it easy but return in 2 weeks. The hospital discharge summary, however, indicated that she was to "return to the clinic" 2 weeks after her discharge to remove packing. Six weeks later she experienced abdominal pain and went to a different hospital. Radiographs of her abdomen disclosed a foreign body. She underwent surgery and an iodoform gauze was removed from her previous incision site. The patient brought suit against the physician for having left the gauze in place. Expert testimony established that it was not customary practice to leave the gauze inside a wound for longer than 1 week.

The physician's faulty explanation of purpose and time of the postsurgical follow-up visits caused the patient to miss necessary aftercare. The physician was expected to reasonably anticipate recognized complications and provide the patient with instructions that would signal the occurrence of complications and instructions to return. To accomplish this, a physician is expected to give the patient sufficient information to prompt return for further necessary care.

What Constitutes Reasonable Instructions?

The patient's first-trimester abortion by suction and curettage had been uncomplicated. When she left the clinic she was given two printed documents that covered what signs she should look for in the following weeks. She was advised that she might experience light bleeding for several days, but continued heavy bleeding, severe cramps, and a high fever could indicate tissue retention for which she could require a repeat procedure. The documents also instructed that if cramps were too severe to respond to medication, or did not improve after rest, she was to call the clinic. She was instructed to "call if you have or suspect any problems." The instructions also said "DO NOT overtire yourself or take up unusual strenuous exercise; DO NOT swim or douche until the bleeding has completely stopped." By the time the patient arrived home from the clinic she was in pain and bleeding. She called the physician, who prescribed methylergonovine (Methergine) and told the patient to call back if her problems persisted. After she took the medication, her pain subsided and the bleeding ceased for the next 5 days. Two days later when she went on vacation, she began bleeding heavily. She was taken to the hospital where exploratory laparotomy uncovered a large peritoneal hematoma and a perforated uterus.

The patient sued the physician claiming that she had received confusing, inconsistent, and misleading postoperative instructions that had urged her to resume a normal life as soon as possible and to avoid strenuous exercise for a few weeks. She attempted to demonstrate inconsistencies in the oral and written instructions.

The physician was required to instruct the patient about postabortion complications, the hazards of future activities, and the need for future care. The physician would be accountable if documents furnished to the patient as part of postoperative care were misleading and consequentially caused the patient subsequent problems. In this case, however, because the perforation was an inherent risk of the procedure, the patient attempted to prove the instructions were negligent to establish liability. When read as a whole, the overriding message was for the patient to call if there were any problems that would appear unusual to a reasonably prudent patient. The instructions were sufficient.

How Much Instruction Is Needed for Patient Safety?

A man was struck in the eye with a small piece of steel that flew off a hatchet he was using. He went to a hospital emergency department, where he was examined by an ophthalmologist. A red spot was noted on the sclera, which might have indicated a contusion or a point of entry of a foreign body. An injury to the lower eyelid was probed and a piece of steel was removed. Although the ophthalmologist thought that this was the only foreign body in the eye, a piece of steel embedded in the orbit had gone unnoticed. The ophthalmologist told the patient the foreign body had been removed. When the patient then asked the ophthalmologist if he needed more treatment, the ophthalmologist told him it was not necessary. The next day the patient's eye pain became worse but he did not know pain was a sign of problems. By the following day, the intensity of the pain had become so bad that the patient returned to the ophthalmologist's office. The ophthalmologist ordered a radiograph, which disclosed a sharp metallic foreign body in the orbit, but by then a serious orbital infection had occurred and the eye was lost. The patient sued the ophthalmologist for failing to diagnose the foreign body sooner by means of appropriate follow-up.

The standard of care for treatment of such patients is to see the physician the following day to further examine the injury. The physician failed to follow up on the case properly and to give proper instructions to the patient to accomplish this purpose. The physician was obligated to advise the patient of the need for ongoing or additional evaluation to effect a complete recovery. Thus the physician had the burden of establishing an understanding with the patient regarding expected recovery or need for follow-up care, and instructions for reporting significant symptoms.

Must All Medical Injuries Be Disclosed?

While excising a suspicious right posterior cervical lymph node, a surgeon negligently injured the spinal accessory nerve. After the operation, the patient told the surgeon that it was difficult and painful for her to raise her right arm and shoulder. Although the physician was aware that the negligent surgery had caused a potentially permanent injury, he told the patient that her postoperative problems would disappear if she would continue the physical therapy he had prescribed. One year later, while still undergoing physical therapy, the patient was told by another physician that her condition had probably been caused at the time of her surgery. The reanastomosis of the severed nerve 3 years after the surgery did not bring about physiologically successful results. The patient sued the original surgeon, charging that he had told her that physical therapy would help, even though he knew it was untrue and that she would rely on his advice. She contended that this fraudulent misrepresentation deprived her of the opportunity for successful repair of the condition initially caused by his negligence.

Ordinarily a physician's concealment of his own malpractice does not give rise to a legal cause of action in fraud distinct from the malpractice action. In this case, however, the physician had reason to know that he negligently injured his patient, and knowingly made material misrepresentation concerning the cause and effect of the injury and the therapy appropriate to its cure. Worse, the patient was diverted from undertaking an available, efficacious remedy in consequence of the misrepresentation. Therefore his misrepresentation to his patient was not merely negligent but intentional and fraudulent.

How Is Reasonable Misdiagnosis Defensible?

A mother took her young child to the family physician because the child had lower abdominal pain, vomiting, and fever. The physician recorded that he had examined the abdomen and found no significant localized tenderness, referred pain, or rebound indicative of an "acute abdomen." He noted that the tonsils were erythematous, and indicated that he believed the elevated white blood count was more compatible with tonsillitis than appendicitis. Although a radiograph of the abdomen disclosed a "reflex ileus," the physician recorded that he believed this was more of a nonspecific finding than an indication of appendicitis. Based on his clinical findings and reasoning, the physician diagnosed "tonsillitis" and prescribed penicillin. A few days later, the child was hospitalized with a ruptured appendix and peritonitis. On behalf of the child the parents sued the physician for negligent misdiagnosis.

The physician's medical record was evidence that he diligently and carefully formulated his diagnosis. The record indicated that he undertook a reasonably skillful formulation of the patient's problem in the exercise of clinical judgment, which in retrospect was erroneous. His record reflected that he had performed the customary methods of diagnosis. The diagnosis of "tonsillitis" was based on clinical findings recorded in the medical record, and was not based simply on intuition or the result of careless assessment. Therefore, even though clinical findings were consistent with other disorders, the physician's judgment was not negligent because it was predicated on the application of careful and diligent methods of diagnosis as reflected by his medical record.

What Function Does Recordkeeping Perform in Claims of Malpractice?

A 2-year-old child was scheduled to undergo surgery for correction of congenital deformities of the feet. The operation had previously been delayed because the child had a persistent upper respiratory infection, was poorly nourished, and underweight. While under general anesthesia, the child died. As a result of her unexpected death, the parents sued the physicians and hospital. The medical records indicated that the procedure had been previously delayed because of her infection. It also noted her weight was still low for her age. The "Nurses' Notes" contained notations of nasal discharges on the day preceding the anesthesia, including one such notation made hours before the child was taken to the operating room.

The child's medical record was used to support the inference that the anesthesiologist negligently failed to delay the operation. The evidence in the medical records suggested the procedure should have been further delayed because of the child's infection. The physician was required to explain and justify the appropriateness of administering anesthesia under the circumstances. In effect, the anesthesiologist had the difficult task of reconciling the decision to put the child under general anesthesia and proceeding with surgery in light of evidence of the child's continuing infected and debilitated clinical state.

How Can an Operative Note Reflect Nonnegligent Injury?

Immediately after a subtotal thyroidectomy, the patient's left vocal cord was totally and permanently paralyzed. A pathologist reported that the excised thyroid gland was three times normal size and was chronically inflamed, but contained no trace of the recurrent laryngeal nerve. The patient sued the surgeon, charging that he negligently severed the recurrent laryngeal nerve, causing vocal cord paralysis. At deposition during the pretrial discovery phase of litigation, the surgeon opined that surgical destruction of the nerve would be negligent unless thyroid disease made dissection difficult, or unless anatomic variations of the nerve through the operative area made injury unavoidable. The surgeon testified that he had no independent recollection of the operation, other than what his records disclosed. The operative report, dictated the day after surgery, did not refresh the surgeon's memory nor could he identify it as being a transcript of his recollection. He could only say that the surgical procedures he used in the patient's case would have been those he routinely followed in excising the thyroid gland, including visualizing the recurrent laryngeal nerve in the operative area where it is most vulnerable to surgical trauma. He admitted that it was good practice for a surgeon to note in his operative report when the nerve cannot be found, or when it has an anomalous course through the portion of the thyroid gland that is to be removed. No mention in the surgical record was made of any problems, variation, or difficulties encountered during the operation. After the operative steps, including visualization of the right recurrent laryngeal nerve through the dissection of the right lobe of the thyroid gland, had been mentioned, the report then stated: "On the left, the same procedure was done." No note was made of anything abnormal in the appearance of anomalous course of the left recurrent laryngeal nerve or that the nerve or the gland presented any problem in connection with the operation.

If the large size of the gland involved the nerve making surgery difficult, the surgeon should have mentioned that fact in the operative report. Ordinarily a thyroid that is markedly enlarged creates particular operating difficulties worth mentioning in the report. If the surgeon had recorded accurately and fully in his operative report everything of consequence that he did and observed during the operation, and if he had dictated the report immediately after the operation, the report would more likely have supplied sufficient facts to support testimony on the question of negligence. Instead, the report was not dictated until the day following the operation, after the surgeon had observed the patient's speech problem. Reports that are not contemporaneous are less reliable about the accuracy of entries and damage a physician's credibility where his conduct is at issue. Although the report did state that the recurrent laryngeal nerve was visualized while operating on the right side of the gland, no mention was made of the operative steps used on the left side. A court will not necessarily assume that the nerve was also visualized on the left side and that the operation was completed with faultless technique. A small percentage of thyroidectomies result in damage to the laryngeal nerve in spite of all precautions. Ordinarily, the surgeon is the person who can report such precautions in a full and accurate report of what was observed and done through the surgical incision. The surgeon failed to prepare such a report. That, coupled with his absence of personal recollection or recorded facts, make it extremely difficult to explain and justify his conduct in injuring the nerve.

What Constitutes a Valid Refusal of Necessary Treatment?

A 33-year-old patient underwent a saphenous varicose vein sclerosing procedure. Immediately after recovery from general anesthesia, impairment of circulation to the patient's lower extremity caused intense pain. Her physician recommended a paravertebral sympathetic block to improve the compromised circulation. Because of her suffering and the administration of drugs, the patient was unable to comprehend the seriousness of her condition. The physician tried to explain things to her but indicated that "she was pretty much hysterical." As a result of her confused condition, she refused to undergo the sympathetic block. Her husband, who was present in the hospital, was not consulted about the need for the procedure. Eventually vascular gangrene developed, requiring amputation of her toes. The patient sued the physician, charging that his negligent inaction caused the partial loss of her foot. The physician contended that the patient's disability resulted from her refusal to submit to a postoperative paravertebral block. The patient countered this contention by charging that the physician negligently failed to advise her of the need for such a procedure.

A patient is expected to reasonably follow appropriate medical instructions or advice. When the patient fails or refuses and an injury results, the patient—not the physician—ordinarily will bear the burden of the damages. Although it is the patient's responsibility to follow the physician's advice, in some situations the patient may be unable to comprehend what the physician is recommending. When the patient is incapable of adequate comprehension but urgently requires a proposed treatment, and the physician is aware of the patient's impaired cognition, the physician's duty to inform the patient of the necessity for the treatment does not end by simply advising the treatment. Depending on circumstances, such as the seriousness and the urgency of the situation, or the patient's mental incapacity, a physician may be obligated to take necessary steps to make the patient understand the recommended treatment.

In this case, the physician did not discuss the urgent procedure with the patient at a time when she was capable of adequately understanding him or when she was sufficiently in possession of her mental faculties. The physician would not necessarily be liable because he could not convince or persuade his temporarily incompetent patient to accept his recommended treatment. However, he would be required to make further effort to communicate with such a patient at a more propitious time or to communicate with the spouse or someone in a position to help communicate with the patient.

Forms

Communication with patients is best done before urgent events are presented. Clearly expressed patient's wishes and designated decisions or a decision maker allow physician and patient to trust that the best and most personally directed actions will be chosen. Too often decisions must be made by physicians and relatives with too little information and preparation. Advance directives, living wills, and durable powers of attorney are all mechanisms to have the patient's wishes known and followed. At a minimum, conversations, if not documents, are advisable to define possibilities and choices if patient consciousness or coherence is impaired.

Advance directives attempt to predict circumstances and to set forth the patient's wishes for decision making. A durable power of attorney may recite certain directives and, more importantly, appoints a person chosen by the patient to take responsibility for decisions that become necessary after the patient cannot personally make them. The patient chooses a person to assure that decisions will be made as the patient would make them. This person may not necessarily be a spouse or family member. In many cases it is better that the chosen decision maker be a close friend who knows the patient's wishes and values intimately but is not as ambivalent about hard choices as are close family members. The guardian for health care decisions appointed may also be better named outside of family members who may have inheritance possibilities or other financial conflicts of interest.

Expressions of patient wishes informally made in the medical context may be recorded in the chart and used where no other indication of patient values has been offered. Each state has different laws on refusal of lifesaving treatment, withdrawal of artificial life support, and effects of advance directives and living wills. A number of state agencies and national societies provide blank forms for durable powers of attorney and advance directives. Direction from legal counsel about the content and effect of directive documents is best followed by opening the subject with patients as early as possible, when urgent decisions have not yet been presented.

Example Form: Durable Power of Attorney for Health Care

Statement of Intent

I am executing this Durable Power of Attorney for Health Care to enable [name], hereinafter referred to as my Attorney, to make health care decisions for me on my behalf in the event that, in the future, I am not able to make such decisions myself.

One of the primary purposes in executing this Durable Power of Attorney for Health Care is to provide for the possibility that, through illness or incapacity, I may lose the ability to care for myself and to interact with others. If I am unable to communicate my wishes, I request my Attorney's decision with respect to my care and to the elimination of extraordinary measures to be guided by my preferences that I have discussed in detail with him/her, in conjunction with the advice and information provided by physicians treating me. In keeping with my preferences, my Attorney may specifically request and concur with the withholding or withdrawal of any care or treatment, including "no-code" (do not resuscitate) orders by the attending or treating physician.

Appointment of Attorney and Recitation of Powers

I, [name], intending to create a Durable Power of Attorney for Health Care, hereby appoint [name] as my Attorney, to make health care decisions for me and in my name. In addition to the powers heretofore conferred on my Attorney, he/she shall have the following powers:

To give consent to or withhold approval for the performance of medical procedures on me, including any or all under consideration by treating physicians or others;

To request, review, and receive any information, verbal or written, regarding my physical or mental health, including but not limited to medical and hospital records, and to consent or withhold consent to the disclosure of this information;

To employ and/or discharge my health care providers;

To consent to and authorize my admission to and discharge from a hospital or care institution;

If I am terminally ill, permanently unconscious, in a persistent vegetative state, or incapable of relating to others, to direct the withholding or withdrawal of life-sustaining procedures or measures that only serve to artificially prolong the dying process, and may include any therapeutic or technologic modality; and

To take any lawful actions that may be necessary to carry out these decisions, including granting releases of liability to medical providers.

This Durable Power of Attorney for Health Care shall not be revoked, impaired, or otherwise affected by any disability of mine that may hereafter occur. This Power of Attorney shall be irrevocable during any period that I am under disability.

I hereby ratify and confirm any and all acts that my Attorney shall do or cause to be done in the exercise of authority and discretion granted herein.

If it should become necessary or advisable to have a guardian of the person appointed for me, I request that my Attorney, [name], be named as guardian, and I waive a jury trial in connection with such appointment.

I do expressly authorize any party dealing with my Attorney to rely implicitly and explicitly on all acts performed by him/her in my name, with no liability or responsibility to that party for such reliance.

[signature]

[witnesses]

Example Form: Advance Directive

Recitation of emotional and mental competence and intent to declare wishes.

Acknowledgment of direction that death not be artificially prolonged under the following circumstances:

> A terminal condition determined by treating physician (with the concurrence of one other physician) with no reasonable hope of recovery and death likely with or without treatment.
>
> A permanently unconscious or persistently vegetative state from which no reasonable hope of return to cognitive and sapient life determined by attending and confirming physicians.

Appointment of guardian to make health care decisions, including decision to withhold/withdraw life support, medication, and artificial nutrition with the exception of therapy for comfort or to alleviate pain even if the therapy will result in death.

Where specified circumstances exist, direction that life-prolonging procedures be withheld/withdrawn, including life support, resuscitation, medication, and nutrition or hydration, with the exception of that therapy necessary to provide comfort or alleviate pain, even if therapy hastens death.

Direction to family, friends, and health care providers to follow directive and acquiesce in guardian's decisions, including transfer to the care of health care providers who are able and willing to do so.

Exceptions for pregnancy.

Expression of partial validity if some directives cannot be followed.

Date for termination of Directive, if any.

Example Form: Refusal by Guardian of Life-Sustaining Therapy for Patient

Acknowledgment of full authority to make health care decisions on behalf of patient named.

Note of medical condition affirmed by attending physician.

Recognition that therapy to be withheld/withdrawn is necessary to sustain life and without therapy, death is expected.

Direction to withhold/withdraw therapy.

Recitation of consequences of decision and full disclosure by physicians of the nature of the illness, the nature of the therapy described, prognosis with and without the therapy, and the fact that death is expected to occur as a result of this decision.

Note of discussion of matter with objective and involved persons consulted for comment and acquiescence but not for consent or concurrence.

Release of physicians and medical personnel and facilities from responsibility as a result of this decision.

Example Form: Refusal by Competent Adult of Life-Sustaining Treatment

Acknowledgment of competence to make health care decisions.

Note of medical condition affirmed by attending physician.

Recognition that therapy to be withheld/withdrawn is necessary to sustain life and without therapy, death is expected.

Direction to withhold/withdraw therapy.

Recitation of consequences of decision and full disclosure by physicians of the nature of the illness, the nature of the therapy described, prognosis with and without the therapy, and the fact that death is expected to occur as a result of this decision.

Note of discussion of matter with objective and involved persons consulted for comment and acquiescence but not for consent or concurrence.

Release of physicians and medical personnel and facilities from responsibility as a result of this decision.

Example Form: Anatomic Gift Declaration

Declaration to make anatomic gift, if medically acceptable, to take effect on death.

Recitation of consent to donated organs or anatomic parts.

Any needed parts

Only listed organs or parts

Recitation of allowable donation purpose: transplantation, therapy, medical research, or education, entire body for anatomic study if needed.

Specific limitations or wishes, if any:

Signature by the donor and witnesses.

Example Form: Living Donor Consent to Donate Organ for Transplant

Authorization and consent to removal of specified organ for the purpose of transplanting it into the body of named individual or another human being or into the storage facilities maintained for transplantation at a later time.

Authorization for surgery by named physician.

Recitation of informed consent disclosures of nature and purpose of the operation, risks involved, possible consequences, and possible complications.

Consent to the administration of anesthetics.

Acknowledge of no guarantee or assurance of success or safety.

Consent to photograph or videotape of procedures performed, including portions of body, for medical, scientific, or educational purposes, provided no identity is revealed by pictures or descriptive texts.

Consent, for medical education purposes, to the attendance by observers to the operating room.

Example Form: General Authorization to Allow Observers

Date of authorization, termination date of authorization, if any.

Patient identification data.

Physician, facility, department.

Acknowledgment of purpose for admitted observers, recitation of expected number and type of observers.

Authorization to specific physician and/or facility to permit the presence of observers for designated purposes in addition to physicians and hospital personnel during surgery, delivery, examination, or treatment.

Example Form: Consent to Taking and Use of Photographs and Images

Date of authorization, termination date of authorization, if any.

Patient identification data.

Physician, facility, department.

Photographer.

Acknowledgment of purpose for photographs or images, recitation of expected number, and type of pictures.

Authorization to specific physician and/or facility to take photographs for designated purposes before, after, or during specified procedures or treatment, surgery, delivery, or examination.

Designation and limits on purpose and use of photographs, medical records, research, education or science, publication in professional journals or medical books, publication in other than professional journals or medical books, or other purpose proper to interests of medical education, knowledge, or research.

Specification of anonymity, with permission to the physician to modify or retouch the images.

Example Form: Documentation of Consent Disclosure and Discussion

Date of disclosures.

Patient identification data.

Acknowledgment by patient that discussion has covered the following topics, with a brief quote of the patient's interpretation of disclosure either written by the patient or transcribed from conversation.

- Diagnosis or diagnostic goal
- Prognosis
- Proposed treatment
  - Anticipated benefit
  - Anticipated risks
  - Anticipated experience
- Alternative treatments
  - Anticipated benefit
  - Anticipated risks
  - Anticipated experience

Patient prognosis if no diagnosis, treatment undertaken.

Patient expectation of effort, suffering.

Residual changes if successful, unsuccessful.

Costs.

Example Form: Refusal of Recommended Treatment

Date of disclosures.

Date of refusal.

Time and place of disclosures and refusal.

Patient identification data.

Acknowledgment by patient that discussion has covered the following topics, with a brief quote of the patient's interpretation of disclosure either written by the patient or transcribed from conversation.

Diagnosis or diagnostic goal

Prognosis

Proposed treatment
Anticipated benefit
Anticipated risks
Anticipated experience

Alternative treatments
Anticipated benefit
Anticipated risks
Anticipated experience

Patient prognosis if no diagnosis, treatment undertaken.

Patient expectation of effort, suffering.

Residual changes, if successful, unsuccessful.

Costs.

Statement of refusal.

Statement of understanding and willingness to accept consequences of refusal.

Release of physician, hospital, and staff from liability for consequences of refusal.

Example Form: Special Consent

Prescription Medication
Placement of Intrauterine Contraceptive Device
Implants and Transplants
Other Special Conditions

Date of disclosures.

Date of consent.

Location and time of disclosures and consent.

Patient identification data.

Acknowledgment by patient that discussion has covered the following topics, with a brief quote of the patient's interpretation of disclosure either written by the patient or transcribed from conversation. Discussion should continue in explicit detail about what the procedure or device or medication will accomplish and what complications or foreseeable events may occur, as well as management, monitoring, and follow-up.

Diagnosis or diagnostic goal

Prognosis

Proposed treatment
- Anticipated benefit
- Anticipated risks
- Anticipated experience

Alternative treatments
- Anticipated benefit
- Anticipated risks
- Anticipated experience

Patient prognosis if no diagnostic, process or treatment undertaken.

Patient expectation of effort, suffering.

Residual changes if successful, unsuccessful.

Costs.

Example Form: Informed Consent for Diagnostic or Surgical Procedure

Date of disclosures.

Date of consent.

Patient identification data.

Authorization to specific physician to perform the operation on named person.

Authorization to physician to use assistants or associates as needed.

Description of expected procedure and authorization to extend or deal with unforeseen circumstances during the procedure, details of the procedure, and anticipated circumstances and possible circumstances explained.

Recitation of choice over alternative methods of diagnosis.

Understanding of relative likelihood of complications, and consequences if complications occur.

Recitation that physician has explained all important matters and answered all questions.

Understanding that a remote risk of death or serious disability is encountered with any procedure.

Authorization for additional services as reasonable and necessary including anesthetic services, radiographs, and laboratory tests.

Example Form: Consent to HIV Antibody Test

Outline of HIV Infection Facts:

The human immunodeficiency virus (HIV) is the causative agent of acquired immunodeficiency syndrome (AIDS) and related clinical conditions. The infection has been shown to be spread by sexual contact, by parenteral exposure to blood and, rarely, by other exposures to blood, and from an infected woman to her fetus or infant. Persons exposed to the HIV usually develop detectable levels of antibodies against the virus within 6 to 12 weeks of infection. The presence of antibodies indicates infection, although infected persons may have no clinical evidence of disease.

Outline of Test Facts:

The HIV antibody test is a simple blood test that detects defensive cells produced by the body after infection with HIV. The HIV antibody test is not a test for AIDS. It is a test to show whether an individual is infected with the virus that can cause AIDS.

The test is done on a small amount of blood from the arm. When the blood sample is drawn, the experience is the same as for all other blood sample tests.

The HIV antibody test poses little physical risk. Because of public fear about the transmission of AIDS, however, testing has serious consequences for persons who test positive for the virus. If test results become known outside the medical context, difficulties in employment, housing, insurance, and other activities can be anticipated. However, no known alternatives other than the HIV antibody test determine the presence or absence of the HIV antibody.

Outline of Disclosures and Consent:

Acknowledgment of false-positive or false-negative blood test results, and that a positive result will require a corroborating test.

Acknowledgment that questions about the test have been answered, and that results of the HIV antibody test will be available with assistance and advice in need for additional testing measures, for prevention of transmission of the HIV virus, appropriate health care and support services, the advisability of locating individuals who may have exposed the test subject or been exposed by the subject.

Specific authorization and release to apply for insurance reimbursement or direction not to seek payment for testing from health insurer. Payment for testing is assured by commitment from test subject if no release is authorized for reimbursement.

Acknowledgment of reports and information that may be required after receipt of positive test results.

Directive to perform test.

Example Form: Notice to Noncompliant Patient

Date of notice.

Patient identification data.

Time and place of last reiteration of advice, recommendations, directives, instructions.

Brief outline of discussion regarding:

Advised treatment, management, monitoring

Anticipated benefit

Anticipated risks

Anticipated experience

Alternative treatments

Anticipated benefit

Anticipated risks

Anticipated experience

Emphasis on patient prognosis if no diagnosis, treatment undertaken, or instructions disregarded.

Patient expectation of effort, suffering

Residual changes if successful, unsuccessful

Outline of patient conduct considered by physician to pose hazard discussed.

Outline of consequences of patient noncompliance.

Expression of urgency of need for appropriate attention to problem.

Directive to return to care or find other physician.

Time limit for patient action or response.

Physician actions to be taken if no response.

Example Form: Notice of Hazards of Patient Decision to Leave Treatment Against Medical Advice

Date and time of notice.

Date and time of departure.

Patient identification data.

Outline, with date and time, of last treatment, advice, recommendations, directives, instructions.

Brief outline regarding:

Advised treatment, management, monitoring
- Anticipated benefit
- Anticipated risks
- Anticipated experience

Alternative treatments
- Anticipated benefit
- Anticipated risks
- Anticipated experience

Emphasis on patient prognosis if treatment or diagnostic process discontinued.

Outline of patient conduct considered by physician to pose hazard discussed.

Outline of consequences of patient departure.

Expression of urgency of need for appropriate attention to problem.

Directive to return to care or find other physician or treatment source.

Statement that patient takes full responsibility for consequences of departure and recognizes what the consequences may be.

A patient may not be forced to sign any statement and cannot be restrained from departure in ordinary circumstances. If the patient refuses to receive and sign the statement, it should be completed, witnessed, and record made of attempts to communicate its contents and the refusal to either take or sign the statement.

Example Form: Release of Liability for Refused Treatment

Date and time of release.

Patient identification data.

Outline, with date and time, of last treatment, advice, recommendations, directives, instructions.

Brief outline of events for which release is executed and disclosures by physicians of consequences of patient choice to decline medical treatment.

Recitation that physicians and facility have made disclosure of every important medical matter for patient consideration in making choices about care. This valuable information and recommendation operate as consideration for the release.

Statement that patient takes full responsibility for consequences of choice and recognizes what the consequences may be.

Agreement to release providers from any liability for any adverse outcomes and commitment to take sole responsibility for outcomes of medical choices.

Refusal to execute a release of liability is distinguished from a refusal to acknowledge medical consequences. The patient can be informed clearly of the consequences of refused care and still decline to sign a release of liability agreement. A patient may not be forced to sign any statement and cannot be restrained from departure in ordinary circumstances. If the patient refuses to receive and sign the release, evidence of medical disclosures can be recorded in the chart.

Example Form: Notice to Patient of Need for Follow-up

Date of notice.

Patient identification data.

Brief outline of last encounter and departure instructions.

Reiteration and emphasis of need to monitor patient condition even in the absence of a currently treatable condition.

Suggest date for follow-up appointment.

Strong recommendation for follow-up by current physician or other physician.

The earliest date for recommended follow-up should be entered in the master calendar and contact with the patient initiated to schedule check-up or to give notice of physician intent to terminate the relationship if urgent care is refused.

Example Form: Notice to Patient Absent from Scheduled Appointment without Explanation or Rescheduling after Phone Inquiry

Date of acknowledgment.

Patient identification data (for minors, add parental identity data).

Recall prior appointment under past conditions, with outline of advice to return.

Inquiry about reasons for absence from appointment.

Statement of patient condition and current need for medical treatment, with commitment to continue care, but also instructions to seek care by another physician if patient intends to discharge physician.

Emphasis expressed for necessity of care and consequences of patient failure to seek treatment for identified problems.

Commitment to transfer records copies and advise new physician of patient history and treatment.

Advice for management of emergencies until other treatment obtained.

Enclose authorization to release records to new physician. Authorization acknowledges receipt of notice of withdrawal.

Example Form: Records Retention Schedule

Business records have a minimum recommended storage and retrieval capability. If possible, all records should be kept permanently. Discard or destruction of specific types of files and documents may be made according to a retention schedule determined by counsel, depending on the jurisdiction. A typical schedule would be:

Type of Record	Years to Date of Discard
Accident reports	7
Accounts payable	7
Accounts receivable	7
Audit reports	no discard
Bank statements	3
Capital stock and bond records	no discard
Cash books	no discard
Charts of accounts	no discard
Checks (canceled)	7
Checks (canceled for important payments taxes, purchases of property, special contracts, filed with underlying transactions)	no discard
Claims (settled cases)	7
Computer backup disks (same as for records backed)	no discard
Contracts and leases	
(expired)	7
(still in effect)	no discard
Corporate minutes, stockholders, bylaws, and charter	no discard

Type of Record	Years to Date of Discard
Correspondence (legal and important matters)	no discard
Correspondence (routine)	2
Deeds, mortgages, and bills of sale	no discard
Depreciation schedules	no discard
Duplicate deposit slips	2
Employment applications	3
Expense analyses	7
Expense distribution schedules	7
Financial statements	no discard
Garnishments	7
General/private trial balances	no discard
Insurance policies (expired)	3
Insurance records, accident reports, claims, policies, etc.	no discard
Internal audit reports	no discard
Internal reports (routine)	3
Inventories of products, materials, supplies	7
Investment transfer registers, records	no discard
Invoices (to customers, from vendors)	7
Journals	no discard
Loans and notes	no discard
Options (expired)	7
Patents	no discard
Payroll records	7
Personnel files (terminated)	7

Type of Record	Years to Date of Discard
Petty cash vouchers	3
Property appraisals	no discard
Property records, including costs, depreciation reserves, balances, depreciation schedules, blueprints, plans	no discard
Purchase orders	no discard
Retirement/pension records	no discard
Requisitions	1
Scrap and salvage records	7
Stock and bond certificates (canceled)	no discard
Tax returns and worksheets, revenue agents' reports and other documents relating to determination of income tax liability	no discard
Time books/cards	7
Trademark registrations and copyrights	no discard
Training manuals	no discard
Union agreements	no discard
Vouchers for payment to employees, etc. (includes allowances and reimbursement of employees officers, for travel, entertainment expenses)	7
Withholding statements	7

Check-up File

5 Medical Disclosures

Confidentiality
Reports and Releases

Indefensible Risks

Unconsented Disclosure, Failure to Warn, Breach of Confidentiality

Practice Objectives

Confidentiality Protection, Appropriate Disclosures

Pattern for Safety

Staff Training, Problem-Handling Protocols, Logs and Files, Access Barriers, Control of Information

Approaches to Medical Legal Safety

Appropriate and Defensible Management of Data

Cases

Waiver of Confidentiality, Release of Medical Information, Conflicts of Confidentiality Interest, Patient Requests for Disclosure, Documentation

Forms

Authorized Release, Computer Confidentiality, Public Disclosures

Indefensible Risks

Unconsented disclosure of medical facts to patient's adversary
Failure of duty to disclose, report, or warn of medical danger
Breach of patient confidence to uninvolved medical personnel
Disclosure of patient medical information in casual communication

Practice Objectives

☐ **Objective:** No patient confidence inadvertently disclosed.

Rationale: Trust obligation is enforceable.

☐ **Objective:** All disclosures of medical records information based on valid legal purpose.

Rationale: Important personal and financial interests depend on record safeguards.

Pattern for Safety

1. Train all staff in confidential record precautions.
2. Rehearse appropriate answers to requests for patient information.
3. List strict protocols for permitted disclosure and release of records.
4. Log and file all requests for records and compliance, with dates and documents transmitted.
5. Adopt effective physical and/or electronic controls and barriers to records access.
6. Exercise the highest control and documentation in transfer of original records.

Bottom Line: When in doubt, head for the high side; never ally with someone who has dirty hands.

Approaches to Medical Legal Safety

Confidentiality

A number of major factors are weighed to determine correctness in safeguarding medical record information:

Medical information gathered for diagnosis or treatment
Patient expectation of confidentiality
Recipient of disclosure
Duties to endangered third parties
Physician right to maintain medical record
Limit of patient privacy
Duty to provide information in court
Interests competing with patient confidentiality
Conditions allowing disclosure
Source of interest or question about records, patient

Specified interests may outweigh patient confidentiality. These include: an endangered identified person who must be warned; children at risk of harm (specific laws often provide immunity from liability for disclosure); medical personnel or family members who should be warned for self-protection and whom the patient refuses to warn; and members of the public (but generally subject to public health–reporting laws). Legal counsel is advisable when weighing confidentiality questions. Disclosure may be limited to the appropriate recipient and the information necessary to protect recognized greater interests as well as to limit damage to the patient.

An example of the balancing of interests that must be made is the tension between confidentiality of human immunodeficiency virus (HIV) test results and public danger from HIV infection. State laws can vary on accessibility of such results, and proposals are numerous in many states to deal with the privacy interests of HIV-infected individuals, which compete with the public health interests of the uninfected population.

Laboratories must report positive HIV tests to public health agencies in some jurisdictions. Failure to report subjects the laboratory supervisor to fines or imprisonment and may also result in liability to third parties.

Recommendations relating to laboratory data in HIV testing may include:

No HIV testing should be performed without verification of informed consent.

Verbal requests for HIV testing should not be accepted. Only those requests that can be shown to have originated with appropriate informed consent should be accepted for analysis.

Informed consent documents should be maintained by the requesting clinician. The laboratory should receive verification of consent that bears the signature of the physician, but not the signature of the patient.

Whenever and wherever practical and when allowed by state law, patient identification should be accomplished without the use of names. Special request forms should be developed that provide laboratory staff with only alphanumeric code numbers.

All records bearing identifiable patient information should be maintained in secured files. Access should be restricted to a need-to-know basis only. Access logs should be maintained and periodically reviewed.

The laboratory should provide the practitioner with necessary documents to ensure compliance with public health–reporting regulations. All information should be completed by code number, and the attending physician should provide patient-specific data. Envelopes should be provided in preaddressed form.

Procedures to maintain confidentiality in insurance claim processing must also be considered by the clinician. This information should also be reviewed with the patient, along with the specific meaning of release of information statements that accompany most insurance forms. The patient should decide if insurance billing is desired for this particular test, and all documents associated with insurance claim processing should be secured.

Reports and Releases

Conditions may alert physician and staff to the need for heightened attention to records safeguards. Special care should be made and advice sought in:

Examinations not for patient benefit
Requests for original records
Medical information detrimental to patient interests or wishes
  Disability, infection, previous diagnosis (for example, disclosure of history of asthma would diminish chances for compensation for lung damage from work conditions)
Requests to limit record release to create false impression

Generally, no disclosure should be made without: (1) patient release; (2) court order; or (3) law requiring specific disclosure. A subpoena may or may not be enforceable. As with receipt of any legal document, call counsel or go to court, but keep the record secure until the patient's interests are determined.

Routine use of medical records information is made with routine patient permission or release of record data with no identification for payment records, utilization review, practice profile, statistical study, or registry/research.

Staff should be prepared with appropriate answers to requests for records or record information. All anticipated requestors—family, friends, employers, attorneys, compensation agencies, public health agencies, and media—must be dealt with appropriately to protect and to serve patient interests.

Unless a significant reason exists not to do so, patients should see all reports and disclosures to others. Without a patient release or law requiring disclosure, a court order will be required. Without an emergency, release of information by phone is unreasonable. Even in an apparent or alleged emergency, when a call from an unknown person requests confidential information, a phone number should be obtained and check made of location before a return call is made to the requestor.

Cases

Does a Patient Waive Confidentiality by Suing a Physician?

A physician received a letter from the attorney of a former patient, requesting copies of the patient's medical records. The request contained a release from the patient. The physician immediately contacted his malpractice insurer and informed them of the request. The insurer instructed the physician to forward a copy of the patient's records to the company, which he did. A copy of the records was not sent to the patient's attorney until 3 months afterward. Half a year later, the patient brought suit against the physician, and died a short time later. The patient's wife as executrix of the estate sued the physician and his insurer for breach of confidentiality.

On just the issue of confidentiality, a verdict was returned for the patient's estate. Because there was no suit for malpractice when the patient requested records be sent to an attorney, records disclosed to the insurer were not protected as attorney work product for defense purposes. A summary of case facts without identification of the patient could have allowed the insurer to begin preparation for any anticipated claim defense. When suit was finally filed, the patient's records would have been permitted to be sent to the insurer's defense counsel. Without a permissible disclosure, the physician was liable for breach of confidentiality.

What Parts of the Medical Record Should Be Released?

After a rear-end automobile accident, a woman complained of head, neck, and back pain. Under the care of a neurosurgeon, she received neck traction and physical therapy for several weeks. Several months later, she was rehospitalized for low back pain and numbness of her left side. At the request of her attending physician, she was examined by a neurosurgeon who concluded that she had sustained a "whiplash" injury of the cervical spine. He was also of the opinion that a marked hysterical element made her symptoms more severe. When the woman brought a personal injury suit against the driver whose automobile had struck her automobile, a physician was employed by the defense attorney to interview the patient's treating neurosurgeon, and to secure a report from him. The neurosurgeon reported that: "There was very mild musculoligamentous strain at the time of the accident, but no permanent neurologic sequela. Although her prognosis for recovery should be very good, her somatic symptoms have been perpetuated by an underlying preexisting anxiety neurosis and hysteria." Although he never received permission from the woman or her attorney to disclose information, the neurosurgeon gave this report to the defense physician, who gave it to the insurance company that employed him. When the woman learned of the neurosurgeon's conduct, she sued him.

The neurosurgeon stood in a confidential and trust capacity to his patient; therefore he owed the patient more than the provision of medical services. He also had a duty to render reports of the patient's condition when necessary. This duty included an obligation to refuse affirmative assistance to the patient's adversary in litigation. Although the neurosurgeon owed a duty to his conscience to speak the truth, he needed to speak only at the proper time and required circumstances in the litigation process. To volunteer damaging information was outside the scope of his duty to release medical information about the injury.

What Interests Outweigh Patient Confidentiality?

A woman was granted a divorce from her husband and was given custody of their children. Over the next few years, however, the father obtained custody of the children, and finally brought a legal proceeding to require his ex-wife to show cause why custody of the children should not remain with him. The ex-husband attached to the motions submitted in this proceeding an affidavit written by the woman's former psychiatrist, which divulged information that he had obtained while treating the woman. The legal proceeding was concerned with exposition of the woman's mental condition and her fitness as a mother to enlighten the court's task of awarding custody of the children. As a result of the psychiatrist's records and conclusions, the woman's ex-husband was awarded custody. The woman then sued her former psychiatrist for breach of confidentiality. The psychiatrist contended that information contained in the affidavit was published in the best interests of the children.

The psychiatrist improperly disclosed information about his former patient's mental condition to her ex-husband. Even the best interests of the children may not be a sufficient reason for the psychiatrist to breach the duty of loyalty owed to the patient. During treatment of the patient, the psychiatrist had not considered reporting suspicions of child abuse or neglect, which would have been a protected disclosure. A duty required the physician to refuse affirmative assistance to his patient's legal adversary. For a physician to be examined and cross-examined about information obtained in the course of a physician–patient relationship may be permissible by an attorney in a courtroom in conformity with the rules of evidence, and with the vigilant surveillance of the patient's counsel under the careful scrutiny of the trial judge. Unsupervised communication of confidential information between the physician and a patient's legal adversary, however, is improper.

When May a Physician Begin to Defend a Potential Malpractice Suit?

A defense attorney persuaded a patient's treating physician to surrender certain confidential information for use in litigation pending against the patient, on the false pretext that the patient was contemplating a malpractice suit against that physician. The patient subsequently sued the physician and the insurance company for inducing the physician to breach his duty of confidentiality. The defendant insurance company argued that the state's privileged communication statute merely precluded a physician from testifying in court about communications received while treating a patient.

A patient's institution of a personal injury suit ultimately will lead to waiver of the privilege of confidentiality on matters relevant to the claimed injury. Thus the privilege would not prevent pretrial discovery of medical evidence that would be placed at issue at a trial. Permission for disclosure of the treating physician's opinion of the extent of a patient's injury, however, does not permit a clandestine conference between a treating physician and the attorney for his patient's adversary. An implied condition of the consensual relationship of physician and patient is the physician's warranty that any confidential information obtained through the relationship will not be disclosed without the patient's permission or waiver.

Are Conservative Evaluations of Patient Conditions for Insurers a Conflict of Interest?

A boy sustained a fractured femur when he was struck by an uninsured motorist. By terms of his insurance policy, the boy was entitled to compensation for damages under a certain policy limit. His parents took him to an orthopedic surgeon for treatment of injuries. The surgeon frequently prepared reports requested by insurance companies regarding his examinations and findings of individuals injured in auto accidents. When the insurance company requested the surgeon to furnish reports containing his prognosis of the boy's injury, the surgeon stated that he did not believe that the patient would have residual impairment or psychologic difficulties directly related to the accident. Based on the report of a favorable prognosis, the insurance company offered one-half the policy limit requested by the parents for settlement. Dissatisfied with the offer, the parents retained an attorney to secure a more advantageous disposition of the claim. Their attorney convinced the insurance company that the medical reports were unduly conservative and inconsistent with the sequela and residuals ordinarily following injuries of the type sustained by the boy. The claim was settled for the full policy limits, after which the parents sued the surgeon, contending that the patient's injuries should have been known to be of a potentially more serious nature with reference to future disability than the physician reported; therefore his drafting an unduly conservative report was negligent. The surgeon contended he owed no legal duty to the patient to prepare medical legal reports in a fashion other than conservative.

The surgeon was obligated to furnish to authorized persons medical legal reports containing his prognosis about residual disability from the accident. The contractual relationship as the boy's treating physician was sufficient to create a duty to furnish an objective prognosis. It might be inferred that the surgeon's objectivity may have been affected by a conflict of interest. This could be true if he frequently prepared reports in a conservative fashion favorable to the insurance companies' positions to minimize in each case the nature and extent of the residual disability, thereby providing insurance companies better negotiating positions. Examinations purely for insurance disability evaluation would be understood by all parties as clearly not for the examinee's benefit and could be as conservative as any medical opinion might be. A duty to the patient of objective evaluation is higher than that owed to examinees.

Is a Patient's Name Medical Information?

A patient sued his physician for injuries allegedly sustained when the physician performed an angiogram, claiming that the physician had failed to obtain proper informed consent for the procedure. During the pretrial discovery phase of litigation, through the use of deposition, interrogatories, and a motion to produce documents, the patient sought to force disclosure of the names and addresses of the physician's other angiography patients. The physician sought a protective order against discovery of these names. The plaintiff then sought an order to disclose the names and addresses of the eight patients who had received an angiogram before the plaintiff and the eight patients receiving an angiogram subsequently, including the names and addresses of the two patients who had developed complications from the procedure. The plaintiff explained that the purpose for seeking the information was the need for the discovery, through the investigation of other patients, of the type of information provided by the physician about his usual practice before performing this type of serious procedure. The patient's attorney contended that patients so identified could, on contact by plaintiff's counsel, claim the privilege and refuse to discuss their particular experience.

When a former patient turned litigant and attempted to obtain information about some of the physician's other patients whose privacy was at stake, the physician was obligated to protect those patients' interests. The purpose for which the patient-plaintiff sought this information was to enable investigators to seek out and interrogate the physician's other patients and try to persuade them to discuss experiences related to their treatment by the physician. Ordinarily a patient, whether or not a party to a lawsuit, has a privilege to prevent a treating physician from disclosing confidential information about the patient. The physician is usually required to claim the privilege on behalf of his patient. Patients who received the specific test, such as an angiogram, from the physician probably communicated to the physician facts indicating the need for such testing. If the physician were required to list persons receiving such tests, he necessarily would reveal those confidential facts and violate the physician–patient privilege. The disclosure of a patient's name does not necessarily violate the privilege if the context of the disclosed information revealed nothing concerning the patient's condition. In this case, however, it is not merely the disclosure of the name and address, but the joining of that information with the fact that these were patients who received angiography. Therefore, a court would probably not require the disclosure of the names and addresses of the physician's patients.

How Does a Physician Comply with Patient Requests for Partial Release of Record Information?

In the course of treatment of a patient, a family physician learned that the patient consumed excessive amounts of alcoholic beverages as a means of dealing with social problems. The patient required repeated treatments for pulmonary problems that the physician opined were secondary to chronic alcoholism. At the behest of the patient, the physician had issued several medical certificates indicating that the patient's pulmonary condition was responsible for his frequent absences from work, which involved nonhazardous activities. Sometime thereafter the physician informed the patient that the latter's employer had requested an explanation of the underlying cause of the patient's condition that was causing the frequent absences from work. The physician related that he intended to respond to the employer's request with a letter establishing that the absences were due to alcoholism. The patient told him not to send the proposed letter. The physician ignored the request and sent the letter. On receipt of the letter, the patient's employer formally notified the patient of his discharge. The employer listed the employee's repeated absences, recited the physician's letter, and rejected the patient's attempt to attribute the absences to a series of misfortunes. The patient sued the physician, contending that he had improperly divulged confidential information. The physician contended that he had an overriding duty to disclose the underlying cause of his patient's absences because he had previously supplied incomplete medical information to the patient's employer.

The delicate balance of this physician's conflicting duties to a patient and an interested third party must be weighed to determine the physician's paramount duty. The prior incomplete medical certificates requested by the patient and supplied by the physician to explain the former's absences justified the physician's full disclosure of those medical facts, superseding a duty to the patient to remain silent. The requested certificates constituted the patient's waiver of the privilege of confidentiality to the extent that they told the reason for the employee's absences. The patient's specific request not to dispatch the letter was invalidated because he had previously asked for and permitted incomplete disclosures as the nature of his illness. Although the patient knew that his illnesses had been set out in the certificates requested by him, he insisted that the underlying cause, alcoholism, could not be disclosed. Under such circumstances he was aware that the certificates were true only as far as they went. Having placed the physician in the position of telling only part of the truth, he was precluded from preventing disclosure of the remainder by putting limitations on the waiver or privilege. The patient also contended that the physician was liable because the letter sent to the employer set forth more than what was required. A narration of less than all the facts requested, however, would have tended to further mislead the employer. In addition, the physician was specifically asked by the employer to clarify the incomplete information previously supplied with the patient's consent.

What Is the Duty of a Physician to a Patient Seeking to Misrepresent Medical Information?

Five months after his infant daughter's birth, her father purchased a life insurance policy for her. The father, who was the beneficiary of the policy, represented to the insurance agent that the baby was in good health. He did not report any possible heart trouble in spite of the fact that a pediatrician had examined the child 11 times during the first 4 months of her life for evaluation of a possible cardiac abnormality. At 8 months of age, the child became seriously ill, was rushed to the hospital, and died a few hours later. An autopsy disclosed a congenital heart defect. During investigation of the claim under the insurance policy, the insurance company requested information from the attending pediatrician who disclosed to the company that the child had suffered from "heart trouble from birth." On the basis of this information, the company denied the claim on the policy, stating that had this medical condition been disclosed, the child would not have been issued a policy. The father then sued the pediatrician for loss of the life insurance benefits, claiming that the physician's unlawful disclosure of confidential information had jeopardized his insurance claim.

Although the pediatrician was obligated not to disclose confidential information about his patient, this duty is subject to exceptions where public interest demands disclosure. This case involved such an exception because of the public interest in an honest and fair resolution of legal claims. Therefore the disclosure of the physical condition of a patient was justified because the condition was a significant factor in a just and fair claim disposition. Otherwise, the physician would be found guilty of fraud and conspiracy to defraud the insurer.

Forms

Authorizations to physicians and hospitals to release medical records or medical reports are legal documents. A "release" authorization is also a declaration by the patient that medical confidentiality is waived. The authorization may be general or specific, and limits should be strictly observed unless a misrepresentation is requested.

Disclosure of fees for writing reports and processing records release should be made at first contact. Commitment from attorneys or insurers to pay for reports and preparation of review summaries can be requested. Fees for composing reports should comport with office visit time charges. To raise substantial income from reports as compared with medical practice detracts from credibility and objectivity. If record information can be reasonably expected to be detrimental to patient goals or prospects, a reminder to the patient of the content of records and verification of patient directive to release the information may be advisable. When examination reports are to be kept from patients, disclosure of this condition of examination is in order before the examination, with release authorized before findings are determined.

Example Form: Authorization to Physician to Release Medical Record

Date of authorization.

Patient identification data.

Introduction summary of purpose of authorization (for example, employment or insurance applications, disability benefit application).

Authorization for copy of records to be furnished, records or summaries or reports relating to specific condition, time period, episode.

Authorization of recipient and method of release, copy, summary, examination, inspection.

Specific limits on authorization.

Release of physician from liability for consequences of release as authorized, waiver of confidentiality to the extent of the authorized release.

Signature with verification as appropriate.

Example Form: Medical Legal Authorization

Date of authorization.

Patient identification data.

Introduction summary of purpose of authorization (for example, claim of personal injuries, potential claim of medical malpractice, determination of mental status, determination of child custody, allegations of criminal responsibility).

Authorization for copy of records to be furnished, records or summaries or reports relating to specific condition, time period, episode, or request for all records.

Authorization of recipient and method of release, copy, summary, examination, inspection.

Specific limits on authorization or disclosure.

Release of physician from liability for consequences of release as authorized, waiver of confidentiality to the extent of the authorized release.

Signature of patient with verification for heightened control.

Example Form: Authorization to Release Findings of Nonpatient Examination

Date of authorization.

Examinee identification data.

Outline of date, place, purpose, and extent of examination.

Summary of purpose of authorization (for example, benefit or employment application, status determination, health screening for sports, employment, professional license).

Authorization for copy of records to be furnished, records or summaries or reports relating to specific condition, time period, episode.

Authorization of recipient and method of release, copy, summary, examination, inspection.

Specific limits on authorization.

Release of physician from liability for consequences of release as authorized, waiver of confidentiality to the extent of the authorized release.

Signature with verification as appropriate.

Example Forms: Confidentiality of Computerized Medical Data

Protect confidentiality of medical records applies to computerized records as any other records. Computer records, however, raise more logistical problems in maintaining confidentiality.

American Medical Association Guidelines for Computer Medical Data

1. Confidential medical information entered into the computerized database should be verified as to authenticity of source.

2. The patient and physician should be advised about the existence of computerized databases in which medical information concerning the patient is stored. Such information should be communicated to the physician and patient before the physician's release of the medical information. All individuals and organizations with some form of access to the computerized data bank, and the level of access permitted, should be specifically identified in advance.

3. The physician and patient should be notified of the distribution of all reports reflecting identifiable patient data before distribution of the reports by the computer facility. There should be approval by the physician and patient before the release of patient-identifiable clinical and administrative data to individuals or organizations external to the medical care environment, and such information should not be released without the express permission of the physician and the patient.

4. The dissemination of confidential medical data should be limited to only those individuals or agencies with a bona fide use for the data. Release of confidential medical information from the database should be confined to the specific purpose for which the information is requested and limited to the specific time frame requested. All such organizations or individuals should be advised that authorized release of data to them does not authorize their further release of the data to additional individuals or organizations.

5. Procedures for adding to or changing data on the computerized database should indicate individuals authorized to make changes, time periods in which changes take place, and those individuals who will be informed about changes in the data from the medical records.

6. Procedures for purging the computerized database of archaic or inaccurate data should be established and the patient and physician should be notified before and after the data have been purged. There should be no commingling of a physician's computerized patient records with those of other computer service bureau clients. In addition, procedures should be developed to protect against inadvertent mixing of individual reports or segments.

7. The computerized medical database should be on-line to the computer terminal only when authorized computer programs requiring the medical data are being used. Individuals and organizations external to the clinical facility should not be provided online access to a computerized database containing identifiable data from medical records concerning patients.

8. Security:

   a. Stringent security procedures for entry into the immediate environment in which the computerized medical database is stored and/or processed or for otherwise having access to confidential medical information should be developed and strictly enforced so as to prevent access to the computer facility by unauthorized personnel. Personnel audit procedures should be developed to establish a record in the event of unauthorized disclosure of medical data. A roster of past and present computer service bureau personnel with specified levels of access to the medical database should be maintained. Specific administrative sanctions should exist to prevent employee breaches of confidentiality and security procedures.

b. All terminated or former employees in the data-processing environment should have no access to data from the patients' medical records.

c. Involuntarily terminated employees working in the data-processing environment in which data from patients' medical records are processed should immediately on termination be removed from the computerized medical data environment.

d. On termination of computer service bureau services for a physician, those computer files maintained for the physician should be physically turned over to the physician or destroyed (erased). In the event of file erasure, the computer service bureau should verify in writing to the physician that the erasure has taken place.

Example Form: Release of Medical Information to the Public

American Medical Association Guidelines for Release of Patient Information to the Media

These guidelines outline specific types of information and encourage cooperation with the press where appropriate. The guidelines state:

A physician should not discuss a patient's medical condition, disease, or illness with the press without the patient's authorization. The patient or the patient's lawful representative may authorize a physician to disclose health information concerning the patient to the press. The physician may release only authorized information or that which is public knowledge.

Because certain news is a part of the public record or is a matter of concern to civil authorities, it is readily available for publication. Physicians should cooperate with the press to ensure that medical news of this sort is available more promptly and more accurately than would be possible without their assistance. News in this category, known as news in the public domain, includes: births, deaths, accidents, and police cases.

The following information in the public domain can be made available without the patient's consent:

a. Personal information: patient's name, address, age, sex, race, marital status, employer, occupation, name of parents in case of births, name of next of kin in case of deaths.

b. Nature of accident: only general information regarding injuries will be released. This consists of the name of the injured portion of the body, such as back injury and the like. The presence of internal injuries may be stated.

If the patient is unconscious when brought to the hospital, a statement to that effect may be made.

Statements regarding the circumstances surrounding shootings, knifings, and poisonings are properly police matters, and questions whether they were accidental or otherwise should be referred to the appropriate authorities.

A statement may be made that the patient was injured by a knife or other sharp instrument, but no statement may be made as to whether it was assault, accident, or self-inflicted.

A statement may be made that the patient received burns and the area of the body affected may be indicated.

No statement may be made that there was a suicide or attempted suicide.

No statement may be made to the effect that intoxication or drug addiction was involved.

No statement may be made that moral turpitude was involved.

c. Diagnosis and prognosis: Inasmuch as a diagnosis may be made only by a physician and may depend on radiologic and laboratory studies, no statement regarding diagnosis should be made except by or on behalf of the attending physician. For the same reason, prognosis will be given only by the attending physician or at his or her direction.

d. Patient's condition: A statement may be made as to the general condition of the patient using the following classifications: minor injuries or similar general diagnosis, good, fair, serious, or critical.

When information concerning a specific patient is requested, the physician must obtain the consent of the patient or an authorized representative before giving information. The patient's decision is final. Physicians are ethically and legally required to protect the personal privacy and other legal rights of patients. The physician–patient relationship and its confidential nature must be maintained. Within these considerations, a physician may assist the representatives of the media in every way possible.

Most hospitals have a designated information officer who can confidently discuss the public interest aspects of patient care and maintain appropriate confidentiality and privacy of patients. Advice or deferral to that person may be the best choice when broadcast or print journalists ask about patients.

Check-up File

6 Office Support

Staff Management
Practice Management

Indefensible Risks

Broken Chain of Communication, Unqualified Staff, Unwarranted Delegation, Unnoticed Hazards, Lost Files, Misinformation

Practice Objectives

Qualified Staff, Tasks Appropriate to Credentials, Errors Caught, Performance Monitored, Corrected

Pattern for Safety

Credentials Review, Training, Monitoring and Correction, Communications Protocols, Fail-Safe Procedures, Performance Standards and Review

Approaches to Medical Legal Safety

Practice Performance Monitored, Controlled

Cases

Staff Role in Instructions, Staff Failures, Prescriptions, Staff Limits, Patient Privacy, Lines of Communication

Forms

Job Descriptions, Standards, Tasks, Credentials

Indefensible Risks

Staff decision not to report symptoms to physician
Medical tasks performed by unqualified person
Unauthorized person allowed access to patient record information
Medical judgment delegated to assistant
Presence of safety or infection hazard
Misplacement or misidentification of patient record or data
Miscommunication or misinformation by staff

Practice Objectives

☐ **Objective:** Duties conform to checked and verified qualifications.

Rationale: Appropriate and valid qualifications allow physician to rely on staff performance.

☐ **Objective:** Risk management tasks assigned and monitored.

Rationale: Risks are not less numerous or serious in a small or limited practice.

☐ **Objective:** No uncorrected failures of administration or identification in care.

Rationale: Checking process can find predictable errors of performance that risk harm.

☐ **Objective:** Physician reviews and corrects any staff judgment errors.

Rationale: Delegated judgment can be validated and corrected before harm occurs.

Pattern for Safety

1. Select staff by effective application of valid criteria to assure performance.
2. Check staff credentials and references.
3. Train, control, and supervise new staff until performance is assured.
4. Check major functions of staff performance periodically without warning.
5. Assure complete and accurate patient communication through staff to physician.
6. Assure complete and accurate physician communication through staff to patients.
7. Require checking of records and data before filing.
8. Plan for foreseeable problems and direct appropriate management by staff.
9. Specify tasks, duties, rewards, and penalties of staff performance.
10. Cross-train staff to fulfill all critical functions.
11. Set performance standards and check for adherence with corrections applied as needed.
12. Maintain master calendar of all future and periodic tasks and follow-up actions.

Bottom Line: Smaller does not mean fewer functions, just fewer functionaries.

Approaches to Medical Legal Safety

Staff Management

Small practices need no fewer functions performed well than large organizations, and have fewer persons to whom to distribute the tasks. Hats include patient management, administration, nursing services, risk management, professional staff coordination, medical records, quality control, utilization review, physical plant maintenance, equipment maintenance, and hospitality.

Staff can be extensions of selected physician capabilities or can compensate for imperfect physician skills or physician aversions. Relentless order in the long run saves time and grief. Disorganization in a medical practice can be fatal. The standard is nothing lost, nothing left to chance, nothing missed. Other zero margins for error are: records or laboratory identification of patients, report of abnormal test results, and transcription of records. Blame is not wholly on staff if staff error should have been apparent to physician review.

Staffing is designed. Persons perform assigned and coordinated functions. Beginning with new staff, work is defined, described, and directed. Performance is monitored for a probationary period; redirection is applied immediately and consistently and repeated until performance is correct. Clarity in supervision, direction, and control is achievable. Investment in early work yields better performance and greater satisfaction for physician and staff. The urge to depend too early and too much on new staff saves time and effort only in illusion. Later difficulties will make the savings insignificant and the costs immense.

Choose staff with help. Arrange with a school that educates medical assistants. Demand attendance records as well as grades and certifications. The school's interests will be aligned with the employer's and they will conduct many screening and verification tasks. Attendance will predict performance and achievement will reflect skills.

Skilled employee management can be learned. Specific description of work tasks must be clear and standards of performance must be appropriate and fair. Instructions about each staff member's functions and requirements for coordination and cooperation should leave no doubt in any staff member's understanding about who does what and which channels are established for communication to, from, and through staff. In short: Tell, summarize, ask for understanding of discussion, copy, check, and monitor. Employees must be treated with the respect due workers, which includes communication of approval of tasks performed well and unemotional discussion of deficiencies. Criticism must be accompanied by a reasonable description of intended performance, with suggestions for achieving success. Known staff deficiencies are a hazard that a physician is responsible to correct.

Employees must be prepared to handle with skill each situation presented. Preparation includes practice for patient emergencies, requests, demands, complaints, or conflicts from many sources. Channels of communication to and from patients, staff, and physician should be defined and discussion of responses to routine and sensitive questions scheduled as part of administrative practice. A physician must know what is being said and done about any contact with patients, prospective patients, other physicians, facility staff, or reimbursement officers. Answers to inquiries from persons other than patients or providers can also be prepared and the right answers made consistently by staff. Early open communication about unpleasant or provocative matters can save time and damage later.

Delegation can promote efficient practice management or may lay a minefield for later problems. If work is assigned to staff, assurance must exist to support the capability of the staff member. Control of the first performance of a task, direction and monitoring of early performance, and supervision of the later performance, with success noted at each stage, supports delegation decisions.

Staff must use limited judgment according to medically and legally appropriate standards. Judgment decisions cannot be prearranged, but the working guidance and protocols can be settled by physician and staff conference. For example, teenage minor patients may request discussion or treatment for unscheduled nonemergency visits. Staff should be able to deal appropriately with the issues of parent notification. Diagnosis or treatment judgment should be outside delegated tasks. Staff role in dealing with patient refusal of tests or treatment must be directed by the physician, with the appropriate response arranged before it is needed.

Channels of communication must have warning bells for matters that cannot wait. "Bells" must be installed for patient dissatisfaction, patient noncompliance, patient failure to keep appointments, take treatment, or any call for clarification or explanation about diagnosis or treatment. Physicians must not remain ignorant while problems grow. Any patient who is misdiagnosed, misdirected, misinformed, or mismonitored by staff will blame the physician who should have supervised, directed, or controlled performance in the practice.

Failures of data gathering are correctable by training protocols with the physician as trainer. Training in medically appropriate and personally preferred ways of doing things can be an investment not only in satisfactory performance but also confident delegation later. Training work may also show faults in current systems and challenge a physician to choose simpler or more effective management practices. Idiosyncratic practice management can multiply problems for new staff, for old staff, and for any coordination work with other practices or facilities.

Staff failures can take many forms:

Error	Correction
Failed courtesy	Practice dialogues
Botched response to legal problem	Training and rehearsal
Triage screening failure	Restriction, protocols, rehearsal

Neglected relay of instructions	Criticism, motivation, monitoring
Failure to notify physician	Redirection, monitoring, probation
Delegation to other staff	Correction, discharge
Practicing medicine	Correction, discharge
Advice on side effects	
Medical jargon	
Cheer-up efforts with medical advice	
Gratuitous or requested medical explanations	
Screening physician too perfectly	Training and reinforcement
Failure of skill or knowledge	Re-education, recertification

Many staff failures are really physician failures. A question about diagnosis or treatment to staff or an assistant is a sign that the physician has not completed appropriate disclosure and discussion with the patient. Communication may have been discouraged by bad response from the physician to "unnecessary" questions or disclosures.

A number of important issues may go without staff discussion because physicians may believe that every professional knows and abides by the same standards. Patient confidentiality may become eroded through habit or failure to perceive its importance. Staff may converse about patients improperly, allow access to patient medical information to improper persons, or fail to notice that confidentiality is even involved—"Don't forget your Dilantin, Mr. Jones." All confidentiality breaches can be controlled by the physician, if the physician in fact notices that confidentiality is in danger. A cavalier attitude toward sensitive medical information may be understandable in busy medical practice; it is never excusable. Discussion, rehearsal dialogue, punishment of infractions, correction and approval for correct, performance will cost time, but much more time will be spent mollifying irate patients or answering questions about treatment that were prompted by a patient's loss of trust.

Practice Management

Hygiene and hazards are two specific areas where the standard is no lapses. Inspection, reinspection, maintenance, and monitoring are achievable. Unlike medical diagnostic and treatment uncertainties, these functions are manageable. Hazard protection precautions serve both staff safety and patient safety. The allowable margin for error in office cleanliness or aseptic practice or infection control is zero. Human immunodeficiency virus or other contagious infections of physician or staff is a perceived danger as well as a real potential danger to patients and workers, no matter how remote the statistics. Disclosure to patients of the risk may be required.

Functional files can be set up by specialists and maintained by the practice staff. Expert file systems can easily be acquired. Reinventing the file wheel is a waste of staff time and will not produce the quality result required. Practice files, practitioner files, patient files, personnel files, vendor and equipment files, medical legal files, and administrative files compete for space and staff time. Any mechanism that reduces error and saves time is worth considering. The staff member who will maintain and use files may not be qualified to design them.

Staff can assure that all records deficiencies are corrected by checking for completeness and accuracy each time a record is retrieved. Checklists should be directed by the physician and all deficiencies remedied:

Legible with no insertions except signed and dated
Errors in recording noted without obliterating the erroneous notation
Patient identification
Designated contact or personal representative
Date, time, and reason for each encounter
Appointment cancellation or failure to keep appointment
Where seen (home, office, clinic)
By whom seen
History

Physical findings
Allergies and drug sensitivities
Diagnostic procedures to be done and by whom, note of disclosure
Diagnostic results reported in writing or by telephone
Medical observations/conclusions, note of communication with patient
Diagnosis, note of communication with patient
Treatment prescribed, discussion documented
Patient instructions (including to whom, and by whom, given)
Referrals and consultations advised, by whom
Reports of referrals and consultations
Consents documented with signature of witness to disclosure and consent
Copies of signed consents
Authorizations
Dates and location of surgery
Dates and location of inpatient admissions
Patient statement of response to treatment
Physician statement of response to treatment reported and observed
Medications given to patient
Prescriptions or treatments written or telephoned
Patient instructions for medications/treatments
Disclosure aids listed: brochures, films, and report of receipt
Record closure note: patient transfer or referral, to whom, when, reason

Logs can provide safety or defense by recording calls and visits, including the content of the contact from patients, laboratories, hospitals, pharmacies, payors or insurers, vendors or suppliers, physicians, family, employers, or attorneys. Control designation can be assigned to records for file or patient management, with management directives for appropriate practice and responses, as routine or heightened control. Designation of each class should be made on specific and clear indications. Files and management for heightened control would be those with legal implications, files for patients with exceptional aspects to treatment, or files with reimbursement problems or complications of patient origin.

Cases

How Can Staff Support Physician Instructions to Patients?

A medical assistant is trained to relay treatment instructions by phone to patients. When one patient misunderstands a dosage order and takes too much medication, serious side effects develop.

If care is questioned, the relay is defensible as long as the assistant confines the communication to explicit instructions, and has been tested to assure that this task is being performed competently. The assistant should always inform patients that the instructions are the physician's and promptly report what the patient has said and make note of the conversation in the patient's record.

Can a Physician Be Responsible for Failures of Facility Staff?

An internist with patients in a nursing home visits them and writes orders for nursing home personnel to carry out. On a visit, the physician prescribes physical therapy for an invalid patient. However, the staff repeatedly fails to carry out these instructions, and the patient's condition worsens.

When the patient's children question care, both the physician and nursing home staff would be accountable. A physician may assume that orders will be carried out; however, when it is apparent or should be apparent that they are not, the physician also has a duty to follow up on the patient's care, and to insist to the proprietors that his patients be treated as ordered. It would also be appropriate after repeated requests, to inform patients' guardians or family as a corrective action to protect the patient.

May an Assistant Authorize Routine Prescriptions?

An architect called a physician's office to have a prescription for diet pills renewed. The physician was away and was not due back for a week. However, the architect was a regular patient, and the assistant knew that the physician had renewed the prescription on a number of occasions, and complied with the patient's request. Several days later, while driving to a building site, the architect suffered a blackout and crashed into another car.

The physician and assistant were named in lawsuits claiming the diet pills had contributed to the condition that brought on the blackout. The assistant could have protected the patient and the physician by referring the request for prescription to the physician covering for the practice, who would have questioned the patient about side effects and other history with the drug.

When Does Staff Practice Medicine?

A patient phoned the physician's office to complain about arthritis pills the physician had prescribed, saying they made her weak and dizzy. She spoke with the physician's nurse. The physician was out of town, but the nurse told the patient that the symptoms were a side effect of the medicine, which was true. The nurse told the patient that other patients had mentioned the same effects to the physician and were not told to discontinue the prescription.

The patient was left with a disabling condition, for which the pills were partly the cause. The nurse was unqualified to practice medicine and the report of complication should have been communicated to covering physicians.

How Must Staff Protect Patient Privacy?

A receptionist left laboratory reports and correspondence on her desk when she left the room. In the time she was gone, another patient happened to see one of the reports, which diagnosed gonorrhea. The patient with gonorrhea was an acquaintance of the one who saw the report and the fact was soon passed around town.

The man sued the physician for invasion of privacy. Similar damage can be done to patients whose identity is displayed on specimen bottles left on technicians' shelves or whose confidential medical files are left where they can be seen by unauthorized persons.

What Is the Physician's Responsibility to Know What Staff Have Been Told?

A newborn was discharged from the hospital the day after an uneventful birth. She appeared fine until 11:30 PM when she moaned and refused to take a bottle. Her first-time parents thought she did not know how to cry. Her mother walked the floor all night to soothe and feed the infant, who refused to eat or sleep. At 6 AM they called their pediatrician's office to report the problems. The pediatrician said that the infant probably was not eating because of gas and was not sleeping because her days and nights were confused. At 8 AM, they called the pediatrician again to report that the baby looked yellow and that her eyes were cloudy. The pediatrician said that the infant had a slight case of jaundice and not to worry. At 3 PM, after the infant had neither slept nor eaten in more than 15 hours, they called the pediatrician again to report that she had purple pinpricks on her hands. The pediatrician's nurse said that the problem was probably a newborn rash. At 5 PM, the baby's lips were purple and she was not breathing. Taken to the hospital, the infant was pronounced dead on arrival. An autopsy revealed that the cause of death was septicemia, caused by a streptococcus B infection she had contracted from her mother before or during delivery. The infection, which is not harmful to the mother, is treatable with antibiotics if detected in time.

No claim was reported in this case. For a successful claim proof would be required that treatment earlier on the day of death would have saved the child. It is possible that, if the pediatrician had been informed that four calls reported a suspicious deterioration of the baby's condition, the infant may have had a small chance to survive if treated.

Forms

Example forms to consider in staffing:

Job description for each staff function. One person would be assigned responsibility for several functions and burdensome or unappealing functions could be rotated.

Patient management
Administration
Nursing services
Risk management
Professional staff coordination
Medical records
Quality control
Utilization review
Physical plant maintenance
Equipment maintenance
Hospitality

Skills or qualities can be defined to assess performance by observable standards. Conversational exchange of definitions and assessments can precede corrections and records of failed performance, or reinforcement of exceptional work.

Dependability
Articulate communication
Firmness
Tact
Common sense
Ethical standards
Compassion
Conscientiousness
Harmonious disposition
Integrity
Stability
Courtesy

The following are example tasks, which should include discussion of standards for acceptable performance:

Accept service of legal documents.
Answer or refer questions about insurance coverage.
Appropriately refer patient questions about treatment.
Cooperate in execution of legal documentation.
Describe the clinical practice for prospective patients.
Explain scheduling to patients.
File correspondence and other documents.
Maintain supplies inventory.
Maintain contacts with medical records at hospitals.
Maintain emergency contacts.
Maintain log of all communications.
Maintain a calendar and reminder system.
Make photocopies.
Obtain patients' written permission for release of records.
Operate system of medical recordkeeping and retrieval.
Operate computer applications.
Place phone calls.
Process incoming and outgoing mail.
Prompt all actions due with notice to physician in time for completion.
Put patients at ease while waiting.
Run office-related errands.
Schedule appointments and other meetings and events.
Screen patients to determine need for immediate attention.
Screen telephone calls; take and relay telephone messages.
Supervise subordinates.
Type correspondence and reports from dictation and handwritten drafts.
Witness informed consent.

Letter requesting assessment for prospective staff from former employer:

Specific questions about professional, personal skills, attendance, problems, achievements, reasons for departure.

Letter checking references of prospective staff:

Specific questions about applicant's stated professional, personal skills, attendance, problems, achievements, reasons for departure.

Sample skills list to check as done within last 6 months, with approximate number of times per month, and skills for which trained but no prior performance required:

Vital signs
Electrocardiogram, other tests
Advanced life support
Catheter placement
Endotracheal intubation
Intravenous puncture

Sample telephone protocols:

Opening and closing scripts for sensitive patient–staff contacts.
Examples of appropriate communications and responses.
Examples of inappropriate communications and responses.
General tone and address, concern, respect, responsive.

Pledge of confidentiality of patient information by staff.

Check-up File

7 Other Providers

Consultation and Referral
Associates and Covering Practice

Indefensible Risks

Unqualified Covering or Referral Provider, Unguided Delegation, Irresponsible Transfer of Care

Practice Objectives

Practice Coordination, Qualified Coverage and Referral Delegation Supervision, Direction

Pattern for Safety

Confirmed Capabilities, Credentials, Coordinated Consultation, Confirmed Arrangements, Prepared Transfer of Care, Thorough Follow-Up, Clear Patient Impressions

Approaches to Medical Legal Safety

Assured, Coordinated Treatment by Multiple Providers, with Patient Understanding

Cases

Patient Misunderstanding, Monitoring Consultations and Referrals, Substitutes' Support, Qualifications

Indefensible Risks

Assigning a resident physician to cover practice
Referral to a physician or facility incapable of referred services
No one in charge of multiconsultant care of patient
Directing assistants to observe and report without guidance
Practice coverage by irresponsible practitioner
Absence of information necessary for patient care during physician absence

Practice Objectives

☐ **Objective:** Patient informed of joint or referred care by qualified physicians.

Rationale: *Mistake or confusion about responsibilities poses risks to patient and physicians.*

☐ **Objective:** Practice coverage offers comparable care in all important aspects.

Rationale: *Substitutes must be qualified to assume practice responsibilities.*

☐ **Objective:** Supervised care is monitored for performance, attention, and skills.

Rationale: *Appropriate supervision, direction, and control are among physicians' duties.*

Pattern for Safety

1. Confirm responsibilities of other physicians in care to both physicians and patient.
2. Coordinate with consultant physicians what specific responsibilities will be assumed and when consultant care will be ended or joined by consulting physician.
3. Confirm reasons for transfers of patient care, to patient and referral physician.
4. Verify qualifications of referred and consultant physicians.
5. Verify qualifications of covering physicians.
6. Introduce and prepare covering physicians before transfer of responsibility for care.
7. Check substitute physicians' method before allowing coverage.
8. Check substitute physicians' findings after coverage with follow-up call to patients, laboratory, and pharmacy.
9. Probe specifically for patient dissatisfaction or complaint after referral, consultation, or coverage.

Bottom Line: Trust but verify.

Approaches to Medical Legal Safety

Consultation and Referral

Major conflicts can occur when several physicians are involved in the care of a patient. Responsibility for others in the treatment process is based on the type of connection between providers. Responsibility can be personal, joint, vicarious, or absent for failures in treatment by other physicians. Basic connections include principle-agent, joint action, or independent action. General practitioners are unqualified to direct the actions of specialists, so agency or employment of specialists is not a likely occurrence. Most disputes over responsibility among physicians relate to which physician had which specific duty to the patient and who had the duty to coordinate care among the physicians.

The duty to consult or refer care is a matter of physician scope of qualified practice. A physician must not practice outside qualifications and capabilities. When more specialized care is necessary, a physician is expected to recognize that need and to obtain appropriate help. Referral is a matter of one physician–patient relationship ending and another beginning. Except for the duty to assure that the referral physician is qualified to provide referred services, the referring physician is not generally connected to the referral physician's performance.

An indication to consult or refer may be a special aspect of the patient's condition or presentation. For patients of a special medical legal classification, such as minors, terminally ill patients, donors and donees, the disabled, those with cognitive deficits, those with cultural or religious limits, or other factors making the patient exceptional, sooner and more frequent consideration of confirmatory consultation or referral may be advisable.

Consultation is a complex arrangement, largely because "consult" is used to describe a number of legally distinct relationships. One type of consult is actually "live research." A specialist or colleague is asked about some aspect of care and gives an answer, advice, or confirmation. Using any source of information, the treating physician must act as a learned intermediary and weigh the "consultation" in terms of clinical judgment. No relationship between the "consultant" and the patient is formed. A cooperative, connected consultation can make two physicians answerable for each other's failures when the consultation describes a legal relationship of joint treatment. Where a consultant physician actually directs care by another, the directed physician is the agent. Agents are responsible for their own failures; principal physicians directing agents are responsible for their own and the agents' failures.

Partially referred care may leave some responsibility on the referring physician, especially if the patient is allowed to consider that the referring physician is still attending. Sometimes what is called a consult is actually a referral for specialized care, such as surgery or therapy, and only the patient is under the impression that both physicians are involved in the procedure. In every circumstance of multiple physicians, a danger arises that coordination will fail, causing the patient injury. Any time additional physicians or providers are connected to a patient's care, a clear statement of purpose, role, and anticipated termination of participation is in order, both to physician and to the patient. Decision making and supervision responsibilities can also be described, with any limits specified that may affect the patient.

Aside from distribution among physicians of responsibilities to the patient, other issues about treatment are raised in cases of consultation and referral:

Standard of care to undertake special treatment
Standard of care to monitor special treatment
Appropriate indications for consultation or referral
Conditions of joint practice
General physician liability for specialist failure
Specialist liability for general physician failure
Duty to oversee or supervise specialist treatment
Duty to evaluate consultant or referral judgment

Referral duties are closely related to qualifications and scope of practice. In addition to medical indications to refer, referral is also indicated when rapport with a patient is poor or when practice overload endangers effective treatment. Handling too many cases indicates a failure of judgment that puts patients at risk. Consultation may be appropriate when limits of capability are reached, when complications arise that change the level of care required, when diagnosis remains in doubt, or when treatment is not effective or the patient is not progressing as anticipated. Also, consultation, second opinion, or referral should be sought at any request from the patient.

Second opinions are intended to confirm an initial finding or judgment. When the second opinion differs from the initial conclusion or recommendation, resolution must be medically sound. The second has more weight if by a specialist; equal qualifications and a difference of opinion indicate a need to reevaluate overall circumstances and obtain a resolving opinion on which action can be based or dismissed. It is a fallacy to think the second opinion is of more consequence than the first, or that if two votes tie, no action is appropriate. Confirmation is still in order. Need for confirmation should also be matched to the intrusiveness and danger of the diagnostic procedure or therapy considered. For invasive or high-risk interventions, indications should rise to high medical confidence. Mismatches of gravity, high indications with no procedure, and low indications for invasive medicine are invitations to adverse outcome with implications of bad judgment.

Clarity of responsibility among consultants and referral physicians should help patients address problems to the right practitioner. Protocols to inform patients about consultation or referral assure that everyone has the same concept of the relationships. Divisions of function should be communicated, summarized, and discussed along with patient questions and problems; copies should be provided of transfer correspondence, and checks made after care for assurance of harmony and success. Asking patients when they return to the practice to comment confidentially about consulted physicians and referred physicians will help identify correctable problems and avoid uncorrectable ones.

Associates and Covering Practice

Questions to staff about referral physicians should be directed to the physician. It is inappropriate for staff to discuss referral or consultant physicians, other than administrative support for connection and location. Transfers of care or coverage in absences should be communicated to patients as early as possible depending on the patient's then-current need for care and the specialty of the practice.

The use of covering services will be a source of problems and disputes—if not liability—if basic connections and communications are neglected. A patient whose current treatment is interrupted by failure of coverage may not appreciate the necessity all physicians have to appoint substitutes for long or short absences from practice. Coverage has to work almost as if there were no absence. The patient is expected only to absorb the difference in practitioner, not practice. Continuity is crucial and attainable. Responsibility for coverage problems can be limited by appropriate selection and adequate coordination. Covering physicians should be prepared for anticipated patient contacts, and should log all contacts, reports, findings, recommendations, and instructions. The covered physician should follow any contacts and verify all events, confirming the covering physicians' practice or changing what should be modified.

Coverage arrangements should assure:

All contacts followed and continuity assured
All logs and records complete and reviewed on physician return
Alternate coverage selected by the covered physician, not the covering physician
Availability to provide care
Background given for anticipated patient contacts
Covering physician of same specialty, qualifications
Hospital privileges at same facility
Notification of answering service and hospital of coverage
Patients notified of long absence and introduced to covering physician
Verified competence and experience

When a patient asks whether another provider has been negligent, an appropriate answer directs the question to the provider in doubt, and redirects the patient to commitment to the current diagnostic situation and need for treatment. Later, a request for expert opinion of the patient's past and future treatment may have to be made; however, the most prudent choice at the outset is to avoid volunteering testimony and focus on the patient's care. Any physician's care can be questioned, and respect for both patient and prior physician may avoid later repercussions of early "taking sides" by concluding that one version of events is accurate. One answer to the query whether another physician's treatment has been negligent or whether malpractice has occurred could be, "If you had any questions about my diagnosis or treatment, I would want you to discuss it with me. There may be many things you are not really aware of and Dr. B may be able to explain to you. You really should ask [him or her] about these issues. I am your treating physician now, and your current condition and treatment are the most important matter for my attention. If you want to discuss legal actions, you should consider consulting an attorney. I am your doctor and we really should focus on your medical care now."

Criticism of other providers should address the specific problem and should be made where correction is possible. The problem could be described in person as objectively as possible to offer the provider awareness that there is a problem. Depending on danger to patients, more action may be required to avoid protection of a physician who should be diverted from harmful practice.

In any current or anticipated legal matter, an early and exploratory session with experienced counsel can prevent missteps and assure physicians about potential problems of involvement with questioned care. Similarly, early legal advice and analysis regarding contract matters and business connections in medical practice can be well worth the time and expense invested.

Examples of situations which counsel could help assure maximum protection for the physician are:

Professional incorporation
Business names and services
Shareholding in other physician enterprises
Employment of physician
Professional partnership
Call-sharing
Overhead, office sharing
Profit sharing
Common billing or letterhead
Advertising listings

Cases

What Is the Importance of a Patient's Impression of the Treatment Team?

A patient sustained a transverse subcapital fracture of the femur. She asked her internist to "take charge" of her case, and also consulted an orthopedic surgeon who recommended surgical repair. Three days after the operation, the internist checked in to reasonably assure that proper recovery was in progress, and told the surgeon that he would return to the case if needed. The surgery was negligently performed, resulting in a worsening of the patient's condition. After receiving a judgment against the surgeon in a medical malpractice suit, she sued the internist in a separate suit on the theory that he was in charge of the case and failed to inform the patient of the nature and risks of the operative procedure proposed and performed by the orthopedic surgeon.

The internist was not liable for the surgeon's negligence in the operation. The internist simply assisted the surgeon casually in preparation for the surgery, but did not determine, select, or perform the surgical procedure. The fact that the internist was asked to "take charge" did not make him responsible for the selection and performance of the surgical procedures used by the orthopedic surgeon. Responsibility to obtain informed consent was not applicable to the internist because he did not choose or advise which surgical procedures should be used by the orthopedic surgeon. He did, however, allow the patient to believe that he would monitor and oversee the performance of the surgeon, a task for which he was unqualified. Clear delineation to the patient of the work of each physician could have removed the patient's impression of oversight by the attending physician.

What Is the Attending Physician's Duty to Coordinate Care?

A young boy sustained a mid-shaft fracture to his femur. He was hospitalized and assigned to an attending physician, who advised the resident physician to place the patient in Bryant's overhead traction. At the end of 3 weeks the attending physician felt that the patient's condition was satisfactory and left orders for discharge. A new resident was then assigned to the service; he examined the patient and determined that the traction had slipped. He therefore reapplied traction, and continued to see the patient daily. Although he knew the attending physician, he did not discuss the case with him. The patient developed a pressure sore on the dorsum of his foot which ultimately resulted in ulceration, necrosis, and permanent tendon injury. The attending physician thought the patient had been discharged because he had left word with the charge nurse that the traction be removed, a splint applied, and the patient be sent home. The discharge order was not recorded, and the discharge order was not discussed with either of the other residents on the service. The patient's parents sued the attending physician, claiming that he had negligently terminated care for the patient. Although pressure sores are common in cases where the patient is in traction, daily examination provides early detection and treatment. Therefore, the injury to the foot was likely caused by the failure to examine at a time when the pressure sore was still superficial and readily treatable.

A staff physician is required to exercise supervision, direction, and control over a resident physician who is treating a patient of the attending physician. If the sole role of the physician is to teach the resident staff, and not to act as a patient's attending physician, however, the physician would not be liable for the negligence of the resident physician. Likewise, an attending physician is not liable for negligence in the performance of routine duties by resident physicians. The attending physician is, however, expected to monitor patient care matters in which his or her presumed superior skill might prevent injury to the patient. Responsibility for supervision does not necessarily extend to duties which resident physicians perform as part of the general hospital routine. The mere fact that the attending physician was on the hospital staff and certain residents were subject to his general supervision did not make him liable for their conduct. Having final responsibility for the care of his patients, however, the physician was under a duty to monitor the patient during the time the patient was still receiving medical care at the hospital. Thus he had a duty to know whether the patient had, in fact, been discharged. If he had properly attended to the patient's care and guided the resident assigned, the foot injury would have been precluded or minimized.

To What Degree May a Physician Depend on the Skills and Knowledge of Assistants or Others?

A man was scraping snow from the windshield of his car, which was parked on the shoulder of a highway. He was struck by a passing car and was taken by ambulance to a community hospital. The emergency department nurse recorded that the man was hit by an automobile and that he complained of right thigh numbness. Although his trousers were not removed, she noted that the patient was able to move the right leg which did not appear deformed. She further noted that his blood pressure was 80/60 mm Hg. Emergency department coverage was provided by private staff physicians "on call" at home on a rotating basis. Fifteen minutes later, the physician on call was contacted about the patient and was told the history and that the blood pressure was 100/60 mm Hg. The physician told the nurse to admit the patient and to administer 100 milligrams of meperidine (Demerol) intramuscularly. An hour later the patient's skin was cool, he was perspiring, and asking for water frequently. The nurse noted a "strong odor of alcohol." His blood pressure was 90/60 mm Hg. The nurse disregarded the patient's hypotensive readings and his requests for water because he had been given meperidine and had been drinking. Two hours later the nurse found the patient in Cheyne-Stokes respiration, pulseless. The physician was notified and cardiopulmonary resuscitation was immediately begun which was unsuccessful. When the physician arrived he observed that the patient's leg appeared foreshortened and externally rotated. Autopsy disclosed a comminuted fracture of the femoral neck and sacrum with extensive hemorrhage around these fractures. The patient's estate sued the physician for not coming to the hospital to attend the patient.

Expert testimonial evidence is not required to demonstrate the physician's negligent failure to attend the patient when common knowledge indicates that without medical attention the consequences of trauma may be serious. When a patient has been struck by an automobile, even a layman is able to conclude that the physician ought to be in attendance to make an informed professional judgment of the patient's condition rather than relying on the observations of a nurse who has less training and expertise in dealing with shock trauma conditions. If a physician must rely on the lesser-trained assistant, a higher degree of supervision, direction, and control is required. This physician failed to ask appropriate evaluation questions and did not direct the nurse to perform a thorough evaluation from which observations could have been accurately reported.

What Is the Physician's Duty to Check and Ensure That Crucial Instructions Have Been Followed?

A woman had premature twins who experienced respiratory distress syndrome. The attending pediatrician gave orders to the nurses to place the twins in incubators and to have oxygen administered in a manner that involved a delicate clinical balance between titration of oxygen concentration and the respiratory distress of the neonates. Although his initial orders comported with the prevailing community standard of care, his instructions about the amount of oxygen to be administered were not properly followed. He did not check on the nurses and thus did not discover their noncompliance. As a result of excessive oxygen administration, the twins developed retrolental fibroplasia, now termed retinopathy of prematurity and resultant blindness. The mother sued the pediatrician on behalf of her twins for failing to adequately monitor the treatment he prescribed.

A specialist, in treating a condition within the specialized area, may be liable if the customary practice of monitoring itself is demonstratably inadequate. In this case, the specialist should have known enough about the care of a premature neonate to realize that ordinary nursing practice was insufficient to adequately protect his patients. It would have been reasonable to check performance, and if checked, the problem in adjustment of oxygen would have been discovered. Thus the pediatrician was negligent for not discovering the impropriety in oxygen administration in a timely fashion.

To What Degree Must a Physician Check on the Work of Other Practitioners?

While on an automobile trip, a woman was injured in an accident and sent to a hospital where a physician suspected a fracture of the distal aspect of her leg and ordered a radiograph of her entire leg. The physician was unaware that the technician did not include the ankle in the radiograph study. Therefore, when he received an oral report from the radiologist that no fracture was noted, he told the patient that she simply had a sprained ankle and instructed her to see her family physician when she arrived home. Subsequently, the physician who ordered the radiograph received a written report of his patient's leg indicating that the knee and upper leg showed no fracture. This report was filed without notice. Three months later, radiograph examination at another hospital disclosed an ankle fracture. By this time the bones had united in poor position, causing permanent ankle dysfunction. The patient sued the treating physician for negligently treating her injury. The treating physician blamed the radiologist group.

When the report subsequently indicated that the patient's ankle was not included in the radiograph, the physician was required to note this and to reconsider the basis of his diagnosis of a sprained ankle. As long as the patient's recovery continued to depend on the accuracy of his diagnosis, the physician's duty of care persisted. Having informed the patient of his diagnosis and directed her to call her own physician, he should have realized that the results of his own diagnosis would be projected into the future care of the patient. Therefore when he subsequently received information indicating that the assumed basis of his diagnosis was mistaken, he was obligated to notify the patient or her current attending physician of his new finding.

What Is a Physician's Duty to Evaluate a Consultant's Advice?

The patient was hospitalized by her family physician for delivery of her eleventh child. She suffered from preeclampsia. Her physician consulted an obstetrician by phone. Although he was the patient's primary physician and directing her medical care, the family physician sought and followed the obstetrician's advice for management, which included blood analysis, urinalysis, and coagulation studies that he knew would take 24 hours to complete. The two physicians discussed several options for the management of the delivery, and the obstetrician favored a conservative approach. About 18 hours after admission, the patient began to suffer seizures. An emergency cesarean section was performed and a viable infant was delivered. The patient's condition, however, continued to deteriorate, and she died that same day. The patient's survivors sued both physicians for malpractice.

The patient was never a patient of the obstetrician and never sought treatment or professional services from him. She was not referred to him for treatment by her physician nor did he send her bills for his services. The obstetrician had never been associated with the attending physician in a professional capacity; he did not cover for him, nor share offices or treatment of patients with him, all of which might be considered to join the two physicians in responsibility. This case is distinguishable from cases in which a physician contracts with another physician to perform services for the benefit of a patient. A consensual relationship between the physician and the patient may exist where others have contracted with the physician on the patient's behalf. The important fact in determining whether the relations are consensual is not who contracted for the services, but whether the service was contracted for with the express or implied consent of the patient or for his or her benefit. In this case, there is no evidence that the obstetrician contracted with the attending physician; the patient was not referred to him for treatment or consultation. The obstetrician's opinions about treatment were addressed to the treating physician, who was free to accept or reject these opinions. Neither physician contemplated that the specialist was directing or exercising any authority or control of the patient's care.

When Is a Consultant Not a Consultant?

A woman who was 22 weeks pregnant was hospitalized because of an incompetent cervix. During hospitalization, her obstetrician was speaking with another physician about a number of patients and asked an opinion about the case. The treating obstetrician did not ask the colleague to take part in the treatment of the patient, but asked generally about the case history without mentioning a name. The colleague responded that the treatment appeared to be correct, without review of the chart. The attending physician recorded the "confirmation" of the physician by name in the chart and told the patient that the consultant specialist had also advised the management plan. Two weeks later, the woman gave birth to a son who now suffers from cerebral palsy, mental retardation, developmental delay, and severe respiratory problems. The woman sued both physicians, charging that her son's injuries were caused in part by substandard advice given and taken during the telephone conversation.

Whether a physician–patient relationship exists depends on the facts in each case, but some facts must support a conclusion that the relationship has been created. In this case, no facts support the conclusion that the relationship ever existed between the consulted physician and the patient. She was not referred to him, nor did she employ him for treatment or consultation. Opinions and advice were addressed directly to a colleague, and not to the woman as a patient. These opinions were not a prescribed course of treatment, but were recommendations to be accepted or rejected. An informal opinion was given to a fellow physician regarding a case with which he had no connection. He did not have any contact with the woman, nor did he see any records relating to the case. He did not know the patient's name, did not consent to treat the patient, and he did not consent to act in a consulting capacity. Therefore, no relationship existed between the consulted colleague and the woman to establish a duty to the infant. The limited and remote connection to the case was not treatment any more than the author of a medical treatise or article which might have been consulted could be considered to have treated the patient.

What Capabilities or Qualifications Should Be Verified about Referral Physicians or Facilities?

The patient, who had collapsed at her job, was hospitalized in a community hospital and given a battery of diagnostic tests by her attending physician. The tests demonstrated the presence of an intracranial hemorrhage. Because her attending physician felt he could not adequately treat the patient's condition, he referred her to a nearby hospital that had a neurosurgeon on its staff. After performing a carotid arteriogram, which disclosed a cerebral aneurysm, the neurosurgeon attempted corrective surgery. He did not use an operating microscope because the hospital did not own or utilize such an instrument. In addition, the anesthesiologist lacked special training in neurosurgical hypotensive anesthesia. During the course of the procedure, difficulty in controlling the patient's blood pressure contributed to complications resulting in the patient's death. The patient's estate sued the neurosurgeon, the anesthesiologist, and the referring physician. Claims against the referring physician alleged that the referral for neurosurgery was negligent.

The referring physician contended that his conduct was not improper because he determined only that he could not provide adequate treatment for the patient and referred her to a neurosurgeon. A referring physician may be negligent if he should have known that he was referring the patient to a facility or practitioner lacking the personnel, equipment, and resources ordinarily considered by the medical profession necessary to safely perform the needed referral procedure. Some jurisdictions may not impose liability on a physician or hospital for referring a patient for treatment elsewhere, or for failing to supervise the care after referral. In those places, a nonnegligent decision to refer ends the physician's duty. Many other courts, however, hold a physician liable for referring a patient in need of a particular type of care to a physician who is unqualified or unequipped to provide it. Such a negligent referral, as opposed to the decision to refer, violates ordinary standards of care and exposes the referring physician to liability.

What Qualifications Must a Covering Physician Offer?

The same day an orthopedist's patient had a cast applied after knee repair, the orthopedist left town for a few days. That evening, the patient called the general surgeon covering to complain of pain under the cast. The surgeon, who was "beeped" in the middle of a concert, asked about the color and temperature of the patient's toes. Reassured by the answers, the surgeon recommended a change in position, elevation of the leg, and more pain medication. He also told the patient to call back if the condition worsened. The surgeon heard nothing further about the case. By the time the orthopedist saw the patient again, necrosis of underlying tissue had developed. This led to exposure of bone, infection, multiple failed attempts at flap coverage, and, finally, amputation of the foot. The patient sued the surgeon for malpractice but also charged the orthopedist with abandonment in assigning coverage of her care to an unqualified physician.

Abandonment is the improper termination of care where a patient is in current need of treatment. Care can be transferred without being considered abandonment if the transfer is to a qualified substitute. When an adverse outcome occurs in the treatment of a less-qualified referral physician, a question may be asked whether care by a more qualified physician would have ended as badly. The physician making the referral will have to show that the general surgeon's method was reasonable or that an orthopedic specialist would have treated the call the same way.

Must a Physician Check Personal Characteristics in Selecting a Covering Physician?

A general surgeon signed out to a general surgeon he did not know very well, then went on vacation. The covering physician was a racing sailor who competed in a race the next day. A call from a woman with symptoms of appendicitis was made to the covering physician, who was by then offshore and out of beeper range. By the time the message was received, the appendix had ruptured. The patient sued her own surgeon for entrusting her care to an irresponsible physician.

Qualifications extend to more than medical training and experience. At a minimum, response to expressed need for treatment is required. An on-call physician who cannot be called is no coverage. By selecting the coverage, the general surgeon warranted at least that the covering physician would respond. Once reasonable qualified coverage is selected, responsibility for patient care is generally transferred to the covering physician.

Can Responsibility for Coverage Be Transferred to Another Physician?

A neurologist on the way to a specialty seminar referred a hospital patient to a neurosurgeon on the hospital staff. The patient, who had been injured in an automobile accident, lapsed into unconsciousness. The covering neurosurgeon was in the middle of a long operation, and referred the case to a colleague. The colleague was a neurosurgeon who had once been a defendant in a malpractice suit in which the covering neurologist had testified for the plaintiff. Although he was not inaccessible, there was a long delay in answering the call. When the patient finally was treated, partial but permanent paralysis had resulted from a subdural hematoma. The patient sued all the physicians for negligent failure to provide needed treatment in time.

The commitment of the attending physician is to arrange for a qualified substitute to provide necessary treatment. The first and second physicians were obliged to arrange for the patient's care. If their conduct could be seen as transfer of the care of the patient from one to the other, referral would insulate them from the third physician's failure. If they were obligated to assure continuity of the patient's care, and only provided someone to call, they each may have abandoned the patient. When the second physician merely put in a call instead of finding a physician to respond to the patient's emergency, a breach of duty occurred. There may be a distinction here between the duty to find a physician and the duty to assure treatment. The patient in need of emergency care cannot be handed down the line by otherwise qualified physicians.

What Capabilities Are Reasonable to Require of Coverage Practice?

For a vacation absence, an obstetrician-gynecologist signed out to a colleague with privileges at a hospital with a religious affiliation. When a pregnant patient consulted the covering physician for vaginal bleeding, the covering physician recommended an immediate dilation and curettage; however, hospital rules at his facility prohibited the procedure. Because the covering physician had no privileges elsewhere, a second covering physician was called on to perform the procedure at a city hospital. By then, however, the patient had bled so much that she needed a transfusion, which transmitted hepatitis. The patient claimed negligent referral by her original physician caused her damage by referral to a physician incapable of providing needed treatment.

If referral is made to coverage with limited capabilities, the patient must be made aware of these and given a chance to agree or to choose alternatives to assuming the risks involved.

What Background or History Is Necessary to Ensure Appropriate Covering Care?

A psychiatrist planning to be away for a few weeks arranged coverage of emergencies with another psychiatrist. A patient called the covering physician, reporting that he needed a refill of antidepressant medication, a new drug with which the physician was unfamiliar. Rather than authorize the refill of the new medication, the physician changed the prescription to a more common and established drug. The patient began taking the substitute but within days committed suicide. The patient's wife sued the original physician for neglecting to inform the other physician about the patient's situation, which included poor response to most drugs and the use of the new drug as the only effective treatment.

By depriving the covering physician of information that would be considered essential to treatment of this patient, the referring physician assumed responsibility for the risk of adverse outcome that occurred.

What Is a Qualified Substitute?

A plastic surgeon took a 1-day trip after doing a facelift on a patient in the outpatient surgery, and signed out to a new resident on the surgery service. The patient called the day of surgery to report considerable swelling of her face. The resident assured her that it was normal postoperative reaction, and no treatment was necessary. The patient called again the following morning to complain that the swelling was worse and black areas had appeared on the skin. The resident saw her immediately and recognized an expanding hematoma with necrosis of the skin that required immediate attention. Although the plastic surgeon treated the hematoma as soon as he returned, the patient was disfigured. She sued the surgeon for negligent transfer of care to an unqualified physician.

The surgeon could have transferred care of this patient to an attending physician qualified to cover. By allowing the patient to be monitored and advised by an unqualified physician, the surgeon took the gamble that the resident would perform up to the standard required of a specialist plastic surgeon. The bet was lost.

What Responsibilities in Transferring Care Can Be Executed by an Assistant?

Successful transfer of care depends on accurate transfer of information about the patient. After 3 days of severe gastroenteritis, a child was brought to a hospital emergency department by her mother at 5:15 AM. The emergency department physician assessed the child's dehydration and admitted her but the patient load in that department prevented an immediate intravenous cutdown to start treatment. Because her family physician was on staff, the emergency department physician asked the nurse to telephone the family physician immediately. The nurse called, relayed vital signs, and described the patient's condition. The physician later maintained he was only told the patient had a complaint of abdominal pain, and was given no impression of the duration of her illness or extent of dehydration. The physician ordered intravenous fluids and told the nurse he would be in soon. The nurse was unable to start the intravenous line, but did not call the physician back. No fluid was administered until the physician's arrival at 9:30 AM, when a cutdown was performed. The patient was in profound shock by then and died 3 hours later. The parents sued the family physician for negligent diagnosis based on faulty communication with the nurse. At trial, testimony supported the conclusion that the family physician would have acted differently if he had had more information about the child's condition, and that death could have been avoided if the family physician had elicited more information from the nurse or had talked to the mother or the emergency department physician.

The family physician had every opportunity to obtain sufficient data to diagnose and treat the patient. Whatever the estimation of the nursing standard of practice, the physician misused the communication device he chose. The emergency department physician had directed the nurse appropriately to call the physician and relied on the family physician's skills to elicit the emergency history which was apparent.

How Can Coverage Monitoring Be Delegated to Nonphysician Staff?

A man was brought to the emergency department of a hospital after being struck in the head with a baseball bat. He was adequately evaluated and then discharged. Eleven days later the patient returned to the emergency department because of increasing lethargy. He was admitted for testing with a diagnosis of suspected subdural hematoma. Because it was too late in the evening for magnetic resonance imaging to be scheduled, and since the patient was alert, his attending neurosurgeon decided the test could wait until morning. When the physician left at 10 PM, he wrote orders for the nurses to check vital signs hourly, but no specific direction was given to check pupils or state of consciousness for alteration. When care was questioned later, the physician contended that such orders were unnecessary, and that nurses should be expected to know to perform those tests. The nurses did not note a progressive deterioration during the night, and the patient was discovered to be profoundly comatose at 4 AM. The neurosurgeon was called immediately and a craniotomy was performed at 6 AM. Death occurred 5 days later. The patient's family pursued several claims of negligence, among which was the failure of the neurosurgeon to give sufficiently clear instructions and the nurses' failure to contact the physician when the patient was obviously deteriorating.

Delegation is not referral. The nurses were capable of following the physician's directions and did so. Some questions could be raised that a reasonable nurse would know that neurologic signs should have been noted and special attention paid to the alteration of consciousness. Nevertheless, the directed care was only as good as the directions, which should have foreseen the danger to the patient of changes that signified intracranial bleeding.

Check-up File

8

Vendors and Suppliers

Pharmaceuticals
Devices, Equipment, Supplies

Indefensible Risks

Prescription Error, Uninspected or Untested Devices, Self-Dealing, Unprofessional Conduct

Practice Objectives

Disclosures, Instructions to Prevent Forseeable Harm

Pattern for Safety

Avoidance of Suspect Business Connections, Fail-Safe Prescription Control, Confirmed Patient Understanding, Systematic Monitoring of Devices, Equipment

Approaches to Medical Legal Safety

Practice Measures, Foresee, Prevent Problems

Cases

Patient Conduct in Prescription Error, Prescription Risks to Physician, Criminal Acts

Forms

Medication, Equipment Logs and Calendars

Indefensible Risks

Prescription dosage error
Prescription drug error
Prescription route of administration error
Prescription patient identification error
Failure to detect apparent defect
Failure to detect apparent malfunction
Use of untested device, material
Use of uninspected device, material
Failure to discontinue use after injury or near injury
Referral to self-interested diagnostic or therapeutic services
Criminal, negligent, or unprofessional use of prescription medication

Practice Objectives

☐ **Objective:** Patient certainty about all aspects of prescription treatment.

Rationale: Mistake or misunderstanding about prescriptions invites adverse outcomes.

☐ **Objective:** No preventable injury or harm occurs.

Rationale: Doing it right is better than having someone to blame.

Pattern for Safety

1. Avoid every real or apparent business connection with vendors, suppliers, and pharmaceutical companies, including gifts, trips, expenses, and honoraria for participation in programs.
2. Ensure completely legible imprint of patient and medication identification on prescriptions; consider credit card-type identification plates such as hospitals use for imprints.
3. Verify understanding of every important detail of patient instructions about medications.
4. Have patients read prescriptions and review what the medication is for, how many should be taken, and what signs, side effects, or complications to monitor for.
5. Keep list of currently prescribed drugs for monitoring updates.
6. Know as much about generic drugs as marketed products.
7. Arrange backup for marginal patient understanding of prescribed medication, such as family or other contact to check and perform appropriate monitoring.
8. Give patients a prescription management chart or book to show what, when, etc., with pictures of drugs as well as names.
9. Foresee each hazard posed by drug, device, equipment, or supplies; establish a system to manage each and prevent the hazard from materializing.

Bottom Line: Investment in prevention and safeguards yields high practical dividends.

Approaches to Medical Legal Safety

Pharmaceuticals

Penalties for prescription practice failures or offenses can be civil liability, privilege or licensure actions, or criminal conviction. Legible prescriptions prevent misunderstanding because checking is possible and convenient. As a check against errors, hospitals require that any orders or prescriptions given over the telephone be signed within 24 hours. Prescriptions and refills made by phone for patients without examinations can be appropriate, but errors in transmitting phone prescriptions are never excusable. A pharmacist could return a written prescription confirmation by sending a facsimile of the generated prescription label. At any sign of prescription confusion or misunderstanding, a verbal clarification may not be sufficient. The transaction should be reissued from the beginning, with data verified and double-checked.

Every patient misunderstanding about prescription medication is an uncalculated risk to the physician. A patient who understands the purpose, action, therapeutic effect, side effect, potential complications, interaction with food, storage, and normal consequences of prescribed medications is an ally. Recording of prescription treatment parallels documentation for all other treatment: indication, intended effect, warnings of hazards, consent, instructions about complications, and explanation of effect on third parties if needed. Departures from manufacturer, practice protocol, or guidelines should prompt a heightened attention in each area.

In medication malpractice cases, the patient's injury often results from a failure to communicate. The cause or causes of the injury are then determined by identifying who had the duty to communicate, when, and what. The communicators involved are the physician, the pharmacist, and the manufacturer of the medication.

Prescription error litigation poses more risk for physicians than for drug manufacturers. Usually, a drug manufacturer can absorb a large verdict without impairing its business capacity. A malpractice claim against a physician can permanently affect reputation, privileges, and insurance. Often, sick patients are provided powerful drugs. If a mishap occurs, the patient usually sues the physician because some states may not recognize a direct cause of action against the drug manufacturer.

An initial claim in prescription liability may be abandonment. In the drug context, abandonment is asserted when a physician prescribes a drug that requires periodic serum test monitoring, but the physician fails to test the patient for adverse effects or reactions. Periodic monitoring looks for toxic levels of the drug.

Defenses are available in claims of failure to monitor. The most effective defense is that testing was offered but the patient refused to submit to it. For example, a patient might decline to be monitored because of a lack of financial resources to pay for the tests. If the physician documented that the patient could not afford the tests, self-monitoring by the patient is a reasonable alternative. The defense is effective if the physician informs the patient of the consequences of not testing. Physicians must provide patients with explicit warnings about the signs and symptoms of toxicity so that the patient will know when to return for evaluation. If the patient experiences the signs and symptoms of toxicity and fails to notify the physician, defense can successfully show that the duty to monitor was met.

Addiction potential of many drugs, especially narcotics, can cause physical and psychologic addiction even when normal doses and specific dose schedules are followed. Malpractice liability can be imposed when a physician causes an addiction through indiscriminate prescriptions or fails to recognize, diagnose, and treat an addiction. Morphine is often an abused drug and its use often results in addiction litigation. Physicians in defense may assert that drug usage was reasonably monitored, or that the patient misrepresented facts to induce additional undetected prescriptions. Because of the difference in medical knowledge, however, patients' solicitation or use of addictive drugs does not constitute contributory negligence.

Patient communications, with emphasis on informed consent and failure to warn, result in most prescription drug–related litigation. In the context of prescription drugs, the duty to inform and warn imposes a communication obligation on the physician to warn of adverse reactions, precautions, side effects, and contraindications. The learned intermediary doctrine exists because drug manufacturers allege that they cannot adequately communicate with the patient. From the physician's perspective, the adequacy of the disclosed information can be successfully defended if appropriate disclosures were made, even when the patient contends that the information was too vague or complex to understand. Once the patient concedes that a disclosure was made, the physician has a significant defense. The patient must then establish that the physician knew or should have known that the instruction or warning was not understood.

Another defense offers to prove that the patient received information regarding the most serious risks and that the poor quality and incompleteness of the history provided by the patient were the cause of the misprescription. The defensibility of an informed consent or failure to warn case can also depend on the use of the product information given to the patient. Different legal weight given to package inserts include: (1) product package inserts do not establish a standard of care but are admissible to show what the physician knew or should have known about the drug; (2) product package inserts are admissible to show the standard of care, if introduced through an expert witness who explains the standard of care to the jury; (3) product package inserts, standing alone without explanation, are evidence of negligence by the physician if the relevant text is "clear and explicit"; and (4) product package inserts can be combined with the "common knowledge" doctrine (no expert needed to prove the case) to establish negligence against the physician.

Diagnostic error can be compounded by inappropriate drug prescriptions. Evidence of misdiagnosis is evident in hospital and office charts by abrupt or premature discontinuation of drug orders. Although the diagnostic mistake will not be erased, the prompt notice and quick correction can prevent or limit damaging injury to the patient.

Medication malpractice claims may significantly involve patient negligence. Drug prescriptions require significant medical and drug history provided by the patient. An inaccurate history can cause the physician to prescribe drugs that are contraindicated and cause harm.

A physician can be held liable for a failure to foresee and prevent misuse of a drug. If a plaintiff ignores the clear and unambiguous instructions provided with the medication, and that conduct causes harm, then contributory negligence exists. If, however, the plaintiff merely fails to report side effects or symptoms, the contributory negligence may not be established unless the physician warned the patient about the side effects and communicated instructions for the patient to return if the symptoms occurred.

Maintenance of pharmaceutical supplies requires attention to the risks of quality deterioration, hazards of poisoning, possibilities of theft, and chance of accidental harmful disposal. The same mechanisms operate to protect against risks posed by other supplies and materials: relentless checking of inventory and age, maintenance of safeguards against improper access, and protocols for discard or destruction.

Devices, Equipment, Supplies

Control systems can be learned or acquired from facilities and suppliers. Where interests of vendors and physician are aligned, control and safe use of resources can be timesaving and dependable. However, physicians must always be alert to compensate for the self-interest of vendors. Interests in high-volume sales may compromise appropriate safety concerns. Physicians will not be relieved of blame or penalties when depending on others to assure patient and staff safety.

Medical devices are treatment as well as products. Knowledge of the implications of device use, just as the implications of prescription drug use, is expected from physicians. A physician may implant a heart valve that operates effectively and corrects a serious cardiac problem. However, when the patient complains that the noise from the device can be heard across the room, questions arise about what the surgeon knew or should have known about the valve. Even though the manufacturer could have such information, the patient sees the physician as an expert agent in the transaction, with a duty to find out what a patient would need to know about treatment by a device to agree to its use.

When information for choice comes from the physician, devices must perform as described to the patient in obtaining consent for the use. Medical devices include hardware used for patient care: x-ray equipment, dialysis, implants, test kits, disposable supplies, medical tools, parts, and accessories. Use by the physician implies a knowledgeable and considered choice for the patient, with safety and effectiveness evaluated and found sufficient. Disclosure of safety risks and risks of failure are crucial to the risk-benefit decision patients must make.

Margin for error in equipment function is none. Equipment failure that harms the patient can be reduced to virtual insignificance by unremitting checking, maintenance, safety devices, and backup systems. Files, logs, and protocols for drugs and devices, and equipment and supplies should be discussed and in place before problems occur. Everyone buys a burglar alarm after a burglary.

Guidelines for maintenance of pharmaceuticals and supplies are easily available. Forms and log books are the type of "free" help that can be obtained and accepted from vendors. Conscious evaluation of the usefulness of promotional practice aids considers patient and staff safety interests first and foremost. What could make such products more useful is a daily, weekly, monthly, semiannual, and annual checklist of safeguard inspections, maintenance, research, and control actions to be ticked off as performed. Computer master calendar programs can easily prompt every appropriate action at the right time. Computer function and support must be assured, buttressed by back-up systems, and checked as well.

Foreseeable problems with equipment must be addressed before harm occurs. Equipment involved in adverse outcomes have often shown repeated patterns of failure:

Failure	Prevention
Faulty operating condition	Testing, inspection
Lacking regular maintenance	Schedule, experts
Noticeable malfunction or improper repair	Inspection, testing, expert source
Prior malfunction or failure	Training, control
Disregard for warnings or specified usage	Training, monitoring
Neglected maintenance or calibration	Training, inspection, expert source
Use after malfunction known or noticeable	Training, inspection, control
Alteration of equipment	Training, monitoring control
Use in manner or purpose not intended	Training, monitoring control
Use after recall or warning without modification	Training, monitoring control
Use by untrained staff	Training, monitoring control
History of alteration or neglect in prior use	Records
Absence of noted precautions	Records

Clinical laboratory operation in medical practice offers many opportunities for error and question. Insufficient training of personnel, incentives for overuse, and lack of adherence to commercial laboratory protocols all expose physicians to problems from many sectors. Clear permissibility for office laboratory services should be established by legal counsel advice, as well as designation of all rules and requirements for laboratory operation to assure compliance with medical testing standards, as appropriate.

In commerce, whenever profit and decision making are connected, suspicion may be reasonable about objectivity of choices. Physicians are understood to have historically devoted themselves to provide medical skills and knowledge where needed. Fees and payments are honorable realities, but patients must be able to trust that financial gain is not an indication for treatment. Connection of any treatment decision to physician gain is intrinsically suspect. Providing needed services for an appropriate fee is not. It is the decision of necessity that must be protected from financial pressures. Financial motives can move decisions to greater use of medical services, as the fee-for-service pattern has been shown to demonstrate, or can discourage utilization of services, as the managed-care and prospective reimbursement patterns may elicit.

Compromised integrity and apparent bias may not be perceived by a physician. A medical journal reported an outbreak of expensive antibiotic use after a lavish promotional dinner for physicians sponsored by the manufacturer of the drug. Whenever a physician is connected to a supplier, vendor, laboratory, or other resource from which income can be drawn by medical decisions for patients, suspicions arise of harmful, unprofessional—if not criminal—acts. This is seen, not as the skilled and honorable practice of medicine, but as the unscrupulous use of medicine for profit.

Cases

How Do Patients Cause Prescription Errors?

Courts and juries need not distinguish intentional from negligent misrepresentations by patients regarding their histories. The physician can testify how prescribing conduct would have been different had the history been factual and complete. Evidence of an incomplete history was effective in defense of a case against an obstetrician and drug company arising from the administration of oxytocin (Pitocin). The physician testified that he would not have prescribed oxytocin because of possible perforation and scarring of the uterus if the patient had disclosed that she had undergone three prior abortions.

How Does Prescription Practice Pose Risks to Physicians?

Prescription practice failures or offenses can result in civil liability and privilege or licensure action and criminal conviction. Elements that must be proved to establish each type of culpability differ, but the same conduct can be involved in each type of questioned practice. A license to practice medicine offers little protection to a physician charged with violating laws designed to restrict the flow of controlled substances. Physicians have been prosecuted and convicted for unlawfully possessing, prescribing, dispensing, selling, distributing, delivering, obtaining, administering, or transporting controlled substances. A physician may dispense drugs only in the context of a physician–patient relationship in accordance with accepted treatment principles. These two conditions are the physician's protection against criminal and disciplinary action.

What Prescriptions of Controlled Substances Can Be Considered Criminal Acts?

A dentist was indicted for felony violations of controlled substance laws in issuing a prescription on behalf of a patient who received the controlled substance from a pharmacist. The prescription was alleged to be intentional or known to be outside the course of professional practice or research, and not necessary in medical treatment and care of patients.

The controlled substance, oxycodone with acetaminophen (Tylox), has accepted uses in treatment but requires severe restrictions because of its potential for psychic or physical dependence. A patient reported severe tooth pain and was diagnosed with abscessed teeth. Extractions were offered and refused. A prescription for 20 oxycodone with acetaminophen capsules was given. During the months after the first visit, a total of 120 capsules of oxycodone with acetaminophen were prescribed without examination or treatment, each time the patient complaining of tooth pain and saying that he would have the dental work done later. Prescriptions for antibiotics given at the same visits were not filled. Similar history was obtained for other patients and the practitioner was also found to have written prescriptions for "patients" that he presented to the pharmacy and took for his own use.

The practitioner tried to defend the practice by contending that even if the prescriptions were not necessary, they were still legitimate treatment of ostensible infections and pain. This was argued to be at most a mistake in treatment choice, not an intentional delivery or transfer of controlled substances. The state was required to prove that the prescriptions were not issued for a legitimate purpose. This proof included evidence and testimony that:

- *No cursory examinations were performed*
- *Prescriptions were issued at intervals inconsistent with legitimate treatment of the recorded underlying condition*
- *No logical medical relationship connected the use of controlled substances and the underlying condition*
- *Large numbers of prescriptions were issued*
- *Large quantities of controlled substances were prescribed*
- *The practitioner wrote more than one prescription on an occasion to "spread them out"*
- *The practitioner warned the patient to fill the prescriptions at different pharmacies*
- *The practitioner knew the patient was delivering the controlled substances to others*

On this evidence, the practitioner was convicted of several felonies.

What Prescriptions of Controlled Substances Can Be Considered Grounds for Revocation of License to Practice?

A physician was accused by the licensure board of prescription of controlled substances for other than legitimate medical purposes. A criminal prosecution had ended with acquittal. The physician defended his practice against revocation proceedings on the grounds of entrapment and double jeopardy. He argued that his acquittal on criminal charges barred the licensure action and that the use of a police officer to pose as a patient and obtain prescription of controlled drugs was entrapment and the state could not revoke his license for an act solicited by the police.

The board charged the physician with numerous prescriptions to three to five persons without medical basis. Evidence of a pattern of intentional or negligent practice included:

- *Issuance of repeated refill prescriptions for controlled substances without explanation over short periods of time*
- *Failure to exercise minimal care to prevent persons from obtaining multiple prescriptions under different pseudonyms*
- *Failure to exercise minimal care in obtaining and recording the addresses of persons for whom controlled substances were prescribed over extended periods*
- *Repeated failure to record appropriate medical history or appropriate physical examination in instances where controlled substances were prescribed*

In one case described, a patient visited the physician on dozens of occasions, giving at least two names and several similar addresses. The patient was over 6 feet tall and weighed more than 300 pounds. Twice in one 6-day period, the patient received prescriptions for methaqualone (Quaalude) or methamphetamine (Desoxyn) under each name. From pharmacy prescription records and the patient cards, prescriptions to this patient were documented as exceeding dosage recommendations by 30% to 40%. Prescriptions were recorded on several patients' cards and some were not recorded at all. Another patient received prescriptions for what would have been 200% of the medically appropriate dosage.

Issuance of multiple prescriptions at short intervals was found to be inconsistent with accepted medical treatment and supported the conclusion that the prescriptions were not intended to serve a medical purpose. Prescriptions without medical examination or diagnosis to the police officer introducing himself as a patient and complaining of pain were not found to be entrapment. Entrapment is a doctrine limiting police abuse in criminal cases, but not generally a defense in delicensure and was not found in this case. The defense of double jeopardy was also not available, because, while the effect of license revocation is punitive to the physician, its purpose is protective of the public. Therefore the acquittal on criminal charges did not bar revocation of this physician's license.

Forms

Medication register for all patients and all medications, made possible by the computer with ease and with paper files with some effort. Dates of refill and dates and quantities expected for use at prescribed dosage. Master medication log and calendar to monitor early requests for refills or late requests indicating failure of medication therapy.

Equipment status register covering purchase, lease, recall, repair, maintenance, training, incidents of malfunction or failure. Numbers and names of contacts and sources.

Practice Setting

Hospital Practice
Managed Care
Physician Contract Obligations and Patient Necessity
Physicians as Independent Contractors or Employees
Concurrent Review of Hospital Stay
Specialty Referral ("Gatekeeping")
Integrated Delivery Systems

Indefensible Risks

Failure to Monitor Care by Others, Inaction in Care Review, Contract Naivete

Practice Objectives

Confident Reliance, Control of Facility Risks

Pattern for Safety

Awareness of Obligations, Facility Capabilities, Staff Work, Avoidance of Suspect Reimbursement Strategies

Approaches to Medical Legal Safety

Advice in Contracts, Patients' Advocacy, No Schemes

Cases

Hospital Staff Failures, Denial of Care by Reviewer, Contracts, Managed Care, Referrals

Forms

Indefensible Risks

Ignorance of notable hospital deficiencies
Failure to compensate for or address noted hospital deficiencies
Errors in medication or directed management of hospitalized patients
Uncertainty about appeal process in denial of patient treatment by payment reviewer
Inaction regarding denial of necessary patient treatment by payment reviewer
Entering a binding agreement for medical services without expert advice about terms, implications, consequences

Practice Objectives

☐ **Objective:** Confident dependence on hospital personnel and systems.

Rationale: *Limited control must be exercised to maximum to balance risks of others' failures.*

☐ **Objective:** Confident knowledge of limits of medical discretion and procedures to achieve maximum effective function.

Rationale: *Control can only be exercised to balance risks of others' failures where the limits of power and discretion are recognized.*

Pattern for Safety

1. Have every contract provision explained and acknowledged as acceptable.
2. Be prepared to look for, note, and act in areas of hospital deficiency.
3. Stay within scope of practice in accepting assignments.
4. Check each major hospital department on which admitted patients will depend.
5. Participate generously where benefit to physician or patient can be seen.
6. Do not participate in practice functions without liability protection.
7. Inquire about hospital track record on indicators of care problems.
8. Prepare and practice how to "go to the wall" on patients' behalf in managed care.
9. Check assets behind any "hold harmless" agreement.
10. Never misrepresent or "game" diagnostic or treatment codings.
11. If choice between economic loss and patient harm, choose loss.
12. Avoid contractual facades contrived to achieve special status for financial gain.

Bottom Line: Counsel early.

Approaches to Medical Legal Safety

Hospital Practice

Medical practice contracts establish agreement to many legally enforceable obligations. During negotiation and before signature, contract duties and implications should be reviewed by counsel. Although a good and fair contract should leave all parties with reasonable benefits, some contracts attempt to "bulletproof" one side at the expense of another. Issues of extreme importance include allocation of fee determinations, control of liability disputes, costs of defense or damage compensation, quality and risk activities, staff or resident supervision, certifications for care decisions or payment approval, cost containment protocols, and compliance responsibilities with peer review and institutional functions.

Personal assessment of major hospital functions on which practice will depend is a prudent step. In hospital practice, many tasks are provided by staff not selected or supervised by physicians. Although changes probably cannot be compelled, compensatory effort by the physician will foreclose potential adverse events. A certain level of communication, monitoring, follow-up, and accountability remain the burden of the physician. Just as office practice requires open channels of communication for positive and negative information, hospital practice calls for direct and objective action in any situation in which patient care may be at risk. Involvement in hospital mishaps taxes physicians as much as questioned personal practice. Typical and numerous hospital incidents injuring patients have been caused by failures to observe or manage conditions appropriately, failures to safeguard patients from anticipated hazards, emergency conditions of overload and confusion, failures of skill in procedures, failures of hygiene, and irrational treatments for patient condition.

Practice agreements with hospitals must be limited to an acceptable scope of practice for physician qualifications and experience. A surgeon in the emergency department may not be able to maintain and titrate sensitive fluid balance and electrolytes in cardiopulmonary support. To accept assignments outside practice scope invites problems. Likewise, actions by physicians intended to serve hospital interests but which are more properly the job of hospital employees should be avoided. For example, release of information about patient or hospital matters should be referred to the hospital officer assigned to do communications liaison.

Hospital performance criteria to assess potential physician risk by association include data on:

Patients with prior hospitalization within the year
Newborns with Apgar scores of 4 or less
Trauma incurred in hospital
Adverse drug reactions
Transfers to comparable care facility
Returns to surgery within 48 hours
Unplanned extensions of surgery
Infection of hospital origin
Unanticipated neurologic deficit
Stays over 90th percentile for diagnosis
Cardiac or respiratory arrests
Fevers on discharge
Discharge of newborns weighing less than 2500 grams
Return for emergency care within 48 hours of treatment

Hospital actions to prevent patient risk from physician-related injuries:

Physician-related incident defined appropriately
Severity scale for physician-related incidents
Early detection of impaired physicians
Scrub-ins or other proctoring routines for high-risk procedures
Second opinions before elective surgery for high-risk procedures
Systems to prevent oversight of abnormal laboratory values, reports
Surveillance of incidence of high-risk procedures
Procedure risk consideration of electiveness, alternative treatment
Informed consent procedures monitored

Patient comments, complaints addressed individually and also aggregated for pattern analysis
Discharges against medical advice immediately reviewed and documented
Staff physicians liability proceedings monitored
Deaths reviewed routinely
Treatment failures or complications reviewed individually and in aggregate
Cases of medication toxicity examined
Systematic control to avoid medication errors
Indicators of systemic problems noted and addressed by action
Ongoing and retrospective drug utilization review implemented

Misuse and mistakes in medication have been closely connected to incidents of patient injury. Several categories of drugs or biologics are most frequently associated with potentially compensable events. The record of adverse reactions to antibiotics commonly used in the hospital occurs with high statistical significance (between 5% and 10%). These are often potent antibiotics used to combat serious infectious diseases and complications. In these situations, adverse reaction rates of 5% to 8% might be justified as clinically acceptable and the liability potential associated with such reactions justified by their effectiveness. However, much antibiotic use in hospitals has been described as "irrational," especially parenteral use of potent and potentially toxic antibiotics. More than 10% of patients admitted may receive at least one parenteral antibiotic, with therapy considered irrational by medical review in over a third of surgical cases, half of gynecologic cases, and a tenth of medical cases.

Managed Care

Managed care presents new and old medical legal concerns. The certainty and clarity of managed care contract terms accompany a more rigid and directive pattern of practice. Managed care is, first and foremost, a payment device for medical care. Payment conditions are the first specific problem, with physicians offered financial connections of variable value.

The key document establishing the relationship between the organization and physician is the participating provider agreement, which sets forth the obligations of each. A preferred provider organization (PPO) agreement among physicians may be interposed as well, with the PPO negotiating terms with third-party payors. The agreements create and define the network of providers offered to the payors.

A key agreement provision is a mechanism for obtaining provider consent to arrangements that specific payors may desire. One alternative is for specific terms to be offered to participating providers, as those terms become required by each payor which contracts for care. Another method is to include in a primary agreement all pricing, participation, and operating terms anticipated to interest all payors to be sought.

In the first method, each time a specific arrangement is negotiated with a payor, the proposed terms are sent to participating physicians, with a limited time to object to the arrangement. Time may be as little as 14 to 21 days. If no objection is specifically registered, the physician is bound by the proposed terms. Each provider must instruct the office manager or educate the staff to identify and retrieve proposed participation arrangements from incoming documents. The provider must then review each offer within a very short period of time. Failure to review and reject a contract offer within the designated time can have quite adverse unintended consequences.

The second alternative, where all of the terms each payor will require are agreed to in a master participating provider agreement. Success of the proposed agreement will depend on how well it attracts payors in a very competitive marketplace. Even this agreement will require amendment, but not generally on such short notice as the first, so-called "messenger model."

Another critical feature of provider agreements is the mechanism to reflect prices that the payors will pay for contract services. The price terms may be a percentage discount off the usual charges of the provider. Discounts from usual, customary charges offer limited opportunities for controlling costs since providers can increase charges to offset the percentage discount. In addition, discounts from usual, customary charges are somewhat harder to administer because costs are less predictable. A fee schedule may be based on Medicare Diagnosis-Related Groups for inpatient services and the Resource-Based Relative Value Scale for physicians' services. A conversion factor may be used or a consultant may develop an alternative fee schedule based on the market.

Aside from the terms of contract pricing, another serious issue is the method physicians use to determine prices, which evokes sensitive antitrust issues. Antitrust risks of the price determination process are outlined in an old but major medical practice case, *Arizona v Maricopa County Medical Society.* Two county medical societies established foundations that could be described as early forms of preferred provider organizations. Expressing a desire to control the costs of medical care, physician participants agreed that they would not charge patients or payors more than the maximum fees developed by the two foundations. The U.S. Supreme Court held that the agreement constituted a self-evident violation of the Sherman Antitrust Act.

While the facts of the situation seen in the case are not likely to be duplicated, some important aspects of antitrust are illustrated. First, the two foundations included an overwhelming majority of physicians, 70% and 80%, respectively, in the area. Second, the foundations did very little other than offer a cap on fees.

The groups offered no credentialing, quality assurance, risk-bearing, or other services common to managed care. Without such procompetitive cost-saving services and amenities, if a large number of physicians agree to maximum or minimum fees, it can be seen as anticompetitive and an exercise of prohibited monopoly power. U.S. law has recognized that when one organization can control virtually all the activity in an industry or business, the temptation to overreach and drain every profit possible is unlikely to be resisted.

Physician Contract Obligations and Patient Necessity

Physicians contracting with managed-care organizations have been faced with pressures from payment review that are seen to compete with patient needs. The payor looks for indications of medical necessity and appropriateness, a minimum standard; the physician looks to provide the highest effective care, a maximum. The physician wants to err on the side of completeness. It is no wonder that questions of diagnostic resources, specialty treatment referral, hospital admission, and length of stay are issues of major contention.

Provisions that exclude experimental modalities, require preadmission certification, concurrent review, and diagnostic-related protocols are typical limits on physician discretion. Physicians are given one tool to modify the operating system—the path of appeal. The payor defense to patient injury will be that the physician failed to adequately inform the managed-care agency of the patient's true condition. The physician's problem is that if needed testing is not ordered because no payment will be made by the managed-care agency, medical credibility is impaired. If a physician complies with limits that harm a patient, the priority duty to the patient has been breached.

Utmost effort to fulfill contract responsibilities should be expended, to the point where patient interests are at stake. At this point, as courts have confirmed, the choice must be made to do all possible to assure that patient needs are addressed. Short of paying the bill personally or resigning from the medical staff, all appeals and documentation must be provided to safeguard physician credibility and patient life and limb. Patients must also be asked to pay for recommended care that is not covered by their benefit contracts.

No matter what the pressure, physicians will not be excused from assuring a reasonable standard of care to each patient. Insistence on needed medical care, documentation of denials, and full effort to exhaust avenues of appeal are required. A final decision by the managed-care agency, overruling the physician to allow risk to the patient, may occur. However, compliance with a directive denial can allocate the burden of harm to the managed-care agency by clear notification by the physician of the risk and its consequences to the company.

Participation in peer review and utilization review activities for an Independent Practice Association (IPA), PPO, or health maintenance organization (HMO) may not be covered by liability insurance procured by the organization. A contract should assure that the managed-care entity provides liability coverage for all such functions if required by participation in the managed care. Contract indemnity of defense cost and liability insurance for compensation are both important to obtain. Immunity is granted by law for much peer review; however, costs are incurred to establish that immunity. "Hold harmless" clauses are also dependent on the financial resources of the entity holding the physician harmless. When payment framework organizations such as managed care entities fail, few assets support many obligations. By default, the physician will be looked to for coverage.

Contracts may appear to confer status of independent contractor by terms and still create an employment relationship. If a medical director in an urgent care facility, for example, has all the duties, benefits, and privileges of an employee, the physician can be found to be an employee regardless of what the contract recites. The significance of contractor versus employee status relates to taxes, investments, pension, and other important financial considerations.

Managed-care contracting offers financial reward pressures as well as cost constraints on providing needed treatment to patients. The temptation to "game" the payment system for optimal reimbursement often backfires. Miscoding diagnoses or treatments for payment leaves a fraudulent medical history to justify. Integrity is lost; liability insurance may be invalid on grounds of misrepresentation.

If integrity lost by use of misrepresented gaming payment codes to maximize patient payment for care is reprehensible, abuse of

the gatekeeper function for personal gain to the detriment of the patient is likely to be indefensible. Both may be unethical and criminal fraud as well. Profit-sharing and specialist fee pool distribution provide physician incentive to forego recommending needed treatment because physician income will be greater for less patient care. When a patient's adverse result is connected to such an arrangement, a conflict of interest is apparent. Likewise, self-referral or referral to any business from which physician profit is to be gained are prohibited acts, if not crimes. Group practice internal referrals are exceptions, but restrictions on billing and location remain.

Any financial investment that could conceivably connect a physician with incentives or inducement to manipulate patient recommendations must be reviewed by counsel for illegality or appearance of illegality. A not-quite-conflict-of-interest and profitable financial arrangement that is not actually illegal, may nevertheless weigh heavily when patient care is questioned after a bad result. Such a potential net loss may make legally marginal contract connections not worth the risk. Other matters for counsel review are payment arrangements that may invalidate qualified retirement plans, liaisons among practitioners that amount to price-fixing, or other prohibited acts.

Physicians as Independent Contractors or Employees

The question of "who is an employee" is not always clearly established before disputes. In questioned care where responsibility follows employment status, whether a physician is an employee or an independent contractor is critical. The key is the degree of control the employer exerts over the physician. Employee status seriously affects physicians' financial considerations of tax, pension, and retirement accounts.

Courts do not look simply at the contract language that specifies that the physician is an independent contractor, but look at the totality of the circumstances to determine the employer's control. For example, a court has held in a case of questioned care, that a physician was employed by an HMO, even though the contract specified independent contractor status. The court focused on the existence of an employment contract between the negligent physician and the HMO. The physician was paid an annual salary, and received fringe benefits, such as sick leave, life, health and malpractice insurance, vacation pay, and professional leave, all typical aspects of employment relationships.

An HMO can be liable for a participating physician's actions. The physician was a specialist and a member of a group that had contracted with the HMO. The court looked at several factors in drawing its conclusion. The contract specified that the physicians' group would abide by the HMO's policies and procedures, and indicated the number of hours the physicians would spend at the HMO. It specified that each physician would spend 1 day per week at the HMO. The HMO controlled the number of patients seen, and maintained all patient charts and records, including the specialists' records. The physicians agreed that they would not let their private practice interfere with the contractual obligations to ensure the timeliness and continuity of HMO patient care. The HMO had control over the laboratory facilities and outside consulting services available to specialists. The specialists were required to use in-house medical services available at the HMO unless a procedure was not available, and specialists could not order outside tests unless an HMO primary care physician approved the tests. HMO clerks and staff physicians scheduled outside testing, handled the paperwork, and arranged billings. The HMO arranged all patient appointments. The HMO had a 24-hour-a-day switchboard to take direct calls from patients to specialists. The employment relationship between the HMO and the specialists lasted for more than 3 years.

It was the regular business of the HMO to provide health services, and this function was performed by the specialist doctors. The patient literature listed the specialist physicians, representing that they were affiliated with the HMO. Patients were not informed of the independent status of the specialists affiliated with the HMO and were not permitted to make independent selections of the consultants or specialists they were to see.

Some courts have found the apparent agency theory inapplicable. For example, a patient contended that the HMO controlled or retained the right to control the medical groups and physicians with whom it contracted by virtue of the quality assessment and utilization review guidelines it used. The court found the HMO's quality assurance compliance program was not the type of control from which an employment agency relationship arises. The HMO required documentation that the physicians were following procedures to assure quality health care, but the HMO did not review the contents of the documentation to assess the accuracy of the medical diagnoses, nor did it assume responsibility for determining the correctness or appropriateness of the medical services provided. Instead, the HMO played only an administrative role in overseeing the process of health care delivery. The court also found no evidence that the HMO had advertised or held itself out as exerting control over its physicians which would support a reasonable conclusion that they were HMO employees. There was no evidence that the patient relied on the HMO for the quality of care received from the physicians. Although the patient was required to choose a primary physician from a limited list, the court noted that all HMOs operate that way. No evidence showed that the HMO controlled or had the right to control the professional treatment of the physician alleged to be negligent.

Concurrent Review of Hospital Stay

A managed-care program's utilization control may expose physicians to liability by denial of payment for necessary health services, including consultation, surgery, or continued hospitalization. The concurrent review process assesses whether treatment, usually a hospital stay, continues to be medically necessary and appropriate. Clinical determinations by plan representatives can result in premature discharge and consequent professional liability exposure.

The primary care physician's role and responsibility have been articulated in this potential conflict of interest situation. The physician who disagrees with the utilization determination and yet prematurely discharges the patient, resulting in harm to the patient, may be liable for the patient's injury. A physician has the responsibility to appeal the payor decision to deny payment, prompting discharge of the patient earlier than the physician considers appropriate. The attending physician's failure to appeal may shift the risk of the patient's treatment to the physician. Physicians may be liable if, against medical judgment, they comply without protest with utilization limitations by payors. Physicians owe a duty to patients to appeal utilization review decisions when a reasonable physician would make calls, write letters, and convene a meeting of the hospital utilization review committee. An appropriate scale of assertive tactics depends on the severity of the risk to the patient of complying with a utilization management decision.

Specialty Referral ("Gatekeeping")

Claims of negligent failure to refer can be anticipated where specialty referral in a health care plan must be coordinated through the utilization review staff. Where economic incentives are coupled with insufficient care, lawsuits may blame the HMO's gatekeeper for the failure to deliver necessary and appropriate medical care if specialty referral was refused for primarily economic reasons. In one HMO, a primary physician "gatekeeper" approach was employed to curb excess utilization. An HMO subscriber could only obtain specialist services on referral by a designated primary physician, who was entitled to a refund of money paid into a "withhold" account for specialist fees, if contributions to that account were not consumed at the end of the contract year. Disclosure of incentives may be required.

Integrated Delivery Systems

Market forces in health care services and payment mechanisms have drawn responses that are largely moving toward consolidation and affiliation among providers and payors. Integrated

Delivery Systems are one form of managed care in which coordination of care and risk-sharing are pursued through comprehensive management and information systems to achieve efficiencies that deliver more cost-effective care.

Strategic alliances are proposed to providers and/or payors. There are many uncertainties in choosing to be on the right team. An alliance declined may grow large enough to close out individual practice by marketing and service contracts with employers. An alliance accepted may go broke trying to provide contract services. The alliances share risk through common ownership, governance, revenue, planning, and management. Integrated delivery can be hospital collaborations, practice integrations, physician–hospital integration, or provider–payor integration.

Whatever financial, corporate, and other arrangements are established, medical services in integrated care can be expected to include: systemized practice by physicians with hospital and all other health care services; system self-monitoring of all services to assure efficient utilization; development and use of uniform clinical guidelines for optimal management of care; and development of common administration in records, enrollment, credentialing, quality standards and measurement.

Legal hazards to integrated delivery systems include malpractice liability exposure, governance and ownership risks, antitrust problems, fraud and abuse restrictions, prohibitions on self-referral, accusations of corporate medical practice, securities violations, tax difficulties, medicare and medicaid reimbursement restrictions, and HMO and insurance laws.

Legal controls on health care delivery innovations challenge experienced attorneys. The utmost care in seeking and agreeing to alliances should be exercised with the most experienced guidance available. Choosing counsel who have successfully organized and negotiated managed-care systems should provide a level of security. Choices about with whom to ally and what contract benefits and concessions will be allowed must still be the physician's.

Cases

What Is the Responsibility of a Physician for Failures of Hospital Personnel?

An obstetrician determined that the patient needed a cesarean section because she had not progressed in labor and the fetus was in stress. The patient and her husband initially expressed apprehension about general anesthesia, but after discussing the procedure they gave their approval. A certified registered nurse assistant (CRNA) was employed by the hospital to administer general anesthesia. The rules and regulations of the hospital provided that the administration and type of anesthesia were scheduled according to the surgeon's request. Hospital-privileged anesthesiologists were private practitioners who charged on a fee-for-service basis and who had no official capacity with the hospital administration or CRNA services.

The CRNA reported to the chief nurse anesthetist who worked for the hospital and made assignments. The CRNA inserted the endotracheal tube and told the obstetrician that he could proceed with the caesarean section. When the initial incision had been made, the CRNA immediately realized that the endotracheal tube had been inadvertently placed in the esophagus, and asked the operating physician for help. The obstetrician responded that he had to deliver the baby. The nurse who was assisting immediately went to the head of the table to assist the CRNA and called for help. Another CRNA and an anesthesiologist attending another patient responded to the call. While they were working on the patient, the obstetrician finished delivering the baby and closed the patient's abdomen. In the meantime, the patient vomited and aspirated, which caused cardiac arrest. By the time she was eventually intubated, she was seriously and permanently brain damaged. The patient's estate sued the surgeon, contending that he was in charge of the operating room, and was vicariously liable for the negligence of the CRNA who was a borrowed servant under his direct supervision.

Although a surgeon may be generally in command from the beginning of the operation to the end as "captain of the ship," surgeon and CRNA work in highly expert fields. Despite the common goal of providing a surgical service to the patient, their responsibilities are not inextricably bound. The role of surgeons in the operating room and the control of hospitals is changing under modern medicine. A legal doctrine that the surgeon directly controls all activities of whatever nature in the operating room is no longer realistic. Modern hospitals hire, fire, train, and provide day-to-day supervision of their nurse employees. Hospitals can and do implement standards and regulations governing good surgery practices and techniques and are in the best position to enforce compliance. Because the surgeon did not actually supervise or control the acts of the CRNA, the "captain of the ship" doctrine was inapplicable. Because the CRNA was neither employed by the surgeon nor a borrowed employee, the surgeon was not vicariously liable for the nurse's actions.

A nurse employed by a hospital but assisting a surgeon or physician under direct supervision would pose a different situation. Here a nurse with specialized training as a CRNA was not under the immediate personal supervision of the surgeon. The CRNA performed duties independently as a nurse anesthetist and was allowed to provide anesthesia according to protocol commonly used at the hospital.

A surgical nurse, under the direct supervision of the surgeon, who acts according to the surgeon's specific directions, is the legal servant of the surgeon and the surgeon would be responsible for performance of the directed acts. The CRNA was not in this category, particularly where there was no evidence that the surgeon directed the procedures to be utilized by the CRNA, or had a genuine opportunity to alter the course of events. The CRNA is not a borrowed servant and could not be characterized as an assistant, which would impose specific responsibilities on the surgeon.

Does a Physician Have a Right or a Duty to Control Hospital Employees?

During a cardiac bypass procedure the patient died of an air embolism, when a noncertified hospital perfusionist, preoccupied with filling out laboratory slips, failed to observe that air was entering the patient's circulation. He was the only perfusionist in attendance. No backup perfusion system was utilized. The patient's estate sued the cardiac surgeon contending that the organization of the perfusion procedure was the cardiac surgeon's responsibility. The suit claimed that it would be negligent to permit the surgery to proceed without some support or backup system to ensure that air did not enter the lines, and that open-heart surgery should not be done with only a single perfusionist in attendance. The suit also claimed that the cardiac surgeon had the ability or opportunity to control the perfusionist's failure to monitor the blood level in the oxygenator to ensure that no air would be pumped into the patient's circulation. It was established that a cardiac surgeon cannot perform coronary bypass surgery without a perfusionist to operate and ensure that the heart-lung machine is functioning properly, that the blood levels in the oxygenator are maintained, and that the patient is receiving an adequate supply of blood.

The liability of a surgeon for the acts of hospital support personnel is often determined using the test of the right-to-control. There is a distinction between services or acts involving professional skill, which would make the assistant subject to the surgeon's control, and ministerial services (such as a sponge count), which are not generally supervised by the surgeon. In performing services or acts not involving professional skill, which are ordinary or routine in character, a hospital employee is not regarded as the agent of the surgeon. In this case, however, it could be reasonably inferred that the perfusionist was acting as the cardiac surgeon's agent at the time of the operation.

A trained professional will not be deemed a borrowed servant of a surgeon unless their responsibilities in caring for the patient are bound together. Although the surgeon in the operating room may be liable for the acts of assisting personnel, a surgeon will not be liable for the negligence of a fellow specialist, such as an anesthesiologist. As part of the overall conduct of heart surgery, the surgeon was vicariously liable for the noncertified perfusionist's failure to observe that air was entering into the patient's blood system. Independent responsibility cannot be borne by a dependent practitioner. Here, the cardiac surgeon was independently negligent for his own conduct as well as vicariously responsible for the negligence of the perfusionist assisting.

What Must a Physician Do When Payment Is Denied for Necessary Patient Treatment?

Reimbursement utilization review about medical necessity after treatment results in disputes and withholding of payment. Errors and disputes in prospective review decision in practical terms result in withholding necessary care, potentially leading to a patient's disability or death.

Five days after undergoing arterial bypass surgery, a patient was required to undergo a lumbar sympathectomy for severe peripheral vascular insufficiency. Although she was scheduled to be discharged 4 days later, her vascular surgeon believed that she needed to remain in the hospital for 8 days to assure medical monitoring of her condition for complications. Relying on information provided by a utilization review nurse screener, a physician utilization reviewer authorized only 4 additional days. Although the vascular surgeon knew that he could attempt to obtain a further extension of the patient's hospital stay by telephoning the physician reviewer, he did not do so. Acting within standards of practice based on length-of-stay norms, he discharged the patient. Nine days later, the patient was rehospitalized because of occlusive thrombosis of her leg. An infection in the graft site had developed, making it difficult for the surgeon to surgically remove the thrombosis because of concern that the surgery would spread the infection systemically. One week later, a below-the-knee amputation was required.

The patient sued, alleging that the failure to approve the surgeon's requested extension of her hospital stay led to undetected complications that resulted in amputation of her leg. The vascular surgeon testified that had the requested 8-day extension been granted, he believed that he would have observed the color changes in her leg and that would have caused him to reopen the graft to remove the thrombosis and to control the infection with the vigorous use of antibiotics. The physician utilization reviewer testified that had the surgeon decided it was necessary to keep her in the hospital for a longer period of time than the reviewer had authorized, he would have expected the surgeon to make such a request. The court declared that the decision to discharge the patient was the responsibility of her attending physician. The court pointed out that although the vascular surgeon may have been intimidated by the third-party payor, he was not rendered powerless to act appropriately if other action was required under the circumstances.

The court declared that the payor did not override the medical judgment of the patient's vascular surgeon at the time of discharge because the surgeon did not protest the utilization physician reviewer's decision. The court also declared that cost-containment programs should not be permitted to corrupt the professional judgment of physicians, and that attending physicians should be encouraged to appeal adverse utilization management decisions with which they disagree. The court pointed out that the physician who complies without protest with the utilization review-imposed limitations when clinical judgment dictates otherwise cannot avoid ultimate responsibility for the patient's care. The physician cannot point to the third-party payor as the liability scapegoat when the consequences of medical decisions harm the patient.

How Can an Agreement Establish Employee Status or Independent Contract Services?

An urgent care center was staffed with physicians who were limited partners, a nonpartner physician serving as the center's full-time medical director, and nonpartner part-time physicians. The center regarded the medical director and the part-time physicians as independent contractors and, accordingly, did not pay any federal employment taxes for them. The Internal Revenue Service determined that those individuals were employees, not independent contractors, for federal employment tax purposes and assessed plaintiff for unpaid taxes, penalties, and interest. The medical director employment contract with the center was executed on behalf of the physician's professional services association, to which he had granted control of his services. The contract stated that the center had no authority to control the director and allocated him no fringe benefits.

Despite the language of the contract, the court concluded that the professional services association had not actually been granted the right to control the director's activities as an association employee which, if true would have indicated that he was an independent contractor under contract to the center. To have the right to control the director's activities, the association needed to have the right to direct his activities in some meaningful sense, and there had to be a contract between the association and the center which acquired association employee services, acknowledging the association's controlling position. The document establishing the association and giving the association control over the director's professional practice were not filed until weeks after the director signed the employment agreement with the center. This was not a valid agreement between the professional service association and the physician; it was a sham. The validity of the employment contract that specified the lack of control over the director's activities was suspect, since the physician signed it as the agent of a not-yet-existing professional association. Even under other conditions of legal analysis, the court determined that the physician was an employee, not an independent contractor, since he was restricted to working for the center, worked full-time, and was subject to peer review procedures. He also received personal leave time, malpractice insurance reimbursement, and moving costs, all of which are traditionally considered fringe benefits provided to employees.

What Process Is Used to Select Plan Referral Specialists?

A patient with urinary stress incontinence was referred by her plan primary physician to a plan specialist. The specialist performed urologic surgery and an adverse outcome caused the patient to sue for compensation. The verdict was awarded on the basis of negligently performed surgery, and the surgeon was held liable, in a separate action. The patient sued the health care plan for the negligence of the surgeon, based on a failure to provide a qualified specialist on referral.

The plan solicited physicians to enter into contracts for their professional services and to thereby be listed by the plan as physicians approved for use by plan members. The contracts did not obligate the physicians to treat only plan members, but where such members were treated, the physicians agreed to observe certain limitations on fees, the use of certain laboratory facilities, and various other conditions intended to minimize costs. A plan member who was treated by one of the contracting physicians was not billed for the services, but fees were paid directly to the physician by the plan.

Listings of physicians indicated either a primary care physician or a specialist. Each plan member selected a primary care physician from the list and consulted the primary care physician for any and all medical services. If specialized services were necessary, the primary care physician referred to specialists on the plan list. The list of plan-approved specialists was provided only to primary care physicians for their use in making patient referrals. Other specialists might, however, be used on a per-patient basis if that specialist would agree, as to that patient, to abide by the regulations of plan and accept its usual, customary, and reasonable fee charges as payment in full. On occasion, the plan paid the fee of a specialist who had not entered into an agreement, but it was not contractually obligated to do so. The plan subscriber who used the services of any physician not under contract with the plan had no enforceable claim under his or her policy for medical expense payments.

The list of plan-approved physicians was compiled by mail solicitation. A physician interested in participating was sent an application form. Review of primary physician acceptance was performed by a credentialing committee of six physicians who accepted applications appearing to be regular in content; if unusual information was submitted, further inquiry was made. A further check was made in all cases of primary care physicians when the physician admitted his or her first plan patient to a hospital.

For specialist physicians, review of applications was done by three members of a Provider-Professional Relations Committee. That committee determined if the applicant was licensed to practice medicine, had admitting privileges to hospitals, and could dispense narcotics. No personal interview was conducted, no check was made of references listed, and no inquiry was made as to the applicant's standing in the medical community. Selection of the negligent surgeon as the specialist for treatment of the urinary problem was made by the plan primary physician. If the plan had made an investigation of the specialist's credentials or reputation, it would have discovered that before the contract with the plan, the surgeon was the object of a number of medical malpractice suits, four of which had already been concluded in favor of the patients. Selection of a specialist to perform the surgery was not made by the patient but by her primary physician, in accordance with the practice dictated under the plan. In making that referral, the primary physician relied on the fact that the surgeon was a listed specialist with the plan, assuming that listing would not have been made unless the plan had made some investigation of credentials.

Supporting the duty to investigate, evidence showed that the plan listed the specialist as approved and circulated that list to primary care physicians, a major reason the patient was referred to him for surgery. If the subscriber is not content with the selection of physicians from the list provided by the plan and a specialist not under contract with the plan is selected, the plan has no duty to investigate because the subscriber has elected to rely on his or her own selection or on that of the primary care physician. In a fashion comparable to the responsibility of hospitals when granting staff privileges, the plan has the duty to conduct a reasonable investigation only in the preselection of specialists it lists in its approval roster. If it is negligent in the preselection, it may be held liable for the failure.

Forms

Full series of forms and records for appeals of denial of payment or prospective review certification approval.

Predrafted emphatic letters that stress the necessity and medical indication for patient care after preliminary denial.

Check-up File

10 Claims and Legal Process

Counsel and Representation
Problem Events
Liability Coverage and Defense
Testimony

Indefensible Risks

Liability Coverage Gaps, Inappropriate Response to Legal Process, Failed Documentation

Practice Objectives

Disaster Planning, Complete Liability Coverage, Medical Evidence to Defend Questioned Care

Pattern for Safety

Dependable Counsel, Practice Audits, Documentation, Instructions for Problem Management, Cooperation with Counsel

Approaches to Medical Legal Safety

Prepare for Foreseeable Legal Problems

Cases

Legal Process Error, Invalidated Liability Coverage

Indefensible Risks

Uncertainty about coverage of medical services or professional activities
Mistakes about period of coverage for medical liability
Failure to recognize legal problems in time to respond appropriately
Inappropriate response which compromises legal interests
Failure to present accessible and persuasive medical evidence
Legal counsel advice after time for effective intervention

Practice Objectives

☐ **Objective:** Safeguards established for preventable or foreseeable legal problems.

Rationale: Disaster planning designs responses to recognize and limit disasters.

☐ **Objective:** At first signs of problems, appropriate communication or action is directed.

Rationale: Inappropriate or tardy response to problems adds more problems.

☐ **Objective:** All professional activities protected by unequivocal coverage for defense and compensation of losses.

Rationale: Protection should not be debatable.

☐ **Objective:** Medical evidence provides effective and persuasive support for positions.

Rationale: In adversary process, full weight of evidence will be needed.

Pattern for Safety

1. Find dependable counsel before necessity.
2. Conduct legal audit on a periodic schedule.
3. File all significant documents meticulously and review them periodically.
4. Classify signal events for application of high control procedures.
5. Train every staff member to recognize significant events and to direct contacts appropriately.
6. Cooperate fully with personal counsel.
7. Cooperate fully with insurance defense counsel if not in conflict with personal counsel.
8. Consider that legal incidents are comparable to medical conditions: some are preventable or avoidable; others can be treated; some must be borne, even with serious losses.
9. Review typical interactions in professional practice without reference to any crisis; discuss with counsel for effectiveness, manner, and credibility.
10. When unfavorable publicity has been given for practice acts, seek reasonable publicity of resolution if resolution is favorable.
11. Combine practice needs for legal counsel by comparing needs with colleagues and negotiating with attorneys as a group, with common access to research about medically significant laws and drafting of practice forms.

Bottom Line: Counsel early; counsel often.

Approaches to Medical Legal Safety

Counsel and Representation

Physicians often see patients who have neglected preventive health measures, have engaged in hazardous behavior, have tried self-treatment for serious conditions, or risked health and life because of a lack of medical sophistication. Poor choices of legal preparation and action can compromise practice health as well. Legal problems can be managed, and early recognition of symptoms will allow maximum effective response. If anticipation of problems is successful, the initial signs are not missed.

Every practice may anticipate the need for legal advice. In contract negotiation and execution, employee or workers' compensation matters, claims of negligent treatment, or involvement in practice connected to other physicians' or health care facility's questioned care, legal disputes arise. Whatever the problem, preparation is less expensive and more successful than crisis management. Patients in urgent need of medical care cannot take time to screen and evaluate the competence of available physicians. Physicians in legal difficulties are at a disadvantage in judging the relative skills of an available attorney.

With time to discuss potential attorney–client relationships and evaluate advice of counsel before events occur, a physician can compare several attorneys specializing in medical affairs. Medical practice counsel need not relate merely to malpractice. Advice in practice legal concerns can be sought from a few firms and a choice made of the best compatible counsel. A small interview cost will be well worth the investment in ongoing legal support. Practice counsel can also select and recommend appropriate estate or investment representation.

Details of what counsel will do should be clear and formal. Legal services may not necessarily be advice or representation. Counsel research capabilities can answer factual questions about the laws in the area where the practice is located. Counsel can draft basic practice documents and agreements, review contracts, and draft legally protective answers to sensitive correspondence. Whatever tasks are assigned to counsel, fees for each function should be set and agreed to at the outset. Unless work is impossible to gauge, a total fee can be negotiated. To ask for legal representation "on-the-clock" without any estimate of total expense invites abuse. Experienced attorneys know what approximate level of effort is required by legal work. Financial incentives should encourage skilled use of time. Agreement on fees is essential and review of bills for excessive charges is customary.

A physician must be confident that advice will be sound and dependable. To evaluate a potential attorney and counselor, specific assurance must be achieved on some important points:

A record of competence and experience in medical issues
Legal work personally performed, not delegated to assistants
Demonstration of clear understanding of medical practice
Demonstration of planning skills in preventive legal counsel
Substantial positive rapport with physician
Freedom from conflict of interest or appearance of conflict

Maximizing success in legal matters requires physician/clients to assist in their own best interests. Some important points in the attorney–client relationship assure the best chance:

Consult legal counsel for planning before problems occur
Cooperate as advised
Give counsel information requested promptly and fully
Never conceal matters from counsel related to representation

Competent attorneys can be depended on for legal expertise and other support. Clients can expect that counsel will:

Provide reports of activities in any matter underway
Explain every phase of the process involved
Prepare clients for whatever participation will be required
Prepare themselves for whatever the matter demands
Objectively evaluate merits and opposition for clients

Dealing with disciplinary process or malpractice without personal counsel may represent a physician's belief that counsel adds weight to the proceedings, making them more serious, or implies culpability. Whatever the motivation, legal problems require expert legal counsel. Physicians may call an attorney after an adverse decision on their license or privileges, often too late to make things better, and sometimes too late to keep matters from getting worse. Counsel can help to maximize effective response and defense only when resources allow full use of evidence and persuasion. Evidence will be found in organized and current files including:

Practice logs and historical files
Unmodified, complete patient records
Insurance applications
Policies and renewal certificates for practice physicians
Insurance documentation for nonpartner physicians and staff
Vendor/contractor insurance certificates
Claim reports
Risk management newsletters/notices

Problem Events

Most legal problems are self-evident. A bad outcome and a surprised or angry patient, lost records, equipment failure, or misidentification error will alert any physician to potential trouble. Any legal document or communication from an attorney is a bell that must be answered. Answers can also be an additional source of trouble if not appropriate. Aside from problems clearly legal, practices can also have symptoms of problems that may or may not grow into disputes. Patients' failure to keep scheduled appointments without notice, or self-referral to a specialist or other consultation, reflect lost confidence and trust. Some other events that should trigger some recognition, assessment, and action by staff and physician:

Patient hospitalization for adverse results of outpatient management

Readmission for complications, incomplete management on previous hospitalization
Operative consent incomplete, missing, different from procedure done, different surgeon, not signed by patient, no note of disclosure for consent
Unplanned events during surgery, invasive procedure, or vaginal delivery
Unplanned return to operating or delivery room
Surgical and other procedures questioned for necessity and appropriateness
- Pathology report/preoperative diagnosis mismatch
- Nondiagnostic tissue

Transfusion reactions, complications, and improper utilization
- Transfusion after iatrogenic bleeding or anemia
- Transfusion not clinically indicated

Nosocomial infection
Antibiotic/drug utilization that is unjustified, excessive, or varies from approved criteria
Transfer from general care to special care unit
- Complication
- Utilization problem

Hospital-incurred patient incident
- Falls and accidents
- Intravenous problems
- Medication problems
- Skin problems
- Equipment problems

Abnormal laboratory, radiograph, or other test results unaccounted for by physician
Development of neurologic deficit not present on admission
Transfer to comparable care facility
Emergency department or outpatient department visit for complications of office treatment
Utilization variations of major degree on review
- Length of stay
- Resource utilization

Poor responses to problem situations include: argument, alibi, blame or antagonism, contrition or confession, self-criticism, preoccupation with personal anguish, and adversary posture in absence of legal adversary.

When unanticipated complications or adverse events occur, even without patient complaint or question, learning and effective management can still cut losses:

Pay extra attention to manage every aspect as perfectly as possible
Contact appropriate counsel, medical or legal to discuss circumstances before acting
Secure every piece of evidence from change or disappearance
Contact attending physician if not attending
Concentrate on an objective report of events and facts
Document every appropriate event or fact in records, including disclosures and discussions
Avoid casual or social discussions of events
Review memory for note of details to be offered when requested
Wait for direction from appropriate sources

Liability Coverage and Defense

Counsel assigned by a liability insurer for defense under policy contract terms should be able to capably serve the interests of the physician/client. Where policy coverage is not in question, defense will be accorded and compensation paid to the policy limits. When a legal dispute involves amounts greater than the policy limits, or disagreement exists over settlement, physician interests are no longer congruent with the insurer's. Settlement disputes involve weighing exposure to high verdicts against the probability that no compensation will be awarded. Quick settlements also limit defense costs, but subject physician defendants to reports of malpractice payments to data collection agencies and public media. Insurance premiums would also reflect claims payout experience.

To maximize protection of insured liability interests, physicians must arrange for full coverage of anticipated exposure and prac-

tice activities. If practice services and policy coverage are not aligned, dispute—if not the loss—will cost a physician dearly. Policy coverage can be extended to apply to every actual practice function or the practice can be curtailed to fit within the policy coverage. Advice of counsel before accepting liability coverage may reveal unconsidered aspects of needed coverage or clarification of defense commitments and concessions.

Two documents from a liability insurer signal important liability insurance problems. When an insurer is presented with news of a possible claim, policy provisions are compared with apparent events and the insurer determines its operating position for coverage of defense or indemnity. Denial of coverage or defense will cite policy provisions on which the denial is based. "Reservation of rights" notification is more-or-less a provisional conclusion that coverage may be denied, but defense will be provided until the issue of liability is resolved. Either document demonstrates that the insurer and physician are no longer of common interests. Control of defense and other matters by an insurer under reservation of rights are very likely to prompt disputes between physician and insurer.

The matter of reporting potential and actual claims should be done strictly by insurance policy contract terms. Counsel is advisable in interpreting contract terms if legal support was not sought at signing. A short consultation with personal counsel will also put the problem in perspective and alert or prepare the physician for coming events.

After a formal claim or suit has been filed, counsel generally advises:

Notify insurer as directed
Notify facility risk/quality organization as required
Avoid contact with patient/plaintiff, but assure that medical needs are being attended to
Begin log and notes of all contacts with case, documents, conversations, phone calls, and facsimiles in a file separate from the medical record

Avoid all informal discussions of case events or claim details
Review the chart without change or alteration
Make a verified and perfect master copy of the complete original record and accompanying exhibits
Verify master inventory and page count of original record; include in file master copy
Put chart and all other records, specimens, radiographs, reports, etc., in secure place
Use the original only when legally required. Copy master copy for routine transmittals
Separate any incoming legal or claim documents from medical records
Log all sent or received materials and communications

Preparing for legal proceedings:

Review all records and reports, etc.
Write a detailed chronology with all recollections for use with counsel
Begin a full medical dossier on the medical diagnosis or treatment in question, with texts, articles, guidelines, commentary, research on every aspect, both favorable and unfavorable to the defensive point of view

Even after the insurer begins formal defense of a claim, a periodic short review with personal counsel can double-check what the insurer's attorneys are accomplishing. Defense control will be determined by the policy terms. Review of the terms with personal counsel will disclose any options the physician may wish to exercise.

Settling claims causes physicians serious anxiety because seldom is the best choice clear. Settling at an affordable sum (within policy limits) is still a settlement. So-called strategic settlements are based on a judgment that the risk of higher payout is too great to continue defense, even if there is a substantial chance that no payout will be required. These are not merely gambles, but calculated assessments based on experience and specific case realities. Pressures to settle may come from the judge, carrier, plaintiff counsel, and defense.

Factors to determine whether settlement is advisable include:

Persuasiveness of medical record evidence
Credibility of defense and plaintiff experts
Total potential loss
Relative affordability of settlement amount
Jurisdiction track record for similar suits
Credibility of defendants
Disputes among defendants about fault

Testimony

Once claims and discovery are over, testimony will be sought. Depositions are preliminary testimony. Trial testimony often reprises the same matters as deposition testimony. The most common error in deposition testimony is failure to appreciate its importance. Many texts and articles offer deposition do's and don'ts. Defendant physicians and expert witness physicians often make the same wrong moves in testimony that impair credibility. They rationalize, blame, explain, or pontificate about the medical circumstances, or express anger, sorrow, shock, or other digressive and harmful demonstrations. Even good testimony can be diminished by excuses or digressions.

Physicians should realize that even key testimony is not the entire case. Scoring a "home run" is not a valid goal. Each question and answer form a piece of the persuasion structure of fact and opinion. A witness need not "win the case" but should give testimony that supports the construction of the case. Testimony at deposition or trial has three main steps:

1. **Listen to the question.** If it is not perfectly clear, say so, and ask for a repetition or clarification. After the question, silently count, "one." The count allows counsel a moment in which to interrupt with objection, comment, or instruction.
2. **Answer the question asked.** Tell the truth, but do not revise the question and answer what was meant. If the answer is not what was desired, another question will be asked. If the

answer appears harmful or misleading, trust counsel to follow up with clarifying questions and explanations.

3. **Stop.** The moment the question is answered, stop talking. Do not continue or expand or explain. Give the answer and nothing but the answer.

A physician who is a party to a lawsuit has a right to attend depositions taken in the case. Even with the constraints of medical practice, it may be useful to attend depositions. The physician's presence may prompt witnesses to tell the truth more persuasively. Attendance at depositions of others may also show how to be more effective in a personal deposition, and assist counsel in questioning other witnesses if asked. Depositions to consider attending include the plaintiff, any involved medical personnel, and opposing expert witnesses. Counsel's advice before attending any deposition should be sought and followed.

Many books have detailed advice about what to do or not do. Some offer lists of "trick questions" and answers. Questions in testimony often follow predictable patterns and questions can be anticipated about payment for expert testimony, instructions from counsel for testimony, and about how much "coaching" was done in preparation for the testimony. Frank answers to such questions can be discussed with counsel, and counsel will object if legal or medical confidentiality is threatened by a question.

Counsel may be able to offer suggestions on the most accurate communication of the physician's position. For example, in answer to a pretrial interrogatory or deposition question such as, "Doctor, do you contend that someone other than you is responsible for the complications in this case?" An appropriate answer for the defense that does not implicate other providers or speculate is, "I don't contend that anyone, including myself, is responsible for the complications."

After legal process has concluded, publicity may have been given to the case and to claims of deficient medical treatment. If the outcome of the legal process is successful for the physician, often little note is made of the event. Some satisfaction may be gained by making appropriate publicity of the favorable resolution. With counsel, write a brief summary of the pertinent points of the decision, especially those that will counteract any false or misleading impressions created by initial publicity. News editors should be contacted to ask for an appointment, but publicity should not be demanded. Take counsel and a well-known colleague for support, and offer newsworthy medical information as well.

Cases

How Can Legal Process Mistakes Be Corrected?

An anesthesiologist was informed by a letter from her malpractice insurance company that an anesthesiology group with which she had formerly been affiliated had been sued by a patient for more than $1 million. The incident had taken place more than 2 years after the physician had left the group to go into solo practice, but she had been named a codefendant. (Apparently, an outdated group letterhead that included her name had been used.) The physician telephoned the local representative of her malpractice insurance company, who gave her the name of the attorney handling the group's defense. The attorney agreed that her involvement was unfair, but felt that a request to drop a named physician would hurt the case. The physician discussed a possible countersuit with colleagues, but decided not to undermine the position of the anesthesiology group. The physician took the problem to her personal lawyer, who cleared the error in a few days. The physician was dropped from the list of defendants.

The next annual premium notice from her malpractice carrier arrived with a notation indicating that a claim had been filed, and a one-third surcharge added to her premium for the next 3 years. After unsuccessful discussions with the insurer's claims and billing offices, counsel was again called. After counsel contacted the insurer with appropriate advocacy, only the original premium was required, and the record of claim was cleared.

What Limits Are Imposed on Insurance Coverage for Medical Treatment Liability?

A psychiatrist was sued for medical malpractice by a former female patient. The complaint alleged that the physician, under the guise of medical therapy to cure the patient's lesbianism, prescribed and personally administered sexual "therapy." The insurer's first notice of claim was its receipt of the complaint, 2 years after the physician began administering "therapy" and 6 months after its last application. After the insurer declined defense, the physician was defended by his own attorney. At trial, the patient was awarded damages, and despite its refusal to defend the physician, the insurer settled with the patient for a reduced amount in return for the patient's agreement not to appeal. The physician then sued the insurer to recover costs and expenses in defending the lawsuit, legal fees for the malpractice suit, and damages for humiliation of having to file for bankruptcy. He also sought punitive damages because of his carrier's refusal to defend him in the malpractice suit. The insurer claimed that the "treatment" that was administered did not constitute medical malpractice and was therefore not covered under the policy, which excluded intentional or nonmedical conduct. The physician argued that the jury found medical malpractice.

The physician admitted that at all times he knew that the therapy he was administering was a violation of professional ethics and not within acceptable medical standards. When the last "treatment" was administered and the physician–patient relationship ended, the physician had reason to believe the acts might lead to a claim against him under the policy. With his admitted knowledge that he had violated medical ethics and deviated from accepted medical standards, he was aware that an event occurred which might lead to a claim. Under the terms of his policy, he was obligated to notify the insurer as soon as practicable. Instead, no notice was provided until 2 years after commencement of the "therapy" and 6 months after the last occasion.

In a factual situation such as this, a distinction is drawn between medical malpractice in the mind of the patient and medical malpractice in the mind of the physician. When the patient submitted to treatment, she believed that appropriate medical therapy was being administered. Only some time afterward did she discover that she had been the victim of fraud. On the other hand, the physician administering the treatment at all times knew that what he was doing was not acceptable within the physician–patient relationship. Active concealment of conditions by an insured physician may be characterized as fraud. Although lateness of notice to an insurer can be overcome, as a matter of public policy, the law resists being used to enforce illicit, immoral, or unconscionable activity. Thus the physician was not entitled to indemnification for expenses of defending his professional fraud.

What Physician Conduct May Invalidate a Policy of Liability Coverage?

A 24-year-old patient went to see a physician to have a wart removed from his thumb. The physician examined the thumb as well as a black lesion on the patient's left leg. The physician told the patient that the lesion looked cancerous and recommended that a biopsy be performed to determine whether it was malignant. The physician's assistant anesthetized the area for a biopsy excision. Because this was the patient's first visit, the physician's secretary also filled out a billing record for the patient and wrote on it "Exc nevus left leg 11 mm, multicolored changing" denoting the excision of the lesion 11 millimeters in length from the patient's left leg. She also noted "Exc wart right thumb" on the billing record, describing the excision of the wart. The wart was removed, but before the physician removed the lesion, the patient said he did not have insurance to cover medical expenses. In response, the physician said that he was so certain the lesion was cancerous that the biopsy was not really necessary and that he could remove the lesion and a section of tissue around it at the same time. This would eventually have to be done, he explained, and it saved the patient the expense of the biopsy.

The patient agreed with this suggestion and the lesion and a section of tissue around it were removed. A copy of the billing record, which was the only record made of the patient's visit to the physician's office, was given to the patient. It was not changed, however, to reflect the procedure that was actually performed. After the procedure, the physician had the lesion and tissue specimen sent for a pathologic examination. The Tissue Examination Report confirmed that the lesion was cancerous and contained a description of the specimen as "a single pinkish tan tissue with a dark brown pigmented center, measuring 20 × 10 [millimeters]." A copy of the report was given to the patient by the physician on a follow-up visit.

Five months later, the patient began to experience swelling in his left groin area, and consulted another physician, who diagnosed disseminating cancer. He informed the first physician of this and told him that he was now treating the patient. The second physician made a notation in his records that the scar on the patient's leg as a result of the physician's excision was 5 centimeters in length, and referred the patient to a surgeon. The surgeon later removed a lymph node from the patient's groin, which was also found to be malignant.

A month after diagnosis, the patient saw a surgical oncologist to whom a copy of the first Tissue Examination Report was sent. The oncologist performed a resection of the original excision on the patient's left leg and removed a lymph node, which was not cancerous. At about this time, the oncologist contacted the first physician and noted that the excision on the patient's left leg appeared to be much larger than 20 × 10 millimeters as stated on the Tissue Examination Report.

Seven months after this contact with the oncologist, the first physician wrote to the pathology laboratory which had performed the first tissue analysis to inform them that the specimen that he submitted to them for testing was much larger than the 20 × 10 millimeters recorded in its Tissue Examination Report. "The specimen was huge . . . I am sure that the total amount of skin was 18 centimeters by about 7 cm," the physician wrote. Four days later, a pathologist with the laboratory sent the oncologist an amended pathology report, which noted that it was made with the aid of the first physician's operative description. It stated that the "[e]ntire specimen measure[d] 18 cm × 7 cm × 7-9 mm in thickness. There is a deeply pigmented slightly elevated lesion in the center measuring 20 mm × 10 mm in size." The first physician then called the laboratory and discussed the amended report. Shortly thereafter, a second amended report that attempted to explain the discrepancy between the original and amended reports was sent to the oncologist by the laboratory. This report, which also described the specimen sent to the laboratory by the physician as 18 × 7 centimeters, explained that the 20 × 10 millimeter specimen referred to in the original Tissue Examination Report was the section used for testing that was cut out of the 18 × 7 centimeter section submitted to the laboratory by the physician. This report also stated that the lesion itself measured 5 × 4 millimeters.

Within months, the first physician was contacted by the patient's attorney, who requested copies of the patient's medical records and bills. The physician sent a letter enclosing what he termed "my operative notes and the pathology report." What was actually sent were copies of the second amended Tissue Examination Report, completed by the laboratory, and a billing record describing the patient's visit to the physician. The billing record enclosed, however, was not the one prepared at the time of the patient's visit, describing the excision of an 11-millimeter lesion from the patient's left leg. Rather, the billing record forwarded to the patient's attorney was prepared by the physician after receiving the letter requesting the patient's medical records, and it described the excision as 18 × 7 centimeters, and recommended that the patient see another physician for follow-up treatment for the cancer. This record, although handwritten by the physician sometime after the records request, was dated for the date of the original excisions on the patient's thumb and left leg. In addition, the physician also sent a letter to the claims department of his insurer, along with a copy of the letter from the patient's attorney, the second amended Tissue Examination Report, and a billing record. This billing record, however, was different from both the original and the one forwarded to the patient's attorney. The billing record sent to the patient's attorney indicated that the physician spoke to the patient about getting follow-up care a week after the first visit and the billing record sent to the insurer stated that this conversation took place on the date of the visit. Furthermore, the physician did not mention to either the patient's attorney or to the insurer the existence of the original billing record. He also later testified that at the time he prepared the second and third billing records, he "had an idea" that the patient might file a malpractice claim against him. In sum, the correspondence that the physician sent to the insurer and the patient's attorney did not mention the existence of the original billing record, nor did it mention the fact that the billing record that was forwarded was not prepared at the time the patient was treated by the physician, but 21 months later and backdated to the time of the treatment.

The patient filed a claim, alleging that the first physician was negligent in failing "to properly excise the malignant melanoma with sufficient margins to prevent recurrence" and in failing "to schedule follow-up examination after the excision for the purpose of early detection and treatment of any recurrence." On the medical facts, this case could have been defensible, either on medical judgment or on causation of damages.

The physician's deposition was taken and the existence of the original billing record, a copy of which was given to the patient at the time of his treatment, was made known to the insurer. Shortly, thereafter, the insurer's claims agent discussed the matter of the different billing records with the physician, who was notified by a claims manager that "the possibility exists that there may have been additions or alterations made by you to your office notes and bills. If these alterations or additions should prove to be prejudicial and material, we reserve the right to withdraw coverage and the defense of this civil action against you."

A Health Claims Arbitration Panel determined that the physician was liable to the patient for negligence in the amount of $650,000. During the course of the hearing, the physician testified that none of the three billing records was accurate. The insurer's attorney and the chairman of the panel informally disclosed that the panel's decision was based on the physician's improper follow-up and the failure of the physician's credibility as a witness.

The insurer notified the physician that his insurance would be canceled for "alteration of records," and the physician filed a complaint with the Insurance Commissioner claiming violation of the Insurance Code, which forbids the cancellation of insurance for any arbitrary or capricious reason or for a reason other than one that involves "the application of standards that are reasonably related to the insurer's economic and business purposes."

The provision in question was: Professional liability insurance will not be provided to any physician who, in connection with a prior claim, materially altered medical records after becoming aware of the possibility of a claim arising from an act or omission in the furnishing of professional services. Alteration includes any addition, correction, or change to, or written supplementation of, the patient's medical records occurring after the creation of those records unless the subsequent addition, correction, change, or supplementation is clearly labeled to indicate that it is not a contemporaneous record.

An appeal was heard in the case, with the physician maintaining that he had not altered the patient's records, that the additional report presented was more complete than the billing record maintained by his office, and that the billing record represented the only record maintained of medical care and treatment given to the patient and was in no way altered. Final review concluded that the records were altered by supplementation and misrepresentation. The contemporaneous record of the physician's treatment of the patient was the one prepared at the time of the surgery, which, due to an oversight by the physician, was not accurate. But when asked to provide the patient's attorney and the insurer with his records of the patient's treatment, he did not send them that record. Instead, he created new, more thorough "records," backdated them to make it appear as though they were prepared at the time of the treatment and transmitted them without indicating that he was withholding the original record. Furthermore, these "records" were created at a time when the physician "had an idea" that the patient was planning to sue him for malpractice, and they were different from the original record in two important, self-serving ways. First, the second set of records described the excision as much larger than the original record did; also, the second set of records contained a recommendation that the patient seek follow-up care, which was not included in the original record. Significantly, whether a large enough excision was made to prevent the recurrence of cancer and whether the physician informed the patient of the need for follow-up care were issues in the malpractice suit subsequently filed against the physician.

The court stated that credible, accurate, contemporaneous medical records are the foundation of the proper defense of a medical malpractice claim. Even if contemporaneous records are not complete, credible testimony of a treating physician may be used to supplement the records and demonstrate compliance with the applicable standard of care. If a physician submits subsequently prepared medical records that are represented as contemporaneous, however, the credibility of the contemporaneous records as well as of the physician will be destroyed. The court found that this standard was reasonably related to the insurer's economic and business purposes. The insurer properly denies coverage to physicians whose medical records cannot be relied on when defending a claim against them.

Glossary

Abandonment Termination of a physician-patient relationship by the physician without the patient's consent at a time when the patient requires medical attention, without making adequate arrangements for continued care.

Abuse of Process Use of legal mechanisms in a manner or for a purpose not supported by law. For example, pursuit of litigation based on little or no legal grounds, intended to harass and cause expense to the defendant. Damages may be recovered for expenses or loss caused a defendant by abuse of process.

Action Legal action, lawsuit.

Affidavit Sworn statement for use in legal process.

Affirmative Defense An answer to a lawsuit which does not deny the alleged conduct or failure, but asserts a legal basis to excuse or foreclose liability. Good Samaritan immunity or a statute of limitations defense are examples.

Agent A person authorized by another, the principal, to act for or represent the principal. Agency relationships may include authority to exercise personal judgment.

Allegation Asserted fact or circumstance that is expected to be proved by legal process.

Appeal A claim to a superior court of error in process or law by a lower court, asking the court above to correct or reverse a judgment or decision. An appellate (appeals) court has the power to review decisions made in the trial court or a lower appellate court. An appellate court does not make a new determination of facts, but examines the law and legal process as applied in the case.

Battery Intentional and unauthorized physical contact with a person, without consent. For example, a surgical procedure performed without express or implied consent constitutes battery. Victims of medical battery may obtain compensation for the touching, even if no negligence occurred. A crime of battery may be defined differently.

Bona Fide In latin, good faith; that is, without deceit, fraud, simulation, or pretense. Pronounced bone-a-fied.

Borrowed Servant Agent temporarily under the supervision, direction, and control of another. For example, an operating room nurse technically employed by a hospital may be borrowed by a surgeon in the operating room to perform certain tasks.

Breach of Contract Failure to perform a legal agreement. If a legally enforceable contract is established, performance of agreed promises may be compelled or adequate compensation for failure to perform may be required.

Burden of Proof Responsibility of proving certain facts required to support a lawsuit. If the burden of proof is not met, the opposing side prevails on that point, even without a defense or response.

Captain of the Ship Doctrine A special agency relationship establishing liability for an employee's or agent's acts. This agency relationship imposes what is called vicarious liability on the one employing the agent. Initially used as an analogy in malpractice cases, it asserts that the surgeon in the operating room has total authority and full responsibility for the performance of the operating crew and the welfare of the patient. By this doctrine, the surgeon may be vicariously liable for the negligent act of any member of the surgical team. The doctrine is not accepted in every jurisdiction.

Case Law Legal principles applied to specific fact situations. Case law is drawn from judicial decisions in similar cases in a jurisdiction. Case law is used to make decisions that are based on precedent, the judicial principle that requires that similar cases be treated alike. Assembled case law principles are also called the Common Law.

Cause of Action Facts or circumstances that support a legal right to seek corrective action or compensation.

Cause Proximate cause. A reasonable connection between an act or failure alleged as negligence and an injury suffered by the plaintiff. In a suit for negligence, the issue of causation usually requires proof that the negligence of the defendant directly resulted in or was a substantial factor in the plaintiff's harm or injury.

Civil Rights Enforceable rights of all citizens guaranteed by several amendments to the United States Constitution and laws passed recognizing specific liberties or privileges. Violation of another person's civil rights may result in criminal or civil penalties.

Civil Action Legal proceeding by a party asking for correction or compensation, distinguished from a criminal action, which is brought by the state to punish offenses against public order.

Civil Liability Legal responsibility to compensate for losses or injuries caused by acts or failures to act. Compensation is awarded as money damages paid by the defendant to the injured party. In contrast, criminal liability is the legal responsibility imposed by the state for violation of criminal laws. Consequences of criminal acts may include death, imprisonment, fines, and loss of property or privileges. Civil liability is limited to monetary damages; however, a single act may be both a criminal act and a civil wrong, also called a tort.

Class Action A legal action instituted by one or more persons on behalf of others in a similar situation. Class actions are used if the same allegations must be proved by many plaintiffs against the same defendant. An example would be litigation over responsibility for a plane crash with hundreds of victims.

Clear and Convincing Evidence A level of persuasion required to support certain noncriminal legal actions. For example, involuntary civil commitment to mental treatment may require clear and convincing evidence of danger to self or others.

Code Collection of laws in a jurisdiction, or on a specific topic area arranged and indexed by subject, with revisions added to reflect the law currently in force. Each state's Code of Laws, the United States Code, or the Internal Revenue Code are examples.

Common Law Case law.

Complaint Initial document filed by a plaintiff, also called a pleading, which begins a civil lawsuit. The complaint is intended to give the defendant notice of facts alleged in the cause of action on which the plaintiff bases a demand for corrective action or compensation.

Confidential Communication Medical information given to health care providers in the course of diagnosis and treatment of an illness or injury. Providers are entrusted with the duty to keep the information from disclosure to third parties, subject to existing requirements of statute and case law.

Consent Agreement to accept the consequences of an action, such as to allow another person to do something or to take part in some activity. Express consent may be oral or written. Implied consent is agreement shown by signs or actions. An example of conduct showing that consent has been given for an injection or blood test is to roll up a sleeve and extend an arm for vein puncture. Consent to the risks of a game, such as hockey, is shown by taking part. Where no actual consent or refusal is possible, for example, the case of an unconscious person in an emergency situation, consent to others' actions to save life or limb is presumed. Consequences of actions taken without consent remain the burden of the one acting without consent.

Consortium Element of damages generally recoverable by one spouse for loss of company, services, and conjugal relations caused by the spouse's injury. Company, participation, counsel, and affection are consortium losses recoverable by other close family members in some jurisdictions.

Consultation Request by an attending physician, generally to a specialist, for information, advice, diagnostic services, or therapy that is indicated or necessary for a patient's condition. A duty to consult may arise when diagnosis is uncertain, therapy is ineffective, or the patient requests a consultation. A consultation that is merely informative does not generally result in a relationship and duties between the consultant and the patient. Other consultations, which require that the consultant examine the patient or records, or provide diagnostic or treatment services, may establish a duty to the patient separate from the consulting physician's. A referral is distinguished from a consultation because it involves transfer of responsibility for the care of the patient to the specialist. In many consultations, the attending physician also retains some ongoing separate responsibility.

Contention Earnest and vigorous assertion of legal significance and interpretation of facts or issues in a dispute.

Contract Agreement by two or more parties to exchange obligations. A contract depends on a similar mutual understanding of the terms of the contract and performance promised. A legally enforceable contract means that compensation for promises not kept can be compelled.

Contributory Negligence Affirmative defense in which a defendant contends that the plaintiff's negligence wholly or substantially caused the injury complained of by the defendant. The effect of plaintiff's negligence on liability or compensation varies among the states, depending on the timing and circumstances of the plaintiff's and the defendant's acts or failures to act.

Counterclaim Defendant's complaint against a plaintiff alleging obligation, failure, and damages for which compensation is demanded. For the counterclaim issues, the defendant is seen as having the burden of a plaintiff.

Covenant Specific agreement or promise to act or refrain from acting in exchange for similar promises or payments. For example, a covenant not to sue one defendant may exchange relinquishment of that claim for a payment or a promise not to counterclaim. However, a specific covenant would not release all persons alleged to have a role in causing the injury and does not accept the payment as full satisfaction for the injury. A covenant with one defendant therefore, does not bar actions against others.

Criminal Liability Responsibility imposed when a criminal statute, regulation, or ordinance is violated. Once criminal liability is established, consequences provided by criminal statute or sentencing codes are imposed. Criminal liability is the legal consequence imposed by the state for violation of criminal law, an offense against the public interest in safety and liberty, and is not directed toward compensating the losses of victims. Consequences of criminal acts may include death, imprisonment, fines, and loss of property or privileges.

Damages Money receivable through judicial order by a person sustaining harm, impairment, or loss to person or property as the result of the intentional or negligent act of another. Damages may be compensatory, to reimburse a person for economic losses such as lost income and medical expenses. Other damages recoverable include noneconomic losses, such as pain and suffering or mental anguish; or hedonic damages awarded for the loss of life's enjoyment, and aesthetic and other pleasures, such as music, athletics, sunsets, or children. Sometimes, token damages are awarded to demonstrate that a legally recognized error has been committed. So-called nominal damages can be awarded even where no actual economic or noneconomic losses are suffered. Punitive damages are those awarded to inflict economic punishment on defendants who have been found to act maliciously or in reckless disregard of others' rights.

Decedent A person who has died, and whose interests are involved in a legal proceeding.

Defamation Intentional communication of false personal or business information that injures the reputation or prospects of another. Spoken defamation is slander; written defamation is libel. Truth is a defense to claims of defamation. Publication of true information may nevertheless violate duties of confidentiality or may be invasion of privacy.

Deposition Part of pretrial process in which a sworn out-of-court statement is taken. In a deposition, a witness is asked questions and cross-examined. The statement may be admitted into evidence if it is impossible for a witness to attend in person. Deposition testimony can also be used to cross-question a witness at trial.

Disclaimer Statement before or after disputed events that announces one party's stance and commitment regarding legal aspects of facts and circumstances in question. A disclaimer could be a statement that no warranties were intended or offered as part of contract terms, or that risks of activities were not assumed by a party. Ordinarily, a disclaimer of responsibility for future negligent conduct is not recognized by the law and would be ineffective as a defense.

Discovery Pretrial activities in the litigation process to determine the essential questions and issues in dispute, and what evidence each side will present at trial. Discovery is intended to narrow trial questions to the absolute minimum, and to allow fair presentation of opposing evidence without surprise during trial. By discovery process, communications and disclosures may also facilitate out-of-court settlement.

Due Care Level of reasonable and ordinary observation and awareness owed by one person to another in specific relationship or circumstances, such as a physician's duty of due care in attendance of patients. Due care anticipates and appropriately manages known, expected, or foreseeable events and complications of the patient's disease or treatment.

Due Process Level of fair method required by the United States Constitution in execution of governmental activities. Due process in legal proceedings must reflect both fair substance—the activity is appropriate and constitutional—and fair means—a method of proceeding that provides parties involved the opportunity to present appropriate advocacy and evidence in any dispute or legal process.

Evidence Beyond Reasonable Doubt A level of persuasion required to support a judgment of criminal responsibility and consequent punishment.

Expert Witness Person invited to testify at a hearing or trial to bring special training, knowledge, skill, or experience to the proceeding where matters in legal dispute are beyond the average person's knowledge. Unlike a fact witness, who is compelled to testify because of involvement in the facts and circumstances of the dispute, an expert witness may be asked for an opinion about specific issues in the case. Fact witnesses testify about what was done, written, or observed, and what occurred. Experts educate the court about the scientific, medical, technical, or other specialized circumstances involved in the dispute. Experts are compensated for their time in court, usually at the rate of income they forego to give time to the court. Fact witnesses are not compensated.

Fiduciary A person in a position of confidence or trust who undertakes a solemn duty to act for the benefit of another who must trust the good intention and performance of the fiduciary. In a fiduciary relationship, virtually all the power reposes in the trusted fiduciary, and vulnerability lies with the beneficiary of the relationship. This disparity of knowledge and power imposes major duties on the fiduciary. Examples of fiduciary relationships are guardian and ward, parent and child, attorney and client, physician and patient, estate trustee and beneficiary, and other financial relationships. In contrast to the marketplace relationship, which may be largely "buyer beware," fiduciary relationships require that the fiduciary never act to the detriment of the trusting party, and certainly not for personal gain or profit. Pronounced fid-dooshi-airy.

Finder of Fact In a trial, the jury, or the judge in trials without juries. Conclusions of fact are not generally appealable. Appeals courts review findings of law, admissions of evidence, and application or interpretation of appropriate legal principles and laws.

Fraud Intentional misdirection, misinformation, or misrepresentation to another person that causes legal injury or loss to that person. Fraud is an intentional wrong, to be contrasted with negligent conduct causing loss. Examples of fraud in medical practice could be to mislead a patient about indicated procedures or therapies; misstate diagnoses or treatment codes to falsely maximize reimbursement; or to conspire with patients to misstate injuries to obtain undeserved benefits.

Good Faith Honest intent to avoid taking unconscionable advantage of another, even if technicalities of law might permit it.

Good Samaritan Statute Law enacted by state legislatures to encourage physicians and others to stop and assist emergency victims. Good Samaritan laws grant immunity from liability for negligence to a person who responds and administers care to a person in an emergency situation. Statutes vary among the states regarding persons covered, the scene and type of emergency, and nature of conduct for which immunity is granted.

Guardian Person appointed by a court to manage the affairs and to protect the interests of a person who is declared incompetent to manage personal affairs. Incompetence may be due to physical or mental status; guardians may be appointed to manage economic or personal matters, including medical treatment choices.

Holding A term for a specific conclusion made by a court in a case, which is used to support the final judgment of the court in the case. A holding may be used to persuade later courts on the same point in similar cases.

Immunity Protection given certain individuals or entities that shields them from liability for certain acts. The individual or entity may be sued, but if immunity is established as an affirmative defense, no prosecution or trial of the dispute will be allowed. Examples of immunity include charitable or nonprofit hospitals granted charitable immunity, government agencies' complete or limited sovereign or governmental immunity, diplomatic immunity, immunity for reporting suspected child abuse, or immunity for peer review comment and activities.

In Loco Parentis Latin phrase for the status of one assigned by law to stand in the place of parents and exercise their legal rights, duties, and responsibilities toward a child.

Incompetence Legal status of dependence on a natural or appointed guardian to make decisions and manage personal and business affairs. Incompetent persons cannot bind themselves by contract, cannot consent to or refuse medical treatment, cannot be held to assume consequences of choices made. Parents are the natural guardians of children, who are legally incompetent until the age of majority or until emancipated. Legally recognized incompetent adults have appointed guardians. Medically, incompetence is the inability of a person to understand and manage personal affairs or to take responsibility for personal choices. Once this status or condition is legally recognized, a guardian is appointed to act in the person's place.

Indemnity State of obligation to reimburse for losses. A person may indemnify another under the terms of an agreement that requires payment of specified losses under specified conditions. Insurance contracts are examples of indemnity agreements, as are hospital agreements to indemnify employed physicians in specific conditions of liability or defense.

Independent Contractor Person who agrees to perform tasks that are completed without direct supervision or control by the party employing the contractor. Ordinarily this arrangement and relationship shield the employer from liability for negligent acts of the independent contractor that occurred during the performance of the work contracted to be performed. Independent contractors are legally distinguished from employees, whose performance is supervised, directed, and controlled by the employer and for whose work the employer is vicariously responsible. Depending on the circumstances, a physician may be either an independent contractor or an employee in practice.

Informed Consent A patient's agreement to permit diagnosis or treatment of an illness or injury based on the patient's knowledge of facts needed to choose whether or not to submit to the medical process considered. Informed consent is a patient's agreement to undergo a medical procedure after risks, benefits, alternatives, and consequences have been discussed and weighed.

Injunction Court order commanding a person or entity to perform or to refrain from performing a certain act. Failure to obey an injunction may result in a citation of contempt of court, and imprisonment until obedience is obtained. The person directed is said to be enjoined by such a court order.

Interrogatories Part of pretrial discovery, interrogatories are formal written questions submitted to an opposing party to be answered before and in preparation for trial. These written answers are signed and affirmed as true by the party or witness in the suit.

Invasion of Privacy Violation of person's right to be free from unwarranted publicity and intrusions. The offense may be unauthorized dissemination of private information about the person or the publication of photographs or records without specific consent. Disclosure of a medical condition without legal justification or release could represent such a violation. Invasion of privacy is a tort, for which civil liability damages are awarded to compensate for mental suffering or humiliation, or other losses of the person whose privacy was violated.

Joint and Several Liability Responsibility shared by a number of persons who are found to have contributed to a plaintiff's injury. Establishment of joint and several liability means that each or any one of those liable can be made to satisfy the whole loss to the patient, and must then sue the other liable parties for contribution to the payment.

Judgment Official decision of a court about the respective rights and claims of the parties to an action or suit litigated and submitted for determination.

Jurisdiction Geographic or subject matter limits to power and authority of courts and other government agencies and officers.

Leading Case Case decision in a specific jurisdiction dealing with specific facts and circumstances that have decided the same issues involved in a later case. A leading case is determinative of the same issues in subsequent cases unless distinctions from the leading case facts are established.

Libel Written defamation by any type of communication or publication, including pictures.

Malice The performance of a wrongful act without excuse, with apparent intent to inflict an injury. Under some circumstances of conduct, the law will infer malicious intent from the evidence of defendant's actions.

Malicious Prosecution Lawsuit or countersuit seeking damages that have been caused to a defendant by a civil suit filed by a plaintiff in bad faith and without probable cause. Ordinarily, the countersuit may not be brought until the initial suit has been found meritless.

Malpractice Professional misconduct or failure to properly discharge professional duties by failing to meet the standard of care required of a professional.

Material Influential and necessary. Material facts or issues concern the substance of the matter in dispute as distinguished from form.

Minor A person who has not yet reached the age determined by law for transactional capacity; that is, a legally incompetent person. Minors cannot generally be held responsible for their contracts or other civil actions. Thus minors ordinarily cannot consent to their own medical treatment. An exception exists for emancipated minors, defined as persons substantially independent from their parents, supporting themselves, married, or otherwise on their own. A statute may also provide exceptions to legal incapacity to allow minors authority to consent to treatment for drug abuse, venereal disease, birth control, or pregnancy.

Misrepresentation Words or conduct that amount to an assertion not in accordance with the existing facts or circumstances. An "innocent misrepresentation" is made by a person who has reasonable grounds for believing that the representation is true. A "negligent misrepresentation" is made when a person has no reasonable grounds for believing that the representation is true, even if the speaker believes it to be true. A "fraudulent misrepresentation" is made by a person who is aware of the falsity of the representation that causes the other party to enter an arrangement or an agreement, or to rely to a detriment on the false representation.

Motion Request to a judge for an order or a ruling.

Negligence Failure to exercise the degree of diligence and care that a reasonably prudent person would be expected to exercise under the same or similar circumstances. Failure that proximately causes an injury is recognized as a basis for compensation owed to the injured party.

Opinion of the Court An appeals court's outline of a case, which states the factual circumstances and the law applied to the case. The opinion also details the legal reasoning supporting the decision and any issues appealed as error. The court's opinion finally affirms, reverses, or remands (sends back for more action) the case appealed.

Ordinance A rule established by the authority of the state. Generally, this is an enactment by the legislative branch of a municipal corporation such as a city council or equivalent body.

Parens Patriae Latin term describing the role of the state as the sovereign guardian of persons under the state's protection. It is the legal basis for the state's power to act to protect the health and welfare of persons who suffer from legal disabilities such as minority or mental incapacity. Pronounced parenz pah-tree-aye.

Party A legal person or entity. Party is a more general term than person and is useful since it can refer to organizations, groups, and legal persons such as corporations and partnerships.

Perjury Willful false testimony under oath, and punishable as a crime.

Police Power Authority granted to the state to restrain personal or property rights of persons within the state for the protection of public safety and health. Police power has limitations imposed by the United States Constitution and by state constitutions.

Preponderance of Evidence A level of persuasion required to award judgment in civil actions for damages. For example, a plaintiff must produce a preponderance of evidence that a defendant failed a recognized duty and that proved losses were caused by the failure. Preponderance is a standard of better-than-equal evidence.

Presumption An initial rational position of law, which can be challenged by evidence presented in legal proceedings. Examples are the presumption of innocence of the accused in a criminal trial, or the presumption of legitimacy of children born in wedlock, or the presumption of competence in adult persons.

Prima Facie Case Latin description for a complaint with supporting evidence that apparently supports all the necessary legal elements for a recognized cause of action. A *prima facie* case is sufficient to produce a verdict or judgment for the plaintiff until overcome by evidence in defense of the case. Pronounced pry-ma-fay-sha.

Privilege Exemption or immunity connected to a specific legal situation. For example, the physician-patient privilege is a rule of evidence by which communications made to a physician by a patient in the course of treatment may not be used as evidence in court. It is the patient's privilege to keep such information from disclosure; it is the physician's duty to resist attempts to compel disclosure. This privilege is conditional and usually subject to certain exceptions. The physician-patient privilege of confidentiality is recognized by statute in most states.

Probable Cause Evidence that would lead a reasonable person of ordinary intelligence to conclude that a cause of action is supportable in a civil lawsuit, or that facts exist to prompt a search or an arrest in criminal matters.

Probate Court Court having jurisdiction over wills and supervision of decedents' estates. In some states, probate courts also have jurisdiction of minors, including the appointment of guardians.

Reasonable Person Hypothetical person used as an objective test or standard against which a defendant's conduct in a negligence suit can be judged. The reasonable person is the figurative standard of care. For example, a standard of care in medical practice could be established by the answer to the question, "What would a reasonably knowledgeable and skilled physician be expected to have done under the circumstances described?"

Regulation A rule or order prescribed for the management of specific activities subject to government control. Regulations can be rules or orders issued by executive authority or by an administrative agency of government.

Release An agreement to relinquish a right or claim against another person or persons, usually exchanged for a payment or a promise, called consideration. A signed release agreement indicates that a claimed injury has been compensated. A release is distinguished from a covenant not to sue by the element of satisfaction of the claim.

Res Ipsa Loquitur Latin for "The thing speaks for itself." It is a legal doctrine sometimes applied in a negligence action when the plaintiff has no direct evidence of negligence but where the nature of the injury under the particular circumstances indicates to reasonable persons that such injuries do not occur in the absence of negligence. The doctrine is applicable to cases where the defendant had exclusive control of what caused the harm to the plaintiff, and where the plaintiff could not have contributed to the injury. Use of the doctrine does not assure the plaintiff a judgment. After proof of the elements of *res ipsa loquitur,* the doctrine shifts to the defendant the burden to prove that conduct was reasonable and appropriate or that other mechanisms caused the plaintiff's injury. Pronounced race ip-sa low-quit-err.

Rescind To nullify a contract by declaring the contract void. A rescinded contract is considered never to have existed. Rescission is distinguished from cancellation or termination, which release the parties to a contract from any additional or ongoing responsibilities, even if the contract terms are not fulfilled.

Respondeat Superior Latin for "Let the master answer." It is the legal doctrine that imposes vicarious liability on the employer for breaches of duties by employees. The duty is the employer's, imposed if the employer engages others to perform tasks on the employer's behalf, which is work within the scope of employment. For example, a hospital is liable for the negligent acts of a nurse it employs, if the acts occurred while the nurse was performing tasks within a nursing job description. Pronounced ress-pon-day-ought soup-eerie-or.

Slander Spoken defamation about one person in the presence of another person that harms the slandered person's income, reputation, or character.

Standard of Care The measure of assessment applied to a defendant's conduct for liability determination, comparing what occurred with what an ordinary, reasonable, and prudent person would have done or not done.

Stare Decisis Latin for "Let the decision stand." This is the principle of case law that requires courts to apply the approach and rationale of previously decided cases to subsequent cases involving similar facts and legal questions. When a point of law has been settled by decision, it forms a precedent that is binding. Later decisions may distinguish their facts or circumstances to come to different results, but otherwise must adhere to the rule of precedent. On rare occasion, precedent is rejected, and a new ruling case decision is adopted. Such a case is called a landmark case. Landmark case decisions have been made in civil rights, criminal law, abortion, and consumer law. Pronounced starry dee-sigh-sis.

Statute A written law enacted by the legislature to achieve a specified legislative objective. Statutes apply legislative prescriptions to some of the same fact situations dealt with by case law and administrative law. Generally, former case law governing the situation is no longer operative in situations in which a subsequent statute is applicable.

Statute of Limitations Laws that specify the permissible time interval between an occurrence giving rise to a civil cause of action and the filing of the lawsuit. Failure to file suit within the prescribed time is an affirmative defense. These time limits for filing suit vary among the states, even for similar legal actions. Most statutes of limitation have exceptions that stop the time from elapsing. Stopping the time is called tolling the statute. In malpractice actions, the time allowed for bringing suit is stopped or does not begin to run until the party claiming injury first discovers or should reasonably have discovered the injury. Fraudulent concealment of an injury by the defendant tolls the statute. Prosecution of some crimes is also subject to a statute of limitations, which elapses while the perpetrator remains within the jurisdiction.

Stipulation Acknowledgment by a party of a specific fact or circumstance that will not be disputed in a case. One party may stipulate that a witness is qualified to testify, or that a physician had been an employee of a facility at the time of disputed care. Stipulations save time and expense by removing certain issues from trial proceedings.

Strict Liability Responsibility for harm caused by special activities or circumstances. This is liability without the need to prove a negligent act or failure. The proof of damages sustained by the plaintiff in connection with the situation and the involvement of the defendant support the finding of strict liability. Examples could be management by the defendant of inherently dangerous activities, placing a defective and dangerous product into commerce, or assembling hazardous substances or mechanisms.

Subpoena Latin for court order requiring a person to appear in court to give testimony or be punished for not appearing. Pronounced supp-peen-a.

Subpoena Duces Tecum Subpoena that requires a person to personally present to the court a specified document or property possessed or under the person's control. Pronounced supp-peen-a deuces tay-cum.

Tort Civil wrong in which a person has breached a legal duty with harm caused to another. To establish liability for a tort, an injured party must establish that a legal duty was owed to the plaintiff by the defendant, that the defendant, breached that duty, and that the plaintiff suffered damage caused by the breach. Torts can be negligent or intentional.

Vicarious Liability Derivative responsibility for an agent's or employee's failures based on the defendant's employer/employee or principle/agent relationship. The responsibility is imposed because the ability to supervise, direct, and control employees in order to safeguard others lies with the employer.

Waiver Intentional and voluntary agreement to forego a known claim or right. For example, a patient could waive the privilege of confidential communication, or a defendant could waive the right to challenge certain testimony. Sometimes, a right may be unintentionally waived if it is not exercised in time. For example, the right to make or amend allegations and claims not disclosed in pretrial discovery and depositions may be considered waived by the court for failure to assert them in a timely manner.

Wanton Act Grossly negligent, malicious, or reckless conduct that implies a disregard for the consequences or for the rights or safety of others.

Warranty Express or implied commitment or promise undertaken as part of a contract, but aside from the central contract purpose. It is to be distinguished from a representation. A warranty is given contemporaneously with the contract agreement as part of the contract. A representation precedes and may be seen as an inducement to enter the contract. For example, a representation would be the disclosed indication for surgery; a warranty would be a promise of a specific result from the procedure.

Index

E

F

Q

R

T

U

V